Advance Praise for # MEDIATED IDENTITIES

"Divya C. McMillin asks vital and compelling questions about the construction of youth identities in an era of postcolonialism, neoliberalism, and transnational media. Her fieldwork in international locales offers insights into the cultivation of a 'global proletariat' in the context of the complex, vibrant, and hybridized youth cultures that crosscut the globe. Along the way, she provides nuanced theoretical insights that bring together cultural studies, theories of gender and identity, and production analysis in new and illuminating ways. Lucidly written and energetically researched, *Mediated Identities* makes an invaluable contribution to the literature on youth and media by taking into account the realities of the twenty-first century."

Meenakshi Gigi Durham, Ph.D., Author of The Lolita Effect: The Media Sexualization of Young Girls and What We Can Do About It

"In this theoretically sophisticated and ethnographically rich book, Divya C. McMillin succeeds in taking the study of youth and media in exciting new directions. Viewing culture as dynamic, and identity as constantly constructed and negotiated, McMillin goes beyond the Euro-American scholarship that has set the agenda for studies of mediated youth culture. Within a framework of postcolonial theory, she rethinks that agenda for the global mediascape, drawing on research with youth across several continents. This book will be welcomed by communication scholars, anthropologists, and all those interested in the processes of media globalization and their role in the cross-cultural experiences of youth."

S. Elizabeth Bird, Professor, University of South Florida

"In this important book, Divya C. McMillin builds on her earlier work in international media studies to explore the complex lifeworld settings in which young people across four continents put media resources to use. Transcending old debates on agency, resistance, and identity, McMillin provides a rich account of young people's work, family, and social contexts under the pressures of neoliberalism and globalization. With much theoretical sophistication, this book sets out a new agenda for youth studies and comparative media studies, and should be widely welcomed."

Nick Couldry, Professor, Goldsmiths, University of London

"Divya C. McMillin takes us on a fascinating, eye-opening journey into the dynamic working of structure and culture through her meetings with youth in their bedrooms, school yards, and cybercafés—as she theorizes about culture and identity in a global world. Empirically grounded, written with an eye sensitive to detail and context, and richly theoretical, this book enables the reader to gain a closer view of the everyday life of urban and rural youth as they negotiate and construct their identities in multicultural environments. While Euro-American readers gain access to a whole new way of seeing and understanding youth, those from non-western traditions will find their many voices represented in a colorful, vivid, and strongly engaging style."

Dafna Lemish, Professor, Tel Aviv University, Editor of the Journal of Children and Media

MEDIATED IDENTITIES

mediated youth

Sharon R. Mazzarella
General Editor

Vol. 6

PETER LANG
New York • Washington, D.C./Baltimore • Bern
Frankfurt am Main • Berlin • Brussels • Vienna • Oxford

Divya C. McMillin

MEDIATED IDENTITIES

Youth, Agency, & Globalization

PETER LANG
New York • Washington, D.C./Baltimore • Bern
Frankfurt am Main • Berlin • Brussels • Vienna • Oxford

Library of Congress Cataloging-in-Publication Data

McMillin, Divya C. (Divya Carolyn).
Mediated identities: youth, agency, and globalization / Divya C. McMillin.
p. cm. — (Mediated youth; 6)
Includes bibliographical references.
1. Mass media and youth. 2. Mass media and globalization. I. Title.
HQ799.2.M35M376   302.230835–dc22   2009027011
ISBN 978-1-4331-0097-0
ISSN 1555-1814

Bibliographic information published by **Die Deutsche Nationalbibliothek**.
Die Deutsche Nationalbibliothek lists this publication in the "Deutsche
Nationalbibliografie"; detailed bibliographic data is available
on the Internet at http://dnb.d-nb.de/.

The paper in this book meets the guidelines for permanence and durability
of the Committee on Production Guidelines for Book Longevity
of the Council of Library Resources.

Printed in the United States of America

CONTENTS

FOREWORD

Ever since movies, comics, and serial adventure and romance stories emerged at the turn of the 20th century in the USA, and young people became enthralled with these media, many (often elite) adults have been worried about the effects that supposedly low-brow forms of communication and entertainment might have on children and adolescents. Over the years, the emergence and global proliferation of radio, television, pop music, video games, computers, and the Internet continued to elicit critical outcries about their influence, and often times led to academic research as well as policy recommendations that might address the "problem" of youth and popular media. More recently, the converged forms of media available—to those with means and access—through cellphones and a variety of mobile and networked communication technologies have likewise prompted debates about their consequences, both positive and negative, for youth learning and development. Adult concerns about youth learning and development are certainly understandable, even desirable and laudable, since youth do need and deserve guidance and nurturing to take on responsibilities as workers, citizens, and possibly, leaders within and across their communities and societies.

But unfortunately, as McMillin and other scholars point out, a good deal of the debates, research, and policymaking about youth and popular media tend to

simplify situations, overlook the specificities of circumstance, as well as, patron-
ize youth—and various regions of the world, too. Simplification, disregard, and
patronization are represented in various scholarly discussions that dichotomize
the relative power of media and youth, the global and the local. These dichotomies are challenged and made contextually complex throughout this book.

McMillin discusses how many theories of youth and media have tended
toward essentialisms and determinisms that are rooted in Western notions of
individualism, capitalism, and liberal visions of development. On the one hand,
youth are regarded as vulnerable and impressionable, and thus susceptible to
the ploys of the contemporary market, a stance that simultaneously perceives
of youth as passive consumers and media as overpowering producers. On the
other hand, youth are regarded as discerning and savvy, and thus resistant to or
at least skeptical about their being consumer targets, a stance that perceives of
youth as active, and media as often ineffective in hitting their intended mark.

At the same time, some theories of identity tend to think of gender, race,
class, nation, religion, and other social positions as fixed and isolated from
one another, rather than constantly in flux and continuously intertwined, and
located in particular places and times. The idea that identities are in flux,
intertwined, and located confronts theories about the hegemonic power of
globalization; while global flows of media do put local identities in contact with
dominant ideologies of the West and of capitalistic markets, the particularities
of identities and the local are not necessarily overcome.

The power and strength of this book is that it complicates and criticizes
any simplistic and patronizing visions of youth and their relations to media,
and thoroughly grounds pertinent arguments that are made about the globalization effects wrought via media. McMillin accomplishes this by providing
vivid descriptions and provocative analyses of the structures that constrain and
shape how young people actually live everyday in various mediated locales, and
by providing extensive quotes from and interpretations of young people negotiating and making sense of their everyday experience of home, school, religion,
peer interactions, and various national/regional realities.

Drawing on postcolonial theories and critical ethnographic research,
McMillin argues that we must marry the macro with the micro, and she does
this effectively by thoroughly and comprehensively describing and analyzing
comparative cross-cultural case studies. Part of the empirical research she presents (in early chapters) grew out of a collaborative project that investigated
teens, identity, and television in four distinct regions of the world: Bangalore,
India; Johannesburg, South Africa; Munich, Germany; and New York, USA.

Researchers in each region conducted a series of in-depth interviews and observations with a small group of diverse teens in each of their locales, asking the teens about their life at home, school, and with peers, and how they identified themselves in terms of their gender, race/ethnicity, class, and various other social and cultural positions. Also, they were asked to talk about their television habits and preferences. In addition, the researchers gathered information on the systems of television the teens had access to in their region. The principal investigators also met as a team in Munich to present the materials they had gathered, to discuss their findings, and to consider publications as well as further research, which appears in later chapters of the book.

I was fortunate to be the principal investigator in New York on this project. Fortunate because that is how I met Divya McMillin and the other researchers on this project. The kinds of critical insights and thoughtful questions she introduced to our collective conversation in Munich, and also via ongoing virtual communications and continued collaborations, are integrated throughout this book. She is always mindful of the roles that context and political, economic, and social power relations play in how young people experience and make sense of their everyday lives and television (and other media). She is also always mindful of how research methodologies are problematic due to issues of context and power relations as well. These issues of context and methodology pertain to all of the case studies, but McMillin highlights them forcefully in the chapter that presents focus group discussions with young people from ten countries who talked and wrote about gender identity and relations, and television representations of gender. She reminds us here that, while it is important to have young people express themselves and to represent their voices, the how, where, and why those voices are prompted and then represented in particular venues have to be taken into account when we put our analyses forward.

And so she concludes this book by looking reflectively and critically at her own work, and by making important suggestions for future research. I hope she will follow up on these suggestions, and that fellow scholars and educators will support and build on this meaningful work in whatever way they can. Because in the long run, our research and teaching should guide us in helping youth make sense of themselves, others, and the world as powerful and successful participants, in all respects. This book makes just such a contribution.

2009
JoEllen Fisherkeller
Associate Professor of Media, Culture, and Communication
New York University

ACKNOWLEDGMENTS

This book is for all the young people who let me into their lives and allowed me to tell their stories. They shared their journals, their thoughts, and television pleasures. Through their eyes the interconnections of globalization moved from abstraction to complex reality. My time with audiences in Bangalore began in 1997, when I started watching television with viewers of varied ages, religions, languages, and socioeconomic levels, at a time when private networks in India were just beginning to pose a serious threat to the state-sponsored Doordarshan. I returned to the field time and again, preoccupied with the ideological entanglements of media, state, and market in postcolonial India. Allowing me to explore these entanglements from sweatshops were hard working young men and women, who shared their stories with me and my sister, Arathi Singh, a doctor who monitored their nutritional needs. I thank her for facilitating access, and all the participants for giving me an intimate look into how labor identities work closely with consumer identities. I thank the call center workers and college students who helped me study the opportunism in mimicry, and the limitations of those very opportunities. The University of Washington's Royalty Research Fund, the UW-Tacoma's Chancellor's, and Founder's Endowment Awards sponsored several phases of fieldwork in Bangalore. Although not included in detail in this book, insights from these explorations primed me for the comparative study of young people in Bangalore, Johannesburg, Munich, and New York.

The two phases of the *TV Characters* project (2003–2004 and 2005–2006, respectively), the first one comparative and the second focusing on Indian teens, were driven by the question of what *meanings* television produces for young people searching for agency. These and the *Exploring Gender across the World* projects in 2007 were sponsored by the Internationales Zentralinstitut für das Jugend-und Bildungsfernsehen (IZI), Munich. Head of the IZI, Maya Götz, organized the first wonderful workshop in Munich in September 2004, when with fellow researchers JoEllen Fisherkeller[1] and Firdoze Bulbulia[2] we hunched over field notes, transcripts, and photographs to discuss ways in which our observations converged and diverged. I thank Maya for initiating these fascinating ventures. In JoEllen I find a true collaborator; Chapters Three and Four are much improved because of her suggestions. I am grateful to Firdoze for generously providing the background material that put the *Exploring Gender* project in context. I thank all these researchers (including Petra Strohmaier and Anita Lakhotia who conducted fieldwork among teens in Munich), for allowing me to discuss the interconnections among our case studies.

A special place will always be reserved in my heart for the eight teens interviewed in the first phase of the *TV Characters* study. Their passion, energy, and honesty inspire me. I thank my mother, Susheela Punitha, postcolonial scholar and colleague, who facilitated the interviews, and played a key role especially in the second phase of the *TV Characters* project. Among the teens in the second phase, we remember one young boy, only 16 at the time of fieldwork in 2005, who died in a tragic car accident in January 2009.

While the IZI-proposed questions from each level of fieldwork resulted in articles and book chapters, only a book-length manuscript could provide the space and freedom to discuss critically how youth lives are implicated in the processes of globalization. I thank Sharon Mazzarella, *Mediated Identities* series editor, for inviting me to write this book. Her support has been unwavering and generous over the years. At Peter Lang, Mary Savigar and Sophie Appel have been so helpful. I thank the copyeditors for their thorough work. Various theoretical insights have been developed through mentors Michael Curtin, Beverly Stoeltje, Anders Linde-Larsen, and Chris Anderson. I especially thank Rey Chow for her incisive writing and her collegiality while this manuscript was in progress. I continue to reach out to her work to keep the critical focus on globalization. My conversations with Nick Couldry, Jeanne Prinsloo, Norma

Pecora, Angharahad Valdivia, Charu Uppal, Ammu Joseph, Sofie van Bauwel, and Marieke Rodenburg have further enriched discussions in this book. Dafna Lemish provided a close reading of Chapter Six, leading to much-needed revisions. I thank my colleagues everywhere in media studies, globalization, and postcolonial theory. I wish I could include every essay and case study I read while putting the chapters together. My debt to this scholarly community is huge; our task is enormous and ongoing, we gain momentum knowing we are all here.

My tightly knit family continued to hold me up through the challenges of producing this manuscript. I thank my mother for being ever present as colleague, adviser, and parent. David, my father, is a significant force in my life; his advice on everything stays strident despite his failing health. My sisters, brothers-in-law, niece, and nephews, all kept me plugged into myriad worlds, providing me a welcome seat at the Skype table when I needed a break. In particular, my niece Koel and nephew Shaurya kept me supplied with Web links and YouTube clips of the latest pop culture trends in India. I thank Sitara and Suneri, my precious daughters, for the delight they bring to each day. I reserve a special thank you for my neighbors Sandy and Mel Caviezel. Sandy's cheerful babysitting gifted me many valuable hours of writing and, more importantly, freed up time for me to play with the girls. My deepest gratitude goes to my husband Andy who took over running the household while I wrote in peace. This book could not have been written without his tremendous support.

Divya C. McMillin
April 24, 2009

· 1 ·
POINTS OF DEPARTURE

High school students filed into the small assembly hall of Ryan International School in Bangalore, India, whispering nervously. It was a sunny summer afternoon in June 2007. Within minutes, the interschool debate competition was to start. Regional winners from such cities as Hyderabad, Secunderabad, and Mangalore had been bused in to the school, where the finals were to take place. I sat among the young girls and boys on the folding steel chairs to watch the debate. Although this was the start of the school year, the participants on stage and the audience were all too aware of the impending, dreaded, 10th grade nationwide Central Board of Secondary Education (CBSE) and Indian School Certificate Examinations (ICSE) exams in March the next year. They probably felt the burden of the topic "Today's Parents Want Prodigies, Not Children." I was a casual visitor, tagging along with my mother, a professor who had been invited as a judge. I was among the audience for many reasons: a sense of nostalgia for my own days as an interschool competitor, an interest in the issues facing urban Indian youth, and a deep curiosity about how this population spoke and behaved as members within a system that placed high priority on academic success.

The rules were simple: each candidate had four minutes to make her or his case. A warning bell would ring at the end of three minutes. Each then had two minutes to respond to rebuttals from other candidates on stage. From the swirl of ideas presented—some focused, some rambling, some factual, most opinionated—a scaffolding of a youth world order awkwardly emerged. Receiving heavy weight at the top was the notion that the competitive world that lay beyond the 10th grade exam was predatory. To quote one of the participants speaking for the topic, a girl from Bishop Cotton's High School, "Everyone is looking for youth. The highest bidder gets the opportunity. Talent is manufactured." Backing her statements with anecdotes about the immense pressure high school graduates faced to get into the nation's top schools for engineering, medicine, and business management, she noted that only a tiny percentage of students actually get into those schools. This is indeed true. A variety of sources note that the Indian Institute of Technology Joint Entrance Examination (IIT-JEE) is probably the toughest engineering exam in the world. Students passing the exam could expect to be admitted to one of the nine leading engineering colleges in the nation. The college entrance exam is a vital experience for teens in East Asian countries and among the middle class in India (Verma, Sharma, & R. Larson, 2002). The CBSE and the ISC (the latter is offered after the 10th grade ICSE examination) curricula provide an early start (as early as 6th grade in some states such as Andhra Pradesh) to train for these entrance exams. The consequence of such pressure, as noted by many speaking against the topic, was a complete annihilation of leisure time. Children were showing signs of stress right from around the 5th grade. Many went from the school day right into evening tuition and from that to late-night studying. All these pressures notwithstanding, the judges spoke at length about the challenges Indian youth need to rise up to in an era of globalization. One judge in fact spoke longer than the entire duration of the debate to urge students to recognize that they were growing up "within internationalism. We *have* to rise to be a super class. We *have* to set standards for those results."

Students of the expensive Ryan International School are generally from upper-class or upper- middle-class backgrounds. Debate participants were mostly from other elite schools in the city and neighboring states. Those few who were from schools where English was not the medium of instruction were at a clear disadvantage in their struggles with grammar and inability to immediately translate into English their responses to rebuttals. Singh and Doherty (2008) observe that the anxieties of the middle class to meet the challenges of globalization are acute: "The young person's progress is now being carefully and 'prudentially' engineered through strategies of choice and the investment of capital by 'anxious' middle-class parents intent on reproducing their class advantages in the face of risky global markets that make such status less secure" (p. 119). On that stage where the debate unfolded, marked discrepancies in *agency* that the participants exhibited were also laid bare, based on the school they attended and their command of spoken English. The judge's challenge to them to rise to be leaders of a technological world was heady; which of them could answer that call is another story.

My mother and I received bouquets for our presence and were thanked graciously by everyone. But we were silent on our way home. We were both educators. We too were raised in middle-class households with immense pressure to perform academically. This urban Indian environment of international schools, of globalized curricula that prepared students for transnational mobility, and of grooming them with an urgency and desperation to be a *super class*, this was new. The debate tapped into an ongoing economic trend to position India and China as the next hot spots of not just outsourced labor, but of research and development as well. Perhaps it also anticipated the economic crisis in the United States just a year later.

The U.S. economic crisis, now part of the 2009 landscape, is just beginning to roll out in all its complex manifestations. Newspaper and television stories about financial scandals and national debt have become taken-for-granted wallpaper in North American urban and rural homes. Even the *Multinational Monitor* that takes on the noble task of publishing the list of 10 Worst Corporations of the year had to admit "we've never had a year like 2008. The financial crisis first gripping Wall Street and now spreading rapidly throughout the world is, in many ways, emblematic of the worst of the corporate-dominated political and economic system that we aim to expose ... " (Weissman, 2008, p. 10). The report briefly discusses the climate that led to this mess: inadequate political influence on business practices and lack of regulation and sanctions against improper lending. In this generally unchecked corporate environment, the denial of the impending housing bubble, financialization of the corporate sector, and the aggressive focus on profit over social purpose, accompanied by foisting of costs on workers and general public, has demonstrated graphically, that "corporations—if left to their worst instincts—will destroy themselves and the system that nurtures them" (p. 11). While a bewildered American proletariat attempts to understand the connection between complex implosions of such corporations as AIG, Cargill, and Chevron and their disappearing jobs, the educational institutions its children attend are back to the drawing board, feverishly reworking curricula to make it more relevant to a country in crisis. It is clear in every financial and scholarly commentary that America's youth will bear the burden of the over $800-billion stimulus package that will unravel over the next few years. Many fear that young people in the country lack the basic education and skills to meet this challenge. On March 10, 2009, U.S. President Barack Obama proposed increasing the number of instruction days in the school year, and providing top teachers merit pay to train students to be competitive in the global economy. The United States' high school dropout rates are among the highest and students consistently rank below their peers in other Western countries in reading and math (Colvin, 2009). Across the globe, urban youth in India, such as those in Ryan International School, get it. The importance of education is part of their national fabric, a priority defined in large part by India's position in the world order.

India and China have long been the focus of global economic growth. U.S. relations with these countries have necessarily been as cordial as they could possibly be. China's lack of transparency and its state-controlled system have bolstered U.S. interest in India, causing each nation to see its future profits in the other. Indian youth, groomed for centuries under the British colonial system have seen, most pressingly since the implementation of India's 1991 economic liberalization policy, a call to labor in multinational industries like never before. The October 2003 Goldman Sachs BRIC's (Brazil, Russia, India, and China) Report published the astonishing results that India's economy could be higher than that of Japan by 2032 and China's higher than the U.S. economy by 2041. Assuming development proceeds at an even pace, the report shows that India is the only BRIC country that would evidence growth rates well above 3% through 2050. Growth rate does not translate into better standard of living however, and it is projected that individuals in BRIC countries will continue to be poorer on average as compared to their counterparts in the G6 countries, which are the United States, Japan, UK, Germany, France, and Italy (Wilson & Purushothaman, 2003). In early 2009, the conditions of the poor in BRIC countries weren't so distant from those in the United States as evidenced by the numerous newspaper cartoons that followed in the wake of the movie *Slumdog Millionaire*'s momentous win of eight Academy Awards. Although vast discrepancies exist between the poor in developed and developing countries, the cartoons expressed that, perhaps in the face of catastrophic failures within U.S. financial institutions and the Bush administration, India's slum children may have indeed scored a better deal. The victory of the protagonist on India's version of the television franchise, *Who Wants to Be a Millionaire*, may very well be more plausible than economic recovery in the United States.

With these macro shifts in interconnected and interdependent economic systems where youth are centrally implicated, and where the mass media play a significant ideological role, it is remarkable that scholarship on youth and media focuses largely on youth as consumers and on media as forms of entertainment. The introductory description of the current economic and political global moment places youth as key agents in weathering the mistakes of the current generation. It signals to us a reorientation in economic power, and presses us—as media scholars—to study youth not just as users of media but as key players in the labor market. We need to *get it*, as did the students in the assembly hall at Ryan International School, that adolescence is not just a time where identities are expressed and constricting structures are resisted. It is a time where media and market pose strong interpellatory forces that shape the nature of the emerging subject. A study of how youth respond to those forces and what cultural reservoirs they tap into will provide important insights into the youth bodies produced through the conditions of globalization. The challenge is to trace the intricate weavings between structure and culture, keeping in focus the location of the historical subject in a dynamic world system.

This is where the book begins.

We start our journey through the lives and passions of youth in various parts of the world by first mapping the world order they inhabit. We enter the study of youth and media globalization from the ground itself, starting from living rooms, bed rooms, school yards, and cybercafes, to name a few spaces. We sit with them as they watch television, chat with them as they sift through magazine clippings and articles of their favorite pop culture celebrities, and share pastries and coffee with them in the heart of the city. We evaluate the *mission civilatrice* of colonialism in developing economies and the benefits and challenges facing youth in these postcolonial nations. We therefore weave in the structural environment that textures the ground. This results in the showcasing of a variety of empirical research on youth and media while raising serious questions about method, theoretical frameworks, and relevance for postcolonial contexts. The point of entry therefore is the local, hybrid, and shifting ground. Case studies gathered during fieldwork among youth in various venues—urban and rural homes in Bangalore, India, among teen delegates at the 2007 World Summit on Media for Children in South Africa, and collaborative analyses with youth and media researchers in Germany, South Africa, and the United States—will be highlighted. For each study discussed in this book, several layers of research were undertaken. Apart from participant observation and lengthy interviews in the sites mentioned above, the author spent extensive time traversing the urban spaces in which the teens lived. As much of the "moment" of fieldwork as possible was recorded through videos and photographs, and extensive notetaking. Methods of fieldwork are described in relevant chapters. The book also draws on rich ethnographies by various scholars around the globe to illustrate the intricate workings of global and local cultures.

Discussion of case studies is closely informed by postcolonial theory. Although only India, of all the countries included, may be considered the poster child of postcolonialism, the theory serves in the study of "cultural legitimation," that is, how terms and conditions acquire validation (Chow, 1998, p. 162). The study of globalization has to draw in centrally how systems of exclusion and inclusion are constructed (Young 2003). The postcolonial attention to difference as a reaction to theoretical tendencies to group together vastly disparate populations and places (Vickers & Dhruvarajan, 2002), and its intimate engagement with political histories (Chow, 2000) makes it a compelling framework through which to study youth and globalization. The struggles of the South African people as the nation reconfigures itself after the abolition of apartheid in 1994 have been likened to that of postcolonial nations where the malevolence of fixed identities are giving way to recognition of rich diversity (Zegeye & Harris, 2003). The resistance and forced compliance, in ideological terms, of European nations to the precepts of the European Union in 1991 have also been paralleled to the trauma of the postcolonial condition, where, to use the example of Malta (see Grixti, 2006), citizens were abruptly exposed to an aggressively commercialized media environment even as nation-states attempted to contain the imaginations of its people and shepherd them into a narrow representation of national identity and citizen privilege. The book does not equate the experiences of teens in the varied locales with one another, nor does it generalize the postcolonial condition as universal (a tendency in postcolonial studies that has been critiqued elsewhere; see Chow, 2000). It uses central features of postcolonial theory to address how neocolonial practices of globalization implicate youth, and how structured realities in various urban centers flow to produce the young, urban subject. Interconnected circuits of globalization bring populations "closer" than ever before; such proximity, while tantalizing in a "constant-contact" generation, also triggers alarm, exacerbating or revitalizing old barriers to redefine material and ideological distance between centers and peripheries (Abélès, 2007).

The objective of the book therefore is to examine, empirically, how youth identity is constructed and negotiated in urban and rural spaces where social, cultural, economic, and political forces compete for the allegiance of the young consumer and worker. It acknowledges that identity is always incomplete and, in this sense, is always a hegemonic project (Butler, 2000). Identity simultaneously is formed by and expresses relations of power (Dolby, 2006). This is where we spend considerable time and attention. We reject essentialist notions of culture and identity. We shall see, in the review of theoretical approaches that dichotomic positions abound in both youth and global media studies. Most prominently criticized is the construction of culture as something that is in crisis—or not—when foreign media products infiltrate its marketplaces (as also argued in Tomlinson, 1997, for example). Globalization is assumed to fragment or connect experiences (see also Applbaum, 2000). There is an urgency to uncover the authentic culture *without* or *before* mediation, as if such a condition exists. This "authentic"—an ideological construction in itself—is actually what savvy transnational corporations attempt to partner with, providing the hybrid local, sometimes convincing consumers and theoreticians alike, that in this intimate, intricate understanding of their audiences, their fingers never leave the pulse of local desire.

Rather than occupy the substantialist position where, for example, local and global television programs are seen as synonymous with local and global culture as if these are concrete, W. Mazzarella (2004) argues that we should approach the study of culture as a simultaneously ideological and social process that is produced through changing relations, practices, and mediating technologies. What we need then is "to attend to the places of mediation, the places at which we come to be who we are through the detour of something alien to ourselves, the places at which we recognize that difference is at once constitutive of social reproduction and its most intimate enemy" (p. 356). Conversations with teens in Bangalore, New York, Johannesburg, and Munich recounted in this book resulted in stories of teens' multiple interests and the places of mediation that informed these interests. Mediating systems are discussed here not just as conventional media technologies, but, as structures of family, peers, school, and religion as well. Far from arguing for "authentic" cultural positions and how these are altered or not by global and local media products, we slip into each space mindful that while the teens themselves may have argued for or against essentialist notions of gender, ethnic, religious, or national identity, the places and practices of mediation revealed dynamic flows between how they lived their lives and the structures that influenced them. What we have then are the stories of the processes of mediation that "always grapple with internal indeterminacies as well as external provocations" and we attend to how "social actors—consciously or unconsciously—try to manage or fix these indeterminacies and provocations by means of reified schemes of cultural identity and cultural difference" (W. Mazzarella, 2004, p. 360).

The book marks a considerable shift from Euro-American approaches to the study of youth and media that have dominated the field. Primary features of such approaches are mediacentrism and the assumption of the modernity of the consuming subject. The trend is to address the globalized and networked environment as the next step of modernity, without problematizing its conditions in the first place. If we are to engage in any critical, *globally relevant* discussion of youth and globalization, we have to take into account colonial histories, development inconsistencies, and the ideological underpinnings of modernity. Postcolonial theory provides a useful way to draw in the political and economic environments that texture how culture is lived and how media courses through and conditions it. It draws us into an engagement with the positioning of audiences from varied locales and questions the romantic notion of the active agent or autonomous consumer. Although postcolonial theory derives from Marxist structuralism, in this book, we highlight the limitations of an uncritical adaptation of such structuralism that can order the world through the "prism" of European development (Serequeberhan, 2007, p. 132).

The concept of *agency* is a much debated one in audience studies. When used to refer to youth choices, the term becomes highly controversial and is regarded as the catchword of a corporate environment rather than that of an analytical one. It is often used in audience and consumer studies quite uncritically. Youth studies, in particular, herald agency in all its forms: formation of subcultures, representations of resistance in popular music and dance, and in consumer choices in urbanized, globalized environments. In this book, we examine the implications of globalization for youth agency. We explore the dynamic cultural processes that inform and are informed by structural hierarchies. While definitions of globalization and modernity and the ideological frameworks of audience and political economy studies have been mapped out elsewhere (McMillin, 2007), this book poses several sets of questions to draw out how youth are implicated in globalization.

The first set pertains to theoretical frameworks that characterize the field of youth studies. The question that forms the basis of Chapter Two is this: what theoretical and methodological tools do we have to study youth and globalization? The chapter describes what we mean by a grounded approach to youth studies (taken up again in Chapter Seven) and the postcolonial lens that draws us into a clear vision of context. It then traces various theoretical strains pertaining to youth culture in British cultural studies. In so doing, it argues for a shift from a Eurocentric construction of youth toward a more inclusive analysis in globalization.

A second set of questions pertains to the conditions of globalization. These are as follows: What are the local mediating systems that contribute to a sense of youth agency? What is the nature of this agency and how is it articulated? How are youth lives connected to the structures of globalization? Chapters Three, Four, and Five address these questions. Chapter Three argues for beginning analysis with context, a shift from mediacentric audience studies. Highlighting qualitative fieldwork conducted during the *TV Characters and Cultural Identity* study[1] in Bangalore, Johannesburg, Munich, and New York from February through August of 2003, the chapter opens up new theoretical directions in that it advocates putting the media in their place, within a larger social context of activities and circuits of identity from which the teen develops a sense of self. Through a careful discussion of the gender, class, caste, and religious identities of the teens and the cultural positioning of television in their homes, the chapter demonstrates that television is used as an extension of ongoing journeys toward selfhood.

Continuing in this vein, Chapter Four engages in a critical discussion of youth and subjective agency in the global marketplace. Media usage has to be studied as part of everyday rituals (Ginsburg, Abu-Lughod, & Larkin, 2002) where audiences are dynamic individuals, possessing a subjective agency in how they consume what they watch. Subjective agency, as opposed to the romanticized active audience of North American cultural studies, is a concept from critical studies that addresses how individuals may experience autonomy and even empowerment within structures that essentially limit the same. Adopting the postcolonial, critical approach to the study of media reception, Chapter Four addresses the flow between television and perceptions of agency among teens in Bangalore, Johannesburg, Munich, and New York.

Chapter Five engages in a critical discussion of viewing contexts. Fieldwork from the 2003–4 *TV Characters* study revealed that Indian teens were experiencing a different level of what could be termed *global anxiety*. The rapidly changing landscape of their neighborhoods making way for multinational corporate headquarters and the transformation of local sheds and warehouses to sweatshops, was conveying to them, in very immediate terms, that their labor was in demand. What type of labor depended on their social and economic positions. Chapter Five, in its discussion of fieldwork among teenagers in Bangalore as a follow-up[2] to the first phase of the *TV Characters* project, explores how these young people accommodated the pressures of school, home, *and* marketplace. The purpose is to study the place of family and social structures in shaping teen identity and media preferences, particularly as they were positioned within a dynamic urban environment that increasingly looked toward the global for icons of success and desirability.

The third set of questions taps into the correspondence between production and consumption of youth media. Ideologies of gender and class in such robust formats as soap operas, game shows, and talk shows endure because of their resonance with entrenched systems of patriarchy across national boundaries.

Pertinent questions here are as follows: How has television responded to the changing opportunities and increased choices available to young people across the world? What are the responses of youth to representations of themselves on television? How may these responses serve as a form of activism for better television worldwide? Chapter Six describes the *Exploring Gender and Media Across the World*[3] project undertaken in March 2007 at the Fifth World Summit on Media for Children in Johannesburg, South Africa.

The final chapter urges inquiry along new and varied trajectories. The question posed here is, how may we meet the needs of youth studies particularly in developing economies where youth are deliberately groomed for a service-providing environment, where dependency means sustenance, and servility to the world order means upward mobility in one's immediate context? Chapter Seven tackles the challenges of conducting fieldwork among youth. As various field-weary researchers have succinctly documented over the years, anonymity of the ethnographer is elusive and the interface between researcher and researched can be quite jarring and abrupt. Much scholarship has been devoted to strategies to ease the raw edge of the encounter, to lay down soft silk cushions of context for interviewer and interviewee to communicate within. The study of the cultural accommodations of globalization, and of the reception of transnational television programs by third world audiences in particular, reeks of smug pedagogical politics. When the respondents under study are teenagers, the imbalances between researcher and researched are even more obvious: differences in age, level of education and experience, who asks and who answers, who seems to know and who doesn't, and finally, who publishes in the core and who is written about on the periphery. The chapter outlines the basic tenets of critical media ethnography. It lays out points to be considered in "studying" youth cultures ethically. It describes the responsibilities of the activist researcher in exploring youth experiences with media and things to keep in mind while writing up field notes.

As Foucault (1970) has famously theorized, modernity produces its subjects; the self develops in relation to structures of power and knowledge. The questions raised in this introduction coalesce into a central one: what bodies does globalization produce? In its questions regarding postcolonial framework and discussion of qualitative fieldwork, the book goes against the grain of the dominant construction of youth as a category that emerged with the development of capitalism (Parsons, 1963); as an assertion of individuality and difference from other development stages such as childhood or adulthood (Grossberg, 1992); and as a working-class creation of yet another consumer market (Hebdige,

1988). It asserts that in developing nations particularly of the global south, *youth* is also a prime developmental arena for the cultivation of a global proletariat. Youth are regarded both as a threat to monolithic constructions of the mythical "golden past" and as highly desirable workers of a techno-rich future.

Scholarship on youth and consumer culture identify global products as connectors of urban youth to transnational communities defying local political structures that may urge them to identify with a constructed past. It may be tantalizing to think of youth as mobile beings, driven by a "libidinal economy (consisting) of social and market structures and dispositions that release, channel, and exploit desires and feelings (intensities), although never fully controlling them" (Kenway & Bullen, 2008). Transnational media flows, in particular, may facilitate participation in various rituals of realization, where viewers attempt to see themselves in the tales of growing pains unfolding on television. Such a conceptualization of youth and consumption as swirling identities and processes limits the analysis of what transactions actually occur between the consumer and market and what struggles ensue within the consumer as a consequence. In its attention to case studies, context, and connections to theory, the book carves a new direction for global youth studies. Its use of postcolonial theory to examine the dynamic interplay among youth, television, and culture draws us directly into an analysis of the ideological positioning of youth in the hybrid, neocolonial processes of globalization.

· 2 ·

TRACKING THEORY

Navigating through theory on youth and media is much like traveling second class on a train in India. It is not for the fainthearted. Crowds surging in at every station and vendors who miraculously balance hot snacks and transport steaming tea over moving bodies orient you to the vibrance of life that theory draws from. The train itself, coursing through lush, green rice fields and over smelly backwaters reminds you that the vehicle from which you are observing life is a product of ideological struggle. The Indian railways was the crowning glory of British rule in India until 1947; yet its connections to primarily British cantonment stations in the country even after 60 years of independence is a testimony to the robustness of the machinery of colonialism itself. In studies on youth, we don't often stray from time-tested tracks to explore where exactly the vibrance of the ground comes from; we just know it's there.

This chapter keeps us close to the ground in the study of youth and media globalization. It raises the train windows, most sticky and clumsy from not being used, and allows gusts of air in—some fresh, some dank. The metaphor helps us pull away from the trend in theoretical critique, particularly in global media studies, to denounce Eurocentric Western theory and privilege non-Western experiences (Chow, 2002). We begin to see that the fields of youth and global media studies are full of divergent tracks, each arguing an essentialist position without adequate lines that examine how they converge or inform one another. Using postcolonial theory, this chapter takes us directly to connections between world order and cultural practice and argues that the dichotomic tracks along which youth and global media studies rumble along limit how and what we view in these areas. It will argue for a *pull-chain* whereby we stop, get off, and wander into more inclusive analyses in the context of globalization. Does this mean we are moving into less rigorous territory, wandering as explorers with heightened senses without much direction? On the contrary, this chapter develops a useful framework by which we understand youth as embedded within context and as visible in their own representations, not just by whether they are "seen" by us from a speeding train window.

A broad survey of theory in youth and global media studies reveals a mine-field of dichotomies. With respect to youth studies we have the child versus the adult, the obedient versus the deviant youth, and the active versus passive audience. Similarly with global media studies, we have the active versus passive audience, the global versus local media network, the media conglomerate ver-sus the victimized consumer, the Western versus non-Western subject—each component of the dichotomy is studied as a closed-off system in itself, or the opposition is examined as if it is a real or given. Gunn and Brummett (2004) summarize that long-standing anxieties about high and low culture with mass media transforming audiences into mindless consumers are renewed in global-ization, where the battle continues between the authentic versus the commer-cial as if each is a monolithic unit.

Trends in Youth Studies

It is widely acknowledged that the study of childhood and adolescence have been the prerogative of psychology and education (Balagopalan, 2008). Vastly different cultures adopt dominant Western theory in these fields to chart the development of their own young people. Historicization of these developmental phases within national and cultural contexts is not given as much credibility, exacerbating the shortsightedness with which we view the development of non-Western individuals. Historian Fass (2008) points out that childhood and youth are studied through a Western lens because it is in the West that theory in the field has emerged. So, for example, dominant thinking on the possibilities of the human being is influenced by such thinkers as John Locke (1632–1704) and John Dewey (1859–1952). Locke's *An Essay Concerning Human Understanding* positioned the human mind as a blank slate at birth; experience defined cogni-tive development. Observation of such cognitive development provided a way to understand processes of knowledge acquisition. Dewey's collection of essays titled *Thought and Its Subject-Matter* provided insights on how children learn. His 1899 work, *The School and Society*, is still considered an authority on how democracy can be achieved in society, and, Fass (2008) argues, shaped social development in the Western world.

In psychology, Jean Piaget (1896–1980) proposed the cyclical and dialec-tical stages of individual cognitive development (sensorimotor, preoperational, concrete operational, and formal operational) stages. Erik Erikson (1902–1994) identified eight phases of psychosocial development, as a departure from Sigmund Freud's (1856–1939) psychosexual stages of oral (birth–two years), anal (two–four years), genital (three–six years), latency (six years–puberty), and mature genital (puberty to adulthood and beyond). Erikson's phases are as follows: basic trust versus mistrust (infancy); autonomy versus shame and doubt (toddlerhood); initiative versus guilt (kindergarten phase); industry versus inferiority (six years–puberty); identity versus role confusion (teenage years); intimacy versus isolation (young adulthood); generativity versus stag-nation (midlife adulthood); and finally, ego-integrity versus despair (old age). Taken together, these theories regard the child as an autonomous individu-al who develops cognitively through a logical sequence of "ages and stages" toward the achievement of adult maturity and rationality. Childhood then is a process of becoming. Adulthood is the finished state where development is regarded as having ceased. Childhood is measured against adulthood standards of rationality, morality, and restraint.

It was Philippe Ariès (1914–1984) who created a shift in the biological determinist approach. In his *L'Enfant et la Vie Familiale sous l'Ancient Régime* (1960) translated as *Centuries of Childhood* (1962), Ariès argued that childhood was a historical construction, quite absent as a concept in medieval times and at best, a notable phase among the upper classes. Among the lower classes, young children were very much part of the labor force, socialized to adult roles and responsibilities out of economic necessity. The industrial environment of mid-1800s Europe is a stark example of the exploitation of children for facto-ry labor. In a nutshell, children and childhood are what adults make of it. In the early twentieth century, *Coming of Age in Samoa* (1928) by anthropologist Margaret Mead (1901–1978) placed culture, not the individual, at the heart of how development should be understood. She noted that the socialization of children is crucial to sustain a culture from generation to generation. Although both Ariès and Mead have been widely criticized for the validity of their data and interpretations, they contributed to a fundamental shift in how individual development was studied. Their emphasis on context and culture as opposed to biological determinism marked an invaluable turn in the study of childhood and adolescence. Adding substantively to the effort to move away from the stage-obsession in psychology is Carol Gilligan, whose colleague at Harvard, Lawrence Kohlberg is noted for the construction of three stages of moral development, deriving from Piaget: preconventional (birth–nine years), conventional (nine–twenty), and postconventional (twenty years and beyond).

Gilligan's *A Different Voice* (1982) argued that not only did Freud, Piaget, Erikson, and even Kohlberg limit into narrow stages how development actually occurs, they also based their observations primarily on males. Girls were quite excluded from these theories of development causing many of their differences from the norm to be characterized as aberrations or instabilities. As Wall (2006) affirms, "The issue here is whether childhood is better understood through generalized stages of individual, cognitive, emotional, and moral development or through wider, diverse meanings and constructions of childhood in history, culture, and society" (p. 526).

Balagopalan (2008) addresses the implications of linear conceptualizations of development where the child is viewed as a presocial being, in international human rights. The 1994 Harkin Bill in Bangladesh prohibited young children from working in garment factories. This led to children finding employment in seamier venues to fulfill their economic roles within the family. The idea that children are isolatable and transferrable from an exploitative condition to a redeeming one, as if they are unattached agents, is a direct outcome of theory that regards the child as without history or contemporaniety, and with only a future. In other words, rather than measure individual development against the linear stages of development, the environment within which the individual exists may provide a better reading on her or his development. Approaches to the study of childhood and youth are now increasingly international and inter-disciplinary. Anthropology, developmental psychology, law, history, education, and sociology are some of the fields that, using the approach of the social sciences, study the various aspects in an individual's journey from childhood to adulthood.

Despite the interdisciplinarity, Balagopalan (2008) states that two trends dominate the field. First, childhood is still measured universally against a Western bourgeois ideal. Seen in this light, the normalization of the Western bourgeois childhood as a self-evident truth where the child is not seen as an economic contributor to the family but an object of nurture and care labels nonkeepers of this ideal, as abusers of this innocent population. The clear separation between child and adult is a noble concept in theory but is fraught with complexity in practice. The second trend is the focus on the concept of "multiple childhoods" where differences in cultural contexts are recognized. Historical and cultural processes are viewed carefully as having intimate impact on how the child is socialized through various stages. Taken into account here is not just biological age, but the ways in which adults and children are differentiated and how children's work is viewed. The aim of the latter trend is highly relevant to this book, which is "to critically interrogate the hidden assumptions that frame ... representations, thereby facilitating a framing of children's lives as culturally discrete and yet intimately connected to the larger social world through the threads of history and its workings of power, knowledge and violence" (Balagopalan, 2008, p. 270). The normalization of Eurocentric, bourgeois childhood as the norm against which all childhood is measured legitimizes a variety of efforts to standardize language and behavior. What is problematic is the privileging of these images even in marginalized communities that have been historically denied opportunities for advancement.

Theorizing Youth in Media Studies

As we chart how children and youth are theorized, we see corresponding positions in the dominant social science paradigm that views the media consumer as autonomous and isolatable, and the media as self-contained environmental cues that exert influence on their consuming subjects. Conventional ages and stages theories in the fields of education and psychology present the individual as an autonomous consumer. Dominant approaches in communication uncritically use such a construction of the individual and chart behavior in response to a variety of media messages. From biological determinism we see a pathway into media determinism where magic bullet theorists of mass communication and Marxist Frankfurt School theorists position audiences as slaves to all-powerful media, consuming both product and ideological meaning.

The most significant contribution of cultural studies to media studies is its paradigm shift from a behavioral to an ideological perspective. The critical turn in media studies most notably emerged in Great Britain in the mid-1950s with the establishment of the New Left that "was within shouting distance of Marxism" (Hall, 1996, p. 265). Proponents of the New Left problematized the Frankfurt School's privileging of high culture over "mass-produced low culture." The Eurocentrism of Marxist theory was questioned, and the orthodoxy and determinism with which it was applied to the study of society was attacked. At the heart of the issue was Marx's organic view of capitalism, which asserted that a society would develop from its own transformations. When assessed within the historicity of colonialism, the organic nature of capitalism was under question. British scholars under the New Left argued that capitalism simply was enforced with all its economic logics, with devastating consequences, in vast areas of the world (Hall, 1996). They placed the concept of ideology at the heart of analysis.

We see connections here among critical scholars in psychology, anthropology, and media studies, where each group urges the recognition of cultural forces in staging how development is articulated and defined and how hegemonic institutions create classes of individuals, societies, and nations.

Within this context of critique by the New Left, emerged Richard Hoggart's *The Uses of Literacy* (1957), Raymond William's *Culture and Society* (1958), and E. P. Thompson's *The Making of the English Working Class* (1963), which demonstrated lived culture as integrated with political practices. These works set the foundations for the Center for Contemporary Cultural Studies (CCCS) at the University of Birmingham in the late 1970s. Emphasizing the role of culture in domination and resistance, the CCCS' various publications—most notably through its journal—*Working Papers in Cultural Studies*, placed at the heart of analysis the study of ideology not just as a belief system, but how it relates to power (Eagleton, 1991); in other words, how ideology is constructed by a hegemonic elite, as meaning in search of power (J. B. Thompson, 1990). During arguably the most prolific years of the CCCS under the leadership of Stuart Hall between 1968 and 1979, several anthologies were produced that focused on youth as subcultures employing unique forms of expression and style to establish identity through resistance (Hall & Jefferson, 1976; Hall, Hobson, Lowe, & Willis, 1980). Willis' *Learning to Labour* (1977) is an influential treatment of the role of the school in preparing children (in his study, 12 boys) for the labor force in ways that reinforce and perpetuate class divisions. Hebdige's (1979) *Subculture: The Meaning of Style* is an examination of how youth resist social order symbolically; signs of resistance coalesce to produce the subculture. The text is controversial in that it positions subcultures as generators of authentic meanings without relating them to entrenched structures of racism and sexism, for example (see Cohen, 1987). Clarke, Hall, Jefferson, and Roberts (1976), using a Gramscian (1971) interpretation of hegemony, discussed that a ruling class is able to dominate subordinate classes through the circulation of ideologies. These ideologies offer meaningful positions to subordinate classes that support the social authority of the dominant class. The hegemony of the ruling class works through the consent of subordinate classes.

Although providing important and interesting ways to study how youth subcultures in particular resist and live within hegemonic structures, these texts have been criticized for their narrow conceptualizations of youth and class identities. McRobbie's *Feminism and Youth Culture* (1991) argued that work on youth subcultures excluded the experiences of women. The texts were critiqued for their masculinist, monolithic constructions of class issues with ethnic politics hidden and orientalized from the epistemological center. McCarthy and Logue (2008) strike down both *Uses of Literacy* for its nostalgia and *The Making of the English Working Class* for its representation of only the English, not the Scots or Welsh. This they call a "cauterizing reflex" (p. 37) that results in a narrow relevance for class analysis. They revealed how individuals pursued self-interests perpetuating their class positions and becoming *klasse für sich* or *class for itself.* What is not developed is how other shifting and contested positions such as race, sexuality, gender, nationality influence *klasse en sich* or *class in itself.* McCarthy and Logue (2008, p. 37) write,

> Is the working class concept equipped to theorize the collective formation of agents with shared interests as members of interpretive communities comprised of individuals (who) may or may not share the same relation to the means of production?

The inclusion of politics of language, caste, and other sociocultural inequalities are now studied as integral components of how a class maintains its privileged position (Fernandes & Heller, 2006). Although disbanded in July 2002 amid much controversy, the CCCS provides important frameworks by which we understand the ideological contexts of the production and consumption of media texts.

Using the broad tenets of British cultural studies and its attention to context and the power of ideology in creating context, Buckingham (2000) argued for a shift in how children and youth were studied. He summarized that childhood—and by extension, adolescence—is considered a social, not biological, category that is historically, socially, and culturally variable. It is also seen as a class-based phenomenon (where this stage was a prerogative of middle and upper classes), or as a symbol of a mythical Golden Age, a Garden of Eden where children could play freely. The general themes surrounding childhood crept into youth studies: its definition as a development category generating sociological concerns of deviance, legitimizing various "moral panics," and sanctioning multiple strategies of control. Youth have been studied in terms of their responses to and negotiations with popular culture, regardless of their socioeconomic status or geographic location (see also Grossberg, 1984).

What happened, ironically, was that in their denunciation of media-determinist analyses, many cultural studies scholars shifted to the other extreme of celebrating audience choices. Drotner (2000) terms the subsequent development of youth studies along determinist (passive audience) or celebratory (active audience) stances the *cultural pessimist* and *cultural optimist* routes, respectively. As may be obvious, the first promotes a close scrutiny of the structural environment while the second examines the cultural positions of audiences. Dolby (2006) asserts that although scholarship has moved on to more nuanced terrain, conclusions on popular media influences on youth still occupy these two camps.

Cultural Pessimism

Although quite different in theoretical framework, the *cultural pessimist route* revives the *magic bullet* construction of the passive audience from the dominant paradigm of communication theory and, reminiscent of Cultivation and Social Learning theories (attributed most notably to George Gerbner and Albert Bandura, respectively), assumes powerful effects. Studies in this tradition claim, to cite a few recent examples, that television "shapes who and what adolescents want to be" (Botta, 2000, p. 155; see also Harrison & Cantor, 1997; Ex, Janssens, & Korzilius, 2002). Children are positioned as threatened and endangered and as subjects of "moral panics" in their interactions with communication technologies (for a critique see S. Mazzarella, 2007, p. 46). Childhood innocence is constructed as a tangible entity, a certain commodity requiring protection from the depravity that accompanies the onset of adolescence. In a "modern," civilized society, the child is protected from predatory external forces. For example, Neil Postman, in *The Disappearance of Childhood* (1982/1994), has argued that the printing press invented by Johann Gutenberg around 1439 and its development in the decades following practically created childhood. It required literacy and paved the way for a school curriculum. Equating rationality with literacy consistent with the ideals of the Enlightenment and its concept of modernity, Postman notes that desirable childhood became synonymous with the "modern" child. As what he calls a "total disclosure medium," television complicates these goals of literacy and rationality, leading to the degeneration of youth. Joshua Meyrowitz's *No Sense of Place* (1985) is another influential commentary on the unsettling role television plays in tampering with boundaries between private and public, between children and their parents. With its ability to expose "backstage" behaviors, television demystifies authority, tarnishes childhood "innocence," and dismantles lines of segregation between children and adults. Continuing in this vein, Barry Sanders asserts in *A Is for Ox* (1994) that television erodes oral literacy. Representing the alarmist culture of the mid-1990s when new media technologies such as the Internet and video games were just establishing their "mesmerizing" capabilities, the edited volume *Kinderculture*

(Steinberg & Kincheloe, 1997) made its way to the stands, its essays aligning with the popular scholarly opinion that mass media blur lines between adults and children. The editors noted that corporate culture to which children and youth become slaves supports free market principles and right-wing conservatism. It is militaristic, patriarchal, and racist, and ignores oppression and inequality.

There is ample evidence to show that television and newer interactive media technologies reconfigure child-adult relationships. Yet Fass (2008) rightly states that determinist stances are flimsy because too often the tendency is to "misunderstand how children fit into this picture as we are presented with facile journalistic visions of children as supine victims of adult economic behaviour and multinational corporate exploitation" (p. 16). The "moral panic" about children, then, may actually be the anxieties of adults about the ability of media technologies to question and demystify authority. Youth may indeed form a subculture and embody "... a compromise solution between two contradictory needs: the need to create and express autonomy and difference from parents...and the need to maintain the parental identifications" (Cohen, 1972, cited in Hebdige, 1979, p. 77). Yet adults criticize the media habits and lifestyles of youth to allay their own insecurities about being adults and to affirm their own, more controlled way of living (Drotner, 1992).

Cultural Optimism

The *cultural optimist route* positions the audience as active negotiators of mediated meanings. This strain is most present in North American cultural studies, which although deriving from British cultural studies as studied in the CCCS, subsumes the latter's political edge. The active audience premise is often considered suspiciously close to Blumler and Katz's (1974) Uses and Gratifications approach of traditional communication theory. Audiences in this route of enquiry are regarded to be influenced by their own identity positions as they consume media. Several "resistance studies" demonstrate the active audience trend where the respondents in question attempt subversions of capitalism, patriarchy or both. The consumer is viewed as a social agent, observing and responding to a hierarchical world inscribed within power relations. The social agent may both resist and reproduce these relations (see Willis, 2004a). McRobbie's *Postmodernism and Popular Culture* (1994), for example, noted that in postwar British society, girls were very much a part of the teddy-boy culture. Motorbikes, mod, and hippy girls were as integral a part of working class subculture as were their male counterparts. More seriously, the focus on male subcultures in earlier cultural studies negated the serious consequences of male cultural expression on the women in their lives. The critical eye toward unrepresented populations, particularly girls, paved the way for the now thriving field of girls' studies.

Mazzarella and Pecora (2007) summarize in a very useful piece on the emergence of this area of study within North American universities that beginning in the 1990s media messages to girls were scrutinized for their ideological messages of ideal girlhood. In the late 1990s and 2000s, attention shifted to how girls receive these messages (see Durham, 1999) and how girls produce media (Kearny, 2006). The media environment has expanded to include interactive communication technologies. Studies have shown that girls use these avenues with greater frequency and for more varied purposes than boys (Clark, 2005). As Mazzarella and Pecora (2007) have noted, the field of girls' studies, while gaining currency in the United States, does bear a bias toward "middle-class white girls in Western countries" (p. 117). A few scholars are changing this trend (Durham, 2002; McMillin, 2005; Valdivia, 2008), but concepts of childhood and adolescence continue to be drawn from Western theory. A criticism in studies that privilege the active audience is that context is not given as much attention; the practice of consumption is the all-encompassing focus. In other words, the micro workings of consumption practices are generally studied in terms of conformity or resistance without much reference to how interrelated power structures influence these practices.

Girls' studies are not exempt from their proclivity to divergent positions. Gonick (2006) labels these the *Girl Power* (where girls are seen as assertive and dynamic) and *Reviving Ophelia* (where girls are constituted as vulnerable and passive) strains, respectively. Both surfaced almost at the same time in the 1990s. Gonick's point is relevant for youth studies in general, that both strains work together in the production of the neoliberal subject. The first represents the autonomous, self-determining subject, a desirable ideal within a democratic, modern society. The second facilitates anxieties about the subject who is unable to express herself in an individualistic way. Both fend off critical engagement with structural inequities that contribute to differing levels of agency. This resonates with Buckingham's (2000) position on children that the construction of this population as dependent unleashes multiple patriarchal and punitive forces without sufficient attention to social realities that may contribute to their dependency. It is useful to recall here Balagopalan's (2008) point that such a framing has dangerous consequences for children's rights and youth

rights. Without the understanding that these populations are socially, culturally, and politically located, we cannot begin to enter their worlds and discuss,
in any useful way, the implications of what they do and what they consume.
Ultimately, it is essential to note that child, girl, or youth are not biological or
universal categories but developed with shifting sociohistorical discourses. As
youth researchers Hudson (1984) and Walkerdine (2003) have argued, the
fixed victim or agent positions prohibit the subject from achieving autonomy
or authorship within her or his own terms of representation.

How, then, are we equipped to study youth in various parts of the world?
Obviously we need a more critical focus on youth in globalization. Young people, particularly in developing countries, face vast opportunities for employment
in newly liberalized economies; yet these opportunities are for the most part,
casual and temporary connections to the labor market. Ancillary and transient
labor offer agency in their flexibility, but they are also replaceable, making the
agent dispensable. The interconnections and interdependencies of globalization make it imperative to explore how the young worker is produced as a node
of connectivity through which the machinery of global capitalism operates.
Each node of connectivity demands a specific type of labor; who performs it is
irrelevant. In venues of extremely high labor supply, the dispensability of the
body and the essentiality of the labor bear consequences for how youth perceive themselves, their social standing, and their destinies. What is required is
an understanding of youth mobility and the "ways in which they are agents of
change and *produce* the new conditions for their lives" (Dolby & Rizvi, 2008,
p. 5). The dominant strains of youth studies that examine them as consumers or
audiences of popular technologies and media leave little room for the examination of youth as bodies of labor. Developed within mediacentric environments
in developed economies, such studies largely neglect the economic and political
conditions that shape youth identity.

Connecting Youth Studies, Media
Studies, and Globalization

Globalization is an umbrella term for interlinked processes of financial
deregulation and the mobilization of capital across a networked world. In
media studies, its economic interdependencies are not so much the focus of
heated academic debate as its cultural implications. The definition offered by
Robertson (1995) is still widely used in a variety of scholarship on the subject.

Robertson defines globalization as "a concept (that) refers both to the compression of the world and the intensification of our consciousness of the world as a whole" (p. 8). Fisher and Ponniah (2003) group the relentless processes of "capitalism, imperialism, monoculturalism, and the domination of biodiversity" (p. 10) under globalization. The projection of globalization as an empowering space that awards myriad choices in previously constricted environments is now routinely criticized in a variety of scholarship. In fact, the possibilities of an interconnected world where there is a perception of "temporary nearness" can also be discomfiting for Westerners (Abélès, 2007), arguably reinforcing neocolonial tendencies. The flip side of the utopian possibilities of globalization is that resources have to be shared. As a hegemonic mission, the pilgrimage toward modernity was "meaningful" because not only did it lead to the realization of the subject, but it also left the primitive behind. The journey of globalization is far more messy and exposes the ideological character of modernity itself. Not only are societies at varying levels of development linked in real time, the armory of each is exposed, making more strident and embarrassing, complaints of self-absorbed centers unwilling to share with compadres on the periphery (Abélès, 2007). Developing economies are subsequently becoming quite vocal in renewing anticolonialist stances, decrying the aggressive expansion of unscrupulous MNCs in labor-rich, safety-poor environments.

Media scholars note that consumerism advances at a hectic pace even in impoverished environments because so-called new and diverse commodities merely repackage time-tested sexist and racist stereotypes. Youth are considered to be the primary consumers of "universalized" or Westernized modes of dress, speech, and music, imbibing these in the same temporal frame all across the world (Walker, 1996; Real, 1996). The question of youth agency assumes prime importance in this context. Jeffrey (2008) documents that approximately 85% of the world youth population, roughly defined as those between 16 and 30 years, live in the tricontinent, that is, Asia, Africa, and Latin America. Within this population emerges a narrow elite group of mainly young men who have achieved a globally competitive education and who can move across elite institutions for highly paid salaried positions. This class of youth is highly desired by Euro-American businesses and innovative headhunting strategies are launched in the spaces where such youth live in the global south. Of these young people, a small percentage is represented by women, who face complex politics of consumption, where the body continues to be the primary site through which desire and vulnerabilities are conveyed (Lukose, 2005). A second stratum of youth, generally between 15 and 19 years, is denied secondary school education; these are more likely to be poorly paid manual laborers in the industry, urban homes, or agricultural fields. The International Labor Organization reports that of this age group, only 35% of women and 59% of men receive payment for their labor and the rest are unpaid laborers (cited in Jeffrey, 2008). In neoliberal societies in developing economies around the world, what is problematic is the rapid increase in the numbers of youth who fall in between: they are educated, yet unemployed. In sprawling bureaucracies like India, middle-class priorities mandate that the child is educated at the very least, to the high school level. Yet in an overpopulated country where the government still maintains considerable control over industries, jobs are few. Writes Jeffrey (2008, p. 743):

> Economic reforms have reduced opportunities for government employment, historically an important source of salaried work for educated young men, and have often failed to generate private-sector jobs. At the same time, economic reform has led to the proliferation of images of success based on prolonged education and white-collar work.

The disconnect between images of success in the mass media and realities on the ground that prevent the "follower-of-rules" from attaining the rewards is an indication of the inherent inequities of an interdependent global system. The current overcrowding in cities and redundant education converge into a "moment of danger" (Venn, 2006, p. 1) for youth, where the intent and strategies of colonialism are very much alive; their forms are more pervasive, subversive, and totalizing. Understanding the development of theory and policy as responses to material conditions primes us to comprehending how youth are constituted within the conditions of globalization in various parts of the world.

As we enter the realm of globalization theory, we see again that we are limited by binary positions. In other words, the active or passive subject construction in media studies resonates with discourse on globalization, which generally follows either the "fragmentation" or "connectivity" trajectory. Under the fragmentation position, individuals are assumed to occupy a borderless world, able to respond to the tantalizing call of multinational products and job opportunities. Under the connectivity position, the individuals follow market imperatives; endless accumulation of capital is the priority, leading to the degeneration of individuality and heritage (Applbaum, 2000). While women's activities and status were markers of development from the 1960s to 1990s, youth practices, especially their consumerism, is an indicator of the extent and impact of globalization (Lukose, 2005). As we can gather from treatments of dichotomic positions in studies on youth, children, and girls, the development of theory and methodology along the two dominant trajectories has pushed aside crucial questions of structural context and its correspondence with the complexities of subjective agency.

Youth in thriving metropolises around the world no doubt occupy a vibrant, hybrid, and bewildering space with a multitude of glamorous products clamoring consumption and promising membership in various desirable communities. The world occupied by youth is often described as fragmented and shifting, with them simultaneously inhabiting multiple worlds *and* feeling isolated (Nuttall, 2008). Globalization as a process that undergirds urban spaces today offers not just economic and political interconnections and interdependencies, but cultural ones as well. Spaces for the expression of dynamic youth identities that are a complex amalgamation of gender, class, religious, ethnic, national, and orientation positions are plentiful, facilitated by the wide variety of local, national, and global television programming available to the average viewer. Neoliberal market discourse positions young consumers as free agents of choice and shapers of their own destinies. The romaticization of agency does not allow much room for an evaluation of what exactly this agency is about or what it actually *achieves*. In the discussion of how globalization is accommodated, the terms subjectivity, agency, and resistance are used without much theoretical rigor. Subjectivity and agency are seen as interchangeable *and* as entirely separate.

The Postcolonial Approach

To make youth studies relevant in globalization, we need a framework that is global in its vision, scrutinizes history, and flags contemporary practices on a temporal, spatial, and ideological map. Postcolonial theory provides such a framework. It fundamentally exposes the "West" and "East" as ideological rather than geographical categories. Edward Said, whose *Orientalism* (1979) was a thorough treatment of ways by which colonized peoples and their lands were manipulated, tagged, and organized for colonizer psychic and material gain, is credited with laying the groundwork for this theory. Gayatri Spivak (1988) and Homi Bhabha (1985) politicized the concerns of Commonwealth Literature and New Literatures in English that emerged in the late 1970s that signified the experiences of countries formerly under the British throne. Postcolonial studies was developed to address the imprints of colonialism on the culture of postcolonial societies. It was conceived as a methodology rather than grand theory, to analyze how colonized societies have adapted imperial discourse, and how these adaptations are similar or shared among colonized societies (Ashcroft, 2001).

Postcolonial refers to the actual material conditions of formerly colonized societies. It pertains to a global condition after colonialism that produced various blocs of allegiance as, for example, the "third world," and to the discourse about these conditions that offers certain epistemological standpoints and orientations to view the global condition (Mongia, 1996; Dirlik, 1996). Literary critics have used the term since the late 1970s to analyze the cultural effects produced by colonization. Postcolonial theory argues that the conflation of the West with master narratives of enlightenment, rationality, scientific objectivity, and progress has legitimized methods of discipline and punishment on the East in the *mission civilatrice*, or civilizing mission. It is the *ideological nature* of this mission, Lazarus (2002) notes, that accounts for its far-reaching and enduring effects. The term postcolonial itself is under much debate, most specifically under question is whether it should be hyphenated, as in post-colonial, or one word, that is, postcolonial. The angst over the hyphen merits a little explanation here because it is relevant to our treatment of youth located in postcolonial countries. Scholars who argue *for* the hyphen state that the term is not abstract. It is flimsy in its applicability like other "post" terms such as post-structuralism or postmodernism. The hyphen has to be present in recognition of the political and psychic trauma that accompanied phases before and after colonization. Those who argue against it state that the hyphen implies a distinction between the period before and after colonialism, as if what came after was indeed a clear break from the ravages of imperial rule. Ashcroft (2001, p. 11) calls the hyphen "a ghost which refuses to be exorcized." Appiah (1996) objects to the "space-clearing gesture" of the hyphen (p. 240), arguing that societies may have gone through colonialism but they may not be *post*colonial in the sense that they have moved beyond coloniality. Ashcroft (2001) writes, which has great relevance to this book,

> Postcolonial discourse is the discourse of the colonized, which begins with colonization and doesn't stop when the colonizers go home. ... Crucially, words such as "post-colonial" do not describe essential forms of experience but forms of talk *about* experience. Once we see the term "post-colonial" as representing a *form of talk* rather than a *form of experience* we will be better organized to see that such talk encompasses a wide and interwoven text of experiences." (p. 13, emphasis in original)

The term is used here without the hyphen, signaling our recognition of the continuity in phases before and after colonialism, and the deep structures that provide that continuity.

Postcolonial scrutiny on the development of world order intersects with the literature on childhood and adolescence. Natives in the colonies were likened to children, requiring discipline and direction by, for example, the Spanish theologians toward the Indians in the Americas in the sixteenth century or by the Europeans toward Africans in the eighteenth and nineteenth centuries. The evolutionary model placed non-Western "primitives" on par with European children and many of these "Age-based relationships continue today to be centrally connected with the racial/ethnic hierarchies developed under colonialism and imperialism, linking race, gender, and age with far-flung global relationships within the intimate economy of the home" (Cole & Durham, 2007, pp. 7–8).

There are several shortcomings of postcolonial theory. First, it could force a myopic view of the past rather than critically engage in the global present (Loomba, 1994). Second, Lazarus (2002) notes, postcolonial theorists often discuss modernity in essentialist terms, as intrinsically Eurocentric. We then are diverted from understanding Marx's crucial point that the globality of capitalism is a historical formation. The focus on just the cultural aspects of colonialism is another downfall of postcolonial studies and prevents a discussion of how systems of capitalism converge, compete, and are facilitated in various contexts. Lazarus (2002) problematizes such foundational works in the field such as Said's *Orientalism* and Mohanty's *Under Western Eyes* (1988) in that they acknowledge the domination and physical restructuring of the "East" by the "West" but do not adequately engage in its economic administration specifically. The terms "West" and "East" then are used as rhetorical terms and become inefficient analytical tools. Chow (2002) poses an important question with reference to global studies, "If all this (attention to the non-Western subject's difference) is testimony to the hegemony enjoyed by Western theory, why are claims of resistance and opposition at the same time so adamant?" (p. 178). What this actually does is reify the attempt in the social sciences to make real an object of knowledge, by defining its difference from the rest. The delineation of difference of the non-Western subject or theory, from Western subject or theory, results in the production of further essentialized notions of identity, resistance, and opposition. The downfall of the "post" framework then, is that, as Chow (2002) puts it (pp. 181–182),

> what lies "outside" (is) recoded as what is inside. ... Be it temporal, ontological, linguistic, or identitarian, noncoincidence can hardly be considered groundbreaking in the global circuits of colonialism and imperialism because the non-Western others are

already, by definition, classified as noncoincident, discontinuous, and fundamentally
different (from populations in the West, from the times and languages of Western
ethnographers).

Renewed here is the argument to move away from dichotomic analyses
and to avoid endless "similar and difference" studies. The ideological nature
of the referentiality of terms is acknowledged; youth subjects are regarded
as representations of ideologies, and as identities that are always incomplete. Postcolonial theory, used appropriately, pushes for analysis beyond the
limitations of polarities and impels scrutiny of the interrelated mechanisms
that perpetuate the power differentials of colonialism. While postcolonial
scholars seek to revive the political edge in their analyses, many use a cultural
Marxism that does not adequately evaluate or deconstruct the ethnocentrism
of cultural Marxism itself where particularism (as also seen in the work of Max
Weber and Emile Durkheim) was relegated to "third world" societies on the
periphery (McCarthy & Logue, 2008). However, while modernity is deployed
as a project with a linear trajectory toward a certain condition of development, the "becoming of the subject" (Venn, 2006, p. 8) is not really the
imperative of globalization. The subject needs to achieve a level or efficiency
that will make her or his labor compatible with a multinational operating system. While the "being" of the subject in modernity has been problematized
by critical scholars, we remain ill-equipped in our analytical tools to address
the "being" in globalization. Chowdhury (2006) calls for the reinsertion of
Marxist critique in the analysis of anything global and "new." This is done by
attention to the continued accumulation of capital and transnational spread,
the expansion of the working class, the proletariat, and the "potential for crisis
that is endemic to capitalism" (p. 132).

This critique is important because it is the keen attention to class and its
texturing by ethnicity, gender, nationality, and so on that expand youth studies to global contexts. Moving beyond linear conceptualizations of youth and
media, and beyond binary analyses of difference that emerged as a response,
we detect a third strain of inquiry. Still in its fledgling stage, struggling to gain
ground, it attempts to draw connections between structure and agency to strike
a balance between the *pessimist and optimist* approaches. Using qualitative,
ethnographic methods, such studies have shown that the media do not play
an all-powerful role in the lives of their consumers, but are a part of a variety
of spheres that influence the teen's sense of place and identity (see also Clark,
2002; Mayer, 2003). These latter studies point to the importance of addressing

the social, economic, and cultural structure within which media and audiences are situated. Popular culture is also, quite specifically, the space where youth express their citizenship (Dolby, 2006).

The book develops this third strain particularly as it is relevant for postcolonial contexts where the examination of the relationship between structure and agency takes on urgency. Rather than herald globalization as a "new" phase, the relevance of Marxism is underscored as important to understand contemporary conditions. Chowdhury (2006) proposes three premises: First, the production and circulation of commodities is essential for the generation of capital. For the endless accumulation of capital, the process of production has to be revolutionized, labor productivity has to be increased. Extraction of capital takes various unethical forms. Second, the increase in capital means the increase in the working class or proletariat. As we see in the case of the expansion of multinationals into the outskirts of Bangalore, India, landless migrant workers pay a high price: "there is a direct correlation between capital accumulation and proletarian misery" (p. 147). Third, a crisis is inevitable. With crisis comes reinvention. It is at this crisis that postcolonial theory can offer assistance.

This book advances critical postcolonial conversations in that it doesn't just occupy an anticolonial stance but also questions what the postcolonial subject stands to gain from neocolonial structures. As youth in particularly developing economies are drawn into the projects of globalization as service providers, we are reminded of the civilizing intent of colonialism where natives came into being only when they put on the garb laid out for them in terms of language, accent, dress, and so on. The important point here is that such a structure can accommodate the colonized subject *as a colonizing subject* as well. Ashcroft (2001) uses the metaphor of the root derived from Gilles Deleuze and Félix Guattari's (1972–1980) rhizome concept, to explain the complex refractory nature of the interactions between colonized subject and colonizer. Rather than regard imperialist and native as separate, we are attuned to the fascinating, even morbid relationships between the two where each sees a future in the other, a dependence fashioned from loathing and adulation. Such a relationship goes far beyond Bhabha's mimicry as resistance and civil disobedience (1985, p. 162). Ashcroft (2001, p. 52) writes,

> ... the inevitable question arises: What is the agency of the subject in this acutely ambivalent rhizomic structure? Clearly, Manichean binarisms became irrelevant in such a model but we still seem to be left with a picture of discursive relations in which the colonized subject cannot be extricated as an entity.

The poverty of dichotomic constructions of active or passive audience, colonizer or colonized subject becomes apparent. We need to advance postcolonial theory so it adequately addresses the opportunistic intent of both sides of the encounter—the success of globalization in all its ethical and unethical manifestations can be understood only from this point of departure. We journey on to the next chapter to uncover how youth subjects live within and use their environments to make meaning and sustain material benefits for themselves.

· 3 ·
TELEVISION AND
TRANSNATIONAL RELEVANCE

On a cool, rainy morning in September 2004, researchers from Munich, New York, Johannesburg, and Bangalore settled down to a rigorous discussion of fieldwork from these diverse locales. We sorted through hefty folders of field notes, transcribed interviews, photographs, and journals, in a drawing room tucked away in a wing of the regal yet austere Tutzing Castle on Starnberger Lake, Germany. Our materials provided evidence of an elaborate, multisited, in-depth exploration of the lives of six teens in each global city. As we talked over steaming cups of tea about our experiences interacting with teens in their living rooms, bedrooms, community centers, and schools, we were struck by how limited we were in using the media as our point of entry to fieldwork. The contexts of the teens were so different, yet they were bound by their need to feel in control of their environments. In the days that followed, we talked about the various ways in which our fieldwork observations came together and pulled apart.

Chapter Two has oriented us to the binary trends in the intersecting fields of youth and media studies. To arrive at a deep, contextually rich understanding of how teens in the four sites of fieldwork experienced changes wrought by urbanization and globalization, we train our eyes to experience, lived realities, and the variety of mediating systems through which teens negotiated their daily lives. We start from *their* ground in our attempt to understand the bodies that are produced in globalization. The 2003–2004 *TV Characters and the Formation of Cultural Identity* project (see note 1) attempted to understand, through qualitative fieldwork, the meanings favorite television characters had for teenagers in very diverse parts of the world. The focus was the strong correspondence between television and teen viewer; the task at hand was to examine the social and cultural context of the teen and then place within this environment, her or his viewing choices. Researchers participating in the study hoped to gain an understanding of how television informed teens' own sense of self and purpose. Fieldwork included the components of ethnography—participant observation, in-depth conversations, and for most of the researchers who either lived or grew up in the very locales as the respondents, long-term immersion in the field. Locales chosen were Johannesburg, South Africa,[6] Bangalore, India,[7] Munich, Germany,[8] and New York.[9] Six teens in each venue participated in the study.[10]

While the primary research question addressed how favorite television characters helped teens negotiate their experiences (McMillin & Fisherkeller, 2008), what also emerged were the intricate inner workings of how the teens came into a sense of agency and the mediating systems that informed this process. Individual reports of teen lives in each locale have been published elsewhere (see F. Bulbulia, 2008; Fisherkeller & Freud, 2006; McMillin, 2006, 2008c). This chapter examines closely the complex contexts each teen was embedded in; the next addresses their perception of place and future in an interconnected world.

Television and Interpellation

The case studies recounted here demonstrate that globalization should be seen as a process that works in resonance with other local structures to set the parameters of what youth aspire to. The subjective agent that emerges should be seen as performative, protean, opportunistic, both combative and noncon-frontational, depending on the interpellatory stance she or he needs to occupy at any given time. Stepping back from television as a point of entry, we are oriented to how class, gender, religion, family structure, and caste distinctions texture teens' sense of personal freedom and limitations. We then see, with clearer vision, how their television choices are in consonance with other ongoing identity projects in their lives (Fisherkeller, 2002). Their choices sometimes reflected the need to stand up to the pressures they faced. For the most part, the choices allowed them to create—in small and nonconfrontational ways—breathing room for themselves. The stories that follow have to be taken as complex interwoven experiences, their meaning has to be derived from a full sense of their contexts and cannot be reduced to any one constitutive moment (Butler, 2000).

Fieldwork observations illustrated Ashcroft's (2001) *interpolation*, which describes the accesses "interpellated" subjects have to a counterdiscursive agency. Ashcroft builds on Althusser's (1971) concept of interpellation, which refers to a denuding force, shaping subjects as the interpellator wishes them to be. In other words, how one answers is shaped by how one is called. A useful example is in the trademark "Come on down!" interpellation of *Wheel of Fortune* that immediately results in a highly animated participant rushing down from the bleachers to the contestants' row, flushed with the realization that she or he has actually been chosen. The interpellation conveys a larger-than-life sense of agency on the contestant and signals to audiences at home that they too could just as easily be called. The mechanics of the show itself and the probabilities of actually going on to win the grand prize remain hidden. With the behind-the-scene engineering magically removed, the show appears seamless in its spontaniety. Television *works* because the mechanics of production are hidden; other mediating systems such as family and education, for example, do not engender agency as efficiently precisely because the teen is privy to the chaos behind the scenes. Ashcroft's (2001) *interpolation* offers an avenue to observe how subjects at the lower end of unequal relations of power intervene and "interject a wide range of counter-discursive tactics into the dominant discourse without asserting a unified anti-imperial intention, or a separate oppositional purity" (p. 47). The case studies revealed that the teens *did* indeed articulate essentialist positions of gender and authority. It is through the intricacies of fieldwork that a sense of how the teens transformed their realities without necessarily engaging in direct conflict is derived. Such a process relates to the rhizomic structure that Ashcroft (2001) discusses, where authority and subject each see a future in the other.

Phases of Fieldwork

The teens who participated in the *TV Characters* study were from diverse backgrounds, selected through social networking and researchers' contacts with educational and community organizations. Fieldwork encompassed three phases during 2003–2004. In the first phase, researchers identified a pool of respondents, typically around 14–15 teenagers, from which 6 were selected for fieldwork. When researchers met respondents individually for the first time (most in their homes with parents present, some in schools or at after-school programs with supervisors at hand), conversations focused on the purpose of the project. The meeting was lengthy, usually spanning the whole afternoon. During this time, the researcher chatted with the teen and her or his family about general interests, family rituals, and television habits. The goal was to get a feel for how the teens interpreted their lives (see Eder & Corsaro, 1999). Typically, the researcher was able to get a tour of the respondent's favorite spaces: the living room, bed room, and so on, and, in some cases, in the neighborhood, such as the playing field or coffee shop. In the case of the New York teens, fieldwork was conducted at an after-school program site. The respondents were asked to begin collecting photographs that best represented their lives (in terms of family, friends, home, school, and social spaces), and to collect materials of their favorite television shows and characters. Each was told that the main focus of the research was to understand the connection between the teens' real world and the world of television.

The second phase was conducted after the respondents had at least two months to collect material about their real and televised worlds. Researchers or their assistants checked in periodically with the teens, answering questions they had along the way. At the end of this period, researchers interviewed the respondents. Semistructured interviews took between two and three hours each where the respondent answered a variety of questions about what it felt like to be a teen, what pressures and victories she or he had faced, and what she or he felt about favorite television characters. Specifically, respondents were asked to describe what their life was like at the age of 14 or 15, what challenges and victories they had experienced, and who they would describe as key figures in their lives and why. Teens also responded to questions about how they would describe their country and neighborhood to a visiting foreigner, and what was particularly gratifying or difficult about their ethnic, religious, class, region and/ or language experiences. Queries regarding hobbies, interests, friends, school, and so on provided a rich range of materials from which to understand respondents' identity locations. In terms of television characters, questions focused on favorite and least favorite shows and characters, and reasons for these choices. Respondents were also asked what type of show they would develop and what range of characters they would include, if they could produce their own show. Finally, respondents commented on how favorite television characters specifically helped them or supported them in their daily lives. All interviews were informal, in-depth conversations during which the researcher took photographs of the respondent and her or his environment, and browsed through the respondent's collected materials.

The third phase included the opportunity for the researcher to seek clarification after a review of all fieldwork materials. Here the researcher returned to each respondent and discussed the construction of teen identity and favorite television character that emerged from it. After fieldwork was conducted, the researchers met at the workshop in Munich in September 2004 to discuss all that was gathered during fieldwork. The sections that follow focus on how local mediating structures flow with media globalization to produce the teen subject.

Place and Performance

Taking as our starting point youth as interpellated subjects, we see that *how* they are called to produce stories about themselves provided varying portrayals of agency. Individuals are active performers of their lives; their actions and performances are processes of negotiations with their cultural environments. Butler (2005) proposes that an individual emerges as individual-with-conscience when asked to explain her or his role in events and processes. Agency is produced in action and narration. Conscience and narration are not isolatable entities in the individual's linear and rational development as theorized within the discourse of Enlightenment. They should be understood within relations of power and produced as part of a structured reality. Interpellation itself is an incomplete process and what one is called can also be what one resists (Butler, 2000). These theoretical insights inform the discussion of teens' representations of themselves.

Reports submitted from Johannesburg, Bangalore, Munich and New York contained quotes from respondents and brief descriptions of family life. For this book, connecting themes in terms of teens' perceptions of agency within the home, among peers, and in the global community are contextualized through the addition of extensive details regarding neighborhood, nation, and television choices in each locale. Synopses of television and film plots and constructions of characters, are integrated with field notes and anecdotes. Television and film production and distribution information is also inserted in certain instances to enable commentary on the "choices" available to the teens and the diversity of role models at their disposal. In general, the teens repeatedly expressed frustration at not being recognized for who they were. Parents saw them as needing supervision and discipline, peers saw them as weaklings to be bullied—very few emerged confident in how they were perceived by people in their social spheres.

A brief description of where the teens lived and what access they had to media would be helpful at the outset. Mapping authority and structure in teen lives has to begin with the city and the public spaces they inhabit. Adolescence as a clearly defined developmental and consumer category is regarded as an invention of urbanization itself. Adolescent lives have to be linked to the visual culture of the city in its advertisements, movie billboards, and scrolling marquees, all of which provide a sense of "the city moving, the city seen synchronically across space" (Wong & McDonogh, 2001, p. 97). Media globalization makes possible the simultaneous world-wide release of such movies as *Spider Man 3* (to use an example from the moment of fieldwork) possibly contributing to a sense of teen *contemporaniety* and *synchronicity* (to be revisited later in this chapter) displacing time, space, and identities (Morley & Robins, 1995; Murdoch, 1996; Barber, 1996; Boyd-Barrett, 1998). Transnational media corporations could overshadow the political and economic authority of the nation-state (Appadurai, 1996), tossing its developmentalist goals aside (Aksoy & Robins, 1992) for consumerist ones, enhancing the profitability of media corporations anchored in the United States, Great Britain, and Japan (Morley & Robins, 1995). Street children reportedly are familiar with global brand names like Nike™ and Coca Cola™ (Diversi, 2006) and teenagers show increased materialistic interests (Verma & Saraswathi, 2002). Robust television formats such as the soap opera, game show, variety show, and anchored music countdowns reify patriarchal and capitalist ideologies. It is essential as we enter the world of the teens that we understand that although their media environments brought them diversity of programming, each country's television system was integrated with structures of political power. Varying degrees of commercialism notwithstanding, the system, taken as a whole, worked within the imperatives of the nation-state. Their media practices then are not necessarily in opposition to the local and in compliance with the global. In fact, as Ginsburg, Abu-Lughod, and Larkin (2002) in their very useful introduction to the anthology *Media Worlds* discuss,

> ... oppositional logics are insufficient for grasping media practices; rather, our models must allow for the simultaneity of hegemonic and anti-hegemonic effects as we examine how "technologies of power" are created and contested within intimate institutional cultures, shaped by ideologies ranging from public service to audience appeal, to aesthetics, to political empowerment. (p. 23)

In the television environments of South Africa, India, Germany, and the United States, we see a complex amalgamation of national networks, private local networks, and foreign satellite networks, each carrying a further variety of indigenous, coproduced, and foreign programs.

The mission of integration is the challenge taken up by mass media in South Africa still emerging from 300 years under the racist apartheid regime. Zegeye and Harris (2003) document that the nation's 44 million people comprise multiple ethnic groups such as the Nguni people (including Zulu, Xhosa, and Swazi who account for two-thirds of the population); the Sotho-Tswana (including Southern, Northern, and Western Sotho); the Tsonga; the Venda; the Afrikaners; the English; the Coloreds; and the Indians. The nation also includes immigrants from other parts of Africa, Europe, and Asia, and from the Khoi and San ethnic groups. In terms of proportion, Africans comprise 76.7%, Whites 10.9%, Coloreds 8.9%, and Indians/Asians, 2.6% of the population. With the overthrow of the apartheid government in 1994, the official languages listed in the new nation's constitution were: Afrikaans, English, isiNdebele, isiXhosa, isiZulu, Sepedi, Sesotho, Setswanam siswati, Tshivenda, and Xitsonga. Christianity is the majority religion (80%) while other dominant ones are Hinduism, Islam, and Judaism. Discrepancies in income brackets are dramatic. During the 1990s, 60% of the black population was poor compared to 1% of Whites. The top income bracket was represented by 65% Whites, 45% Indians, 17% Coloreds, and 10% Blacks. Unemployment stayed at 40% with crime rates one of the highest in the world (Jacobs, 2002).

Changes in the government brought about changes in the media as well. President Thabo Mbeki's *African Renaissance* sought to reinvent an image of Africa that was progressive and modern (Ahluwahlia, 2003). The 1999 Broadcasting Act underlined the role of the media as educator, national integrator, and community developer. Radio stations received a boost in the latter 1990s with the African National Congress' deregulation of the medium. The South African Broadcasting Corporation (SABC) now operates three national television networks, two pay-TV channels, and Bop TV (a music channel). A foreign satellite channel, TV Africa, broadcasts in English and French to around 26 countries in the continent. The commercial network e.tv competes with SABC and broadcasts U.S. and British programs.

The primary goals of the SABC are to de-essentialize ethnic categories that facilitated the violent rule of the apartheid government and privilege difference as an expression of identity, not ability (Zegeye & Harris, 2003). However, Dolby (2006) writes that global popular culture in South Africa more often reinforces racial divides even as it provides more spaces for connections and changes in racial alliances. Nuttall (2008) summarizes that the current environment

> ... can be characterized by heterogeneity, by a fracturing of the contemporary moment in South Africa, now a place that is moving in multiple and unforeseen directions, splintering into manifold forms of desegregation and resegregation, shaped, increasingly by media cultures and cultures of consumption. (p. 153)

The SABC still struggles to define its goals and role as an independent service public broadcaster.

In Johannesburg, 15-year-olds Rabia, Luke, Nina and 14-year-olds Themba, Keenan, and Kgomotso could receive a wide variety of television channels through satellite and dish, a product of the newly commercialized environment. They could enjoy music and soaps on radio (Strelitz, 2003), most prominently through YFM, created in 1996 by the SABC with stipulations that it should be 80% black owned and 50% staffed by women. The station has popularized *kwaito,* a local music genre that combines *toyi-toyi* (protest chanting and dancing) with a bubble gum pop beat and traces of hip-hop (Nuttall, 2008). The competitive environment because of deregulation meant that the SABC had to step up its commercial character to stay ahead of private commercialized radio stations and the new free-to-air television channel, e.tv. As such, the network finds it challenging to meet its goals of national integration and development while creating programs that have mass appeal (Tomaselli & Teer-Tomaselli, 2003; Barnett, 2004). The SABC faces criticisms that it is focused on a lucrative black youth market; however, it maintains its leader status and its pedagogical function with the broadcast of such programs as *Soul City* and *Khululeka* (N. Bulbulia, 1998).

Soul City, started in 1992, is an edutainment package targeted to low-income black South Africans. It consists of a 30-minute weekly drama dealing with issues of women's health, illiteracy, and development; child abuse, nutrition, and diseases; and sexuality and HIV/AIDS awareness. Such messages are also transmitted in 15-minute daily serials in the Zulu, Xhosa, and Sotho languages and in serialized 36-page booklets in newspapers. *Soul City* has evolved into *Soul City:* Institute for Health and Development Communication (SC: IHDC) and now includes a special division addressing the needs of 8–12-year-olds through its *Soul Buddyz. Buddyz on the Move* is a relatively new addition that portrays the work of clubs in community activism especially related to youth issues. *Soul City* reportedly reaches 79% of the South African population while *Soul Buddyz* reaches 68% of children. The program includes careful monitoring of audience response and attempts to make programs as relevant and realistic to its target viewers as possible (Usdin, 2005). As another example, *Yizo Yizo* (The Way It Is) on SABC1 in the *tsotsitaal* vernacular is a popular soap in the edutainment telenovela tradition set in the fictional township Supatsela High School. The series targeted issues such as violence, rape, drug abuse, and sexual harassment (Barnett, 2004).

Indian television history is quite similar to that of South Africa's, in that the national television network was used as an articulator of national integrationist goals as the country struggled to develop its postcolonial character. In fact, Zegeye and Harris (2003, p. 8) draw strong connections between postapartheid South Africa and postcolonial nations in their focus on antiracism and efforts to recognize *difference* to move away from damning constructions of singularity and fixed identities. While further details of the Indian television environment will be described in the next chapter, at this point, it is useful to note that Doordarshan—India's state-sponsored network—was used, since its first telecast in 1959, to promote images of a prospering and culturally diverse nation. Early broadcasts were primarily about agricultural innovations, regional dances and songs, and the struggle for independence. Telenovelas such as *Hum Log* were designed to bring awareness of domestic abuse, alcoholism, and family planning to the Indian people (Singhal & Rogers, 2001). Broadcasts were subsequently engineered for political purposes, privileging Hindu fundamentalist notions of caste hierarchy and cultural purity (Mitra, 1993; Mankekar, 1999; Rajagopal, 2001). India's 1991 economic liberalization policy coincided with the influx of foreign satellite channels, most notably, Star TV. Indian teens, 14-year-olds Zohrab, Teja, Anujoth, and Ambika and 15-year-olds Ashok and Shubha were exposed to a thriving television environment. The teens each received the national Doordarshan network channels and, based on where they lived, an assortment of private vernacular language channels such as the Telugu language Eenadu, Kannada language Udaya TV, and Malayalam language Asianet. Urban teens Zohrab, Teja, Anujoth, and Ashok received Rupert Murdoch's Star TV network (which includes such channels as Star Plus, Star Movies, and Star Sports). Rural teens Ambika and Shubha received vernacular channels—a factor of clientele interests served by a local head end operator. Examples of top-rated serials were Hindi language dramas such as *Jassi Jaissi Koi Nahin* (There Is Nobody Quite Like Jassi, the Indian version of *Ugly Betty* on Sony ET) and *Kyunki Saas Bhi Kabhi Bahu Thi* (Because the Mother-in-Law Was Once a Daughter-in-Law on Star Plus). Urban teens could also watch American sitcoms such as *Caroline in the City, Friends,* and *The Simpsons* on Star World, while urban and rural teens could receive Kannada language dramas such as *Mangalya* (Marriage) and *Kumkuma Bhagya* (The Blessing of Being Married) on Udaya TV.

In Munich and its outlying suburbs, 14-year-olds Marian, Christian, Nazan, and Verena and 15-year-olds Pascal and Martina received such channels as Russia's International ORT, the Czech TV Puls, Norway's NRK International, Germany's Deutsche Welle, the Portuguese RTP Internacional, and the Irish Tara TV with their cable subscriptions. This is an outcome of the 1991 European Union's (EU) *Television without Frontiers Directive* (TVWF), which decreed that member states could not obstruct broadcasts from member states. Some believe this will result in a declining sense of national identity and crucial state support for ethnic programming (Aksoy & Robins, 1992). Others contend that the EU is able to meet the challenges of a globalizing world through such an arrangement. Some examples of foreign channels reaching European audiences because of the policy are Korea's Korean Arirang channel, Japan's JSTV, the satellite arm of the Japanese public broadcaster NHK, and the Indian Zee TV channels such as Zee TV, Zee Music, and Zee Cinema (Chalaby, 2005). The TVWF became the *Audiovisual Media Services Directive* (AVMS) in 2007, which—in a nutshell—extends responsibilities of information, education, and entertainment to nonlinear services as well such as video-on-demand. It also provides greater flexibility in regulations to accommodate greater commercialization.[11] Through cable operators Primacom, Tele Columbus, and Kabel Deutschland (the latter the only cable operator for most of Bavaria), around 45% of Germans have cable, around 45% have dish, and less than 10% either rely on terrestrial transmissions or don't own a television set.

Much has been written about television in the United States and its relevance and influence worldwide (see, for example, Herman & McChesney, 2003). In New York, 15-year-olds Tia, KD Ann, Shawanna, Dennis, and Luis and 14-year-old Ronald could access a wide variety of programming, both network and cable. Like the Indian teens, the channels available to them depended on their neighborhoods and subscriptions. Network channels are: ABC, NBC, CBS, and the Fox-owned and operated WNYW and WWOR channels. PBS programming is provided through the public television station WNET. New York City audiences receive Spanish-language programming through affiliates of Univision and Telemundo. Cable packages include the HBO, Disney, Showtime, Encore, and Starz array of channels, to name but a few options.

As we shall see in the next section, vast differences in agency were articulated by teens. Their stories are not provided here to privilege one response over another, but to show explicitly, how postcolonial condition, socioeconomic class, and birth order all coalesced to provide a sense of agency. Certain aspects drew them together—their developmental concerns, their roles and responsibilities within the family, and the pressures and victories they faced in school. In the narratives that ensue, we detect the scaffolding of a world order that lies beneath.

Stark Conditions, Activist Choices

Teens living in stark poverty, like 14-year-olds Themba and Kgomotso in the Zevenfontein settlement in Johannesburg, and 14-year-old Ambika and 15-year-old Shubha,[12] living in the outlying villages of Nagundanahalli and Immadehalli of Bangalore, conveyed a passion to succeed that was quite unlike what was expressed by the other participants of the study. As citizens on the outskirts of gentrification efforts, they had to make way for the rising new middle class, a documented trend in globalizing cities (Beng-Huat, 2000). While Themba and Kgomotso were still awaiting improvements to their neighborhoods under the new South Africa, Shubha and Ambika were all too aware of the politics of spatial purification that refers to "middle-class claims over public spaces and a corresponding movement to cleanse such spaces of the poor and working classes" (Fernandes, 2000, p. 2416).

We begin with the teens in Zevenfontein, which is a 10,000-strong informal settlement with a high rate of HIV. It lacks basic amenities such as water, electricity, and sewage management. The zinc and tin shacks offer its residents little protection from the heat and cold (F. Bulbulia, 2004). As with any country ravaged by segregatory politics, the impoverished Zevenfontein borders the very exclusive Dainfern Village. Barbed wires, high walls, and security cameras maintain the demarcation between the very rich and very poor. Under the 1950s Group Areas Act, residential areas such as in Zevenfontein were established by the Afrikaner Nationalists to separate people based on skin color and to manage the ownership and occupation of land. Such separatist policies resulted in "blacks only" and "whites only" zones, providing the white government with total control over black populations. The 1954 Native Resettlement Act allowed the apartheid government to uproot black people from urban spaces and relocate them to so-called township spaces to ensure the "whiteness" of the city. Townships and informal settlements are associated with the impoverished black underclass, a place of violence and criminal behavior, requiring harsh and swift discipline (Ellapen, 2007).

In such a place lived Kgomotso—of Pedi ethnicity—with her mother and two siblings; and Themba, with 10 other family members (F. Bulbulia, 2008). Both children were worried about their mothers who worked hard to keep the family afloat after the fathers left. Fass (2008) discusses that in many societies in the twenty-first century, women are forced to travel for work, sometimes leaving children in the care of extended family and even strangers, to be able to provide for a better economic life for all. While Fass' comments are more directly relevant to immigrant laborers who leave homelands for much better prospects, she makes an important point that the effects of such arrangements on children are not adequately studied. For the two respondents from Zevenfontein, education was a lifeline out of poverty. Kgomotso was determined to finish high school so she could get a job and support the family. Her mother worked as a housemaid as did Themba's. These mothers were among the countless women who often left families and children in rural areas to live in the informal settlements and earn a living as domestic workers.

Kgomotso took care of her siblings, bathing and feeding them, and getting them ready for school. Themba fetched water and did the dishes every evening. His father had left the family when Themba was a baby, and he himself was being raised by his older sister. Themba and Kgomotso had a strong network of friends who shared their circumstances. Both wanted to help those less fortunate and were members of a local youth group run by social worker Ma Jennifer, called *Survivours*. Through this group, they engaged in a variety of activities such as Zulu dancing, painting, organic gardening, and media production. The organic gardening project was started in 2002 as part of the UN World Summit on Sustainable Development (WSSD). This community activity as well as a beautification project where members helped paint the outsides of the shacks gave them a sense of belonging and responsibility. The teens worked with others in the settlement to paint stories on pieces of fabric that were then incorporated into clothing, cushion covers, bedspreads, and so on. Funds from the sale of these items paid for important needs such as books, school uniforms, and fees. Kgomotso participated in an Internet project called *Open the Box* that facilitated communication among children of five southern African countries. The project was particularly exciting for Kgomotso because she loved computers, was interested in meeting people from other countries, and was keen on a career in travel and tourism.

Themba and Kgomotso had erratic electricity, so their television watching was limited to what could be received through battery-operated generators. *Zola 7*—a reality program—was Kgomotso's favorite particularly because the protagonist, Zola (portrayed by Bonginkosi Dlamini), helped disadvantaged people achieve their dreams. Zola himself had been brought up in the Soweto settlement. He was also a singer of *kwaito* music that the teens loved. *Kwaito*, derived from the 1950s gangster group "Amakwaito" and derived from the Afrikaans word, "kwaai" meaning angry, is now synonymous with resistance and local expression. *Kwaito* music emerged in the early 1990s, associated with the antiapartheid sentiment. It is chanted or shouted, usually by males, and incorporates deep bass with a slower tempo than house music in urban streets in the United States, for example.[13] SABC1's youth channel, YoTV, broadcast a wide variety of programs that Kgomotso enjoyed. Topics ranged anywhere from overcoming challenges (*Big Breakfast*) to traveling across the country (*Yo Trip*). Through her media production training with *Survivours*, she could critique production and interview techniques. Because her leisure time was so limited, Kgomotso's television watching was quite purposeful; she used it as a source of information on life strategies. Themba also watched Yo TV and liked to emulate the confident and respectful anchor, Sipho. *Jozi Street*, a local version of *NYPD Blue*, made Themba hopeful that crime would be reduced in his neighborhood (F. Bulbulia, 2004).

Like the two teens in Johannesburg, Shubha and Ambika, both 10th grade students of the Immadehalli High School on the outskirts of Bangalore, India, lived in poverty. Shubha, a first generation learner, belonged to the low-caste flower-seller community. Her father (educated until the 5th grade) was a landless laborer and his income varied with the farming jobs he was able to get. Her mother earned around Rs. 1000 (USD 22) a month as a sweatshop laborer. Shubha and her family often ate just one meal a day. Her mother's steady income helped support her schooling and provided the household rent (Rs. 400 or USD 9 per month). Shubha wanted to work as a skilled laborer in the Industrial Training Institute (ITI) and did not want to get married before she was 25 years old. Her mother wanted her to finish high school and then work in the same sweatshop to help with household expenses. Shubha's feelings of insecurity about her future have to be placed within the context of her elder sister's recent marriage, which (costing Rs. 13,000 or USD 295) plunged the family into deeper debt than before. Shubha suffered from severe migraines but the family was too poor to treat the condition.

Ambika was in a complex bind. Although of the somewhat affluent, agricultural Gowda caste, her family was in financial ruin because of the ongoing drought that had severely limited their crop yield. It was beneath their dignity for her father to seek work or for her mother to work outside the home. Ambika understood she could not take on the stresses of her parents, yet she had to help them by studying hard and getting a job as soon as she graduated. At the same time, she was angry they could not provide a more secure environment and focus on her needs as a growing child.

Both Shubha and Ambika had a keen sense of activism, like Themba and Kgomotso. Shubha spoke strongly about becoming an advocate for women and children. She raged about child abuse and the arrogance of men and their harassment of women in her village. She wanted to be involved in development projects to help the poor and eradicate the stereotype that they were dirty and unintelligent. Caste distinctions were pure evil, she said. She was proud to be from the farming community. We enter into Shubha's narration about farm labor, a woman's place in society, and the difficulty in fighting for the dignity of each. She said:

> For me, working in the farm is *so* important, the whole *nation* stands on the backs of bending farmers. Only if the farmer grows food can the whole nation *eat*. If the farmer has no food, how can people live? How much ever (the farmer) bends that's how the nation grows, but the farmer *also* has to progress.

She was struck by the irony that while the nation as a whole grew rich, those who fed it were below the poverty line. Shubha and Ambika's television choices reflected their passions. Shubha loved patriotic serials and watched anything that had to do with social justice. She said:

> I first watch serials about the nation ... then those about God, and about the mother ... all these I like ... If (there is a movie) about empower(ing) women, if there are serials like that, whatever my mother says, how much ever work I have, first as soon as I come (home), I watch ... Yes it will definitely help us. Women's rights, children's rights, we *need* (them). *Especially* children's rights we *absolutely* need (them) *especially* in this age.

Shubha's favorite television character was Kannada actresss Bhavyashree because of her strong and quiet personality: "She doesn't talk to anyone. Whatever anyone says, she just holds it in." Here Shubha paused, overcome emotionally. She said she was surprised at herself, and realized through her descriptions of Bhavyashree, she was actually talking about herself:

If *her* mother says anything bad to her, she gets angry. Now if *my* mother says anything bad to me, I get so angry and in the same way if her mother tells her anything bad she gets very angry. ... If you have money everyone comes to you. If you don't have money nobody comes to you. She is *very* silent and even if her mother's house (*thavarumane*) hurts her she stays silent.

Television provided her lessons for the future: "I watch on TV whatever there is about a woman, whatever it is. After watching that, if in the future anything similar to that happens to me, then I too feel I should do that." Ambika also provided a direct connection between her television hero, a versatile Kannada and Tamil language action and romantic lead, and herself: "Ravichandra, like me, does not keep anything in his heart. He is very direct and says everything directly. That's why I like him and his directness."

Both Shubha and Ambika enjoyed regional language variety programs such as the Telugu language *Once More Please* (on the Eenadu Channel) and wished the same program could be cloned on the Kannada language Udaya TV. Ambika believed television transformed her life: "After watching TV I learn(ed) about what a woman goes through and endures and I learn that I too should endure like that. I *too* should bring my parents a good name. That's how I feel."

What is offered here is just a very small view into some aspects of the lives of Themba, Kgomotso, Shubha, and Ambika. From our excursions into their worlds and from experiencing with them such realities as erratic electric and water supply and uneven television broadcasts, we see that their choice of favorite characters is not random. Their involvement in television narratives and certain celebrities' lives was because the latter provided them a relevance and possibility beyond what they could see in tangible terms in their own surroundings. They each had very little time to watch television, with evenings being taken up with a variety of mandatory activities such as feeding and putting siblings to bed (Kgomotso and Themba), helping with cooking and housekeeping (Ambika), as well as cleaning the cattle shed (Shubha).

Lutz et al. (2001) document that population increases will be felt most in the already overcrowded, poor areas of the world such as Latin America, Southeast Asia, South Asia, the Middle East, and Africa (cited in R.W. Larson, 2002). In India, by 2020, the demand for grains is expected to increase by 65%. The population in African countries is expected to increase despite HIV-AIDS. Middle-class adolescents in these countries then will continue to fight for their place within the struggle for adequate nutrition and education (R. W. Larson, 2002).

The experience of perhaps growing up too soon, or taking on adult roles and responsibilities in their mid-teens was echoed in the lives of several teens in New York and Munich. And so we move on to our conversations and observations with 15-year-olds KD Ann and Shawanna in New York and 14-year-old Verena in Munich. These teens said they felt grounded within their close-knit families, yet pressured with the burden of caring for siblings, balancing school, and reconciling feelings of resentment toward their absent fathers.

Parenting Siblings and Raising Selves

Shawanna, a positive, smiling teen from a low-income African American family, believed that "…it's all how you take it, how you take things in life. You make a bad thing into a good thing. … You have to look at the upside of things. I could have been dead but I'm here." She was stressed out from balancing school with household work that included taking care of her younger sisters. If they misbehaved, she was blamed. It seemed unfair to her that her 12-year-old brother did not take on any responsibility and in fact had the same curfew of 7 p.m. as she did. Education was very important to her. Like the teens in the previous section, she saw her goal to go to medical school as a lifeline: "I want to go somewhere in my life, and not be like my mother," she claimed. She loved watching dramas on television because "there is a lot of drama in my family." She could relate to the fast-paced humor in sitcoms like *Everybody Loves Raymond* (CBS) and *Steve Harvey* (WB). *7th Heaven* (WB) was a top choice because "it's about family problems and they help other people … they talk about everything. There is everything in it. It reminds you of real life and it doesn't seem phony like reality shows." Fisherkeller (2004) discussed that *Gilmore Girls'* (WB) Lorelei Gilmore was Shawanna's favorite because she was a "friend mom" to her daughter. Television was an activity she shared with her grandmother and they discussed programs together.

KD Ann, also African American and from a low-income background, was the oldest of six siblings. Her father lived in Jamaica, leaving KD Ann to take on the role of surrogate parent within the household. She wished she didn't have to keep initiating phone calls to her father—she longed for him to call her. Her mother served as her role model and despite pressure from friends to smoke or do drugs, KD Ann believed in staying clean and maintaining her individuality. She was attentive to how she dressed and wanted to look smart for her own self, not to attract boys. She hoped to be an entrepreneur someday. Television watching, for around 3–4 hours every night, was a family ritual. Reality shows such as *Amazing Race* (CBS), *The Apprentice* (NBC), and *Survivor* (CBS) were everyone's top choices because they were "about regular stuff, so there is suspense and you just wait for it … it's just happening or it's about things that are going to happen." Of particular interest to KD Ann was *Amazing Race*. She admired Chip and Kim (Season 5), the only African American couple on the show. They provided important lessons for KD Ann: "if someone betrays them, they just move on. They put behind them everything that happened in the past" (Fisherkeller, 2004).

While both Shawanna and KD Ann considered their inner strength and maternal support to be key to advancing their futures, 14-year-old Verena—living in the eastern, rural Waldtrudering district of Munich—who also helped her divorced mother by caring for her siblings, knew that her affluent family would take care of her future plans. Verena's parents were medical doctors and she lived with her 13- and 10-year-old brothers and her mother in an upper-middle-class neighborhood. Yet her sense of vulnerability stemmed from having to step up and help her mother run the house after her father left. This also gave her a sense of direction and motivation to seek a stable life, as it did for Shawanna and KD Ann.

Affluent Lives, Personal Challenges

Verena's parents divorced when she was just six. Her father, a gynecologist, lived in the neighborhood to help take care of the children. Verena was scornful of his presence, recalling that she fell quite ill after the divorce; she believed her father felt no remorse. She related that her father had cheated on her mother and continued denying it despite the evidence. Ultimately, it was her father who left her mother even though her mother was willing to try again. She was bewildered at her mother's position and angry with her father:

> … my father is not a role model for me that I would use to find my own way because he did, well let's say, he did a lot of things wrong. Well he hurt us, he hurt my mother very much and he in fact changed everything in our life totally. I take my mother as a role model because I want to be like her in the future because she was strong enough to survive the divorce and to bring up all the three children by herself and she also had a full time job to do. I find that admirable. Well my mother is indeed one of my role models for sure.

The divorce transformed her into a serious, responsible teen. Like Shawanna in New York, she wanted to make the best of a bad situation. She said,

> There are also children whose parents got divorced who simply lean back in defiance and who are not interested in anything any longer. I however got up and simply took care of my siblings and I also helped my mother and she well told me, well she showed me that one has to be strong when things go wrong and that one has to get on one's feet also when the situation is not that great.

The experience made her feel vulnerable and fearful of losing other dear things in life. She worried that she would lose other family members and fail at school (Strohmaier & Lakhotia, 2004). Like KD Ann, she also faced immense peer pressure to look cool, act hip, and be acceptable within cliques. A way to alleviate these fears, for her, was to seek a stable life partner, "someone who is *always* there for me, when I am doing bad for example. Where you can *always* go to, and also that I am always in close contact with my mother and also with my father." Verena longed to be 18, to be free, and not have to listen to her parents' rules. She understood that her mother in particular knew what was best for her, but she wanted to be treated as an adult, capable of making her own decisions. She described herself as "chaotic and stubborn." With around €25 a month allowance supplemented by income from babysitting when needed, Verena was rarely strapped for cash. During the summer, she spent three weeks at sea with her father and brothers, while her mother vacationed with her boyfriend (who also had an apartment in their neighborhood) in Italy. She often traveled to Vienna with her mother to visit the boyfriend's family.

Verena loved reality shows, particularly *Berlin, Berlin*, which ran from 2002 to 2005 on Das Erste, the public TV network. The lead character Lolle (played by Felicitas Woll), who was clumsy, impulsive, and funny, was quite like herself, Verena said. Lolle showed her "that one should not take it all that seriously (laughs), that one should also give in, and that one should also understand to keep one's life a bit more in a proper order" (Strohmaier & Lakhotia, 2004). Like Shawanna and KD Ann, Verena loved shopping, dancing, listening to music and hanging out with friends. The affluence of her family positioned her in a realm of possibilities that the New York teens could only dream about. Despite failing grades, Verena was quite confident about going to university and studying psychology. This was a stark contrast to Shawanna and KD Ann, who had to rely on their own efforts to take them through to their dreams of higher education.

In the example of 14-year-old Rabia, an upper-income teen in Johannesburg, we see further how income level and family support could bolster a teen's sense of agency even with an absent father. Feelings of frustration and vulnerability remained, but the avenues for development multiplied with the support of other mediating systems. Rabia helped take care of her three younger siblings while her mother worked late. But her involvement with a youth media production group and her interactions with her grandparents who lived with her family brought forth a different sense of agency, perhaps more clearly articulated, than Shawanna and KD Ann.

Rabia, a South African of East Indian heritage, is the eldest of three sisters. Her maternal grandparents lived with them in the Mayfair suburb of the city. Mayfair itself, during the apartheid regime's 1950 Group Areas Act (41) that excluded nonwhites from developed areas and segregated living areas by race, was a "poor white suburb" for railway workers speaking Afrikaans. Mayfair transitioned to a "grey area" in the early 1990s after apartheid when Indian traders who had been hitherto cordoned to Lenasia—around 60 km from their business centers in Johannesburg—began moving to the suburb. Mayfair real estate skyrocketed as white Afrikaners realized the Indian traders would pay dearly to live close to their businesses. Currently the area boasts a number of mosques and temples and very expensive homes that rival white suburbs. Its move from predominantly white to mixed populations has also resulted in a decline in its desirability as a neighborhood for whites; it is currently populated by Muslim Africans and Muslim Indians (like Rabia), and is a combination of very expensive and very poor properties. As in most of Johannesburg, rates of drug trafficking and crime are high.

The inclusion of Rabia's grandparents in the household was not an easy transition. She now had to share her bedroom, follow their rules when her mother was at work, behave conservatively, and perform traditional Islamic rituals. Her mother's two failed marriages pushed Rabia to excel at school and gave her a maturity beyond her years. She took care of her sisters while her mother worked long hours, supplementing her income by catering Indian delicacies to neighborhood clients. Rabia's hobbies were swimming, reading, and listening to music. Like Ambika, Shubha, Kgomotso, and Themba, Rabia had an activist streak, wanting to surge beyond the helplessness she felt under her mother's efforts to keep the family afloat. She was involved with the Children and Broadcasting Foundation for Africa (CBFA) where she had received training in media production. Her team had helped produce such televised documentaries as *The Girl Child, HIV-AIDS in Africa, Poverty in Africa,* and *Leadership in Africa.* Her most recent project included five-minute shorts on sustainable development in informal settlements, aired across Africa during the 2002 UN Summit on Sustainable Development (WSSD). Rabia's participation in this group brought her confidence and hope: she had attended the World Summits on Media for Children in venues such as Greece (2001) and Brazil (2004). As a member of the Afrika Cultural Centre (an NGO) where she worked on an HIV-AIDS book for children, she had visited New York to participate in the UN Special Session on Children. Her position on the board of the children's arm of the Nelson Mandela Children's Fund provided her an experience unusual for youth her age—the ability to actually see her decisions through to action. The path to her desired career in media production or law or politics seemed to have already begun. Within that context, her comments about self and body image take on authoritative subjectivity:

> ... When I think of me being a woman, I get this feeling of euphoria, that I am one of those who has been through a process of being through a lot of pain and a lot of struggle and coming out, probably (a) better (person). ...

She took it for granted that she would grow up to care for her mother. She was not interested in dating just yet because of her age, but more because of her fear of contracting HIV-AIDS.

Rabia's television choices were more akin to Shubha and Ambika's: she sought out news and current affairs programs such as SABC's *Special Assignment* and e.tv's *3rd Degree*. Although she did enjoy animated shows and soap operas (mostly watched while babysitting her siblings), she more often stayed with the news channels because she wanted to learn the skills of a news anchor. She admired *3rd Degree's* Debora Patta, a veteran journalist who grills politicians and celebrities on a variety of issues, often incurring the wrath of conservatives. Rabia occasionally watched *Take 5* (on SABC1 and produced by 24 Frames, comprised of young South Africans). Although a teen magazine program, she said she could not relate to it because "the presenters are typical Township black people, the lingo (language) is typically black and I don't really understand all of it (but) ... it helps me sometimes with school projects because of OBE (Outcome Based Education)." It should be noted here that OBE is a controversial educational method. It is based on behavioral learning premises and standardized outcomes based on specific resources available to the students. Primary criticisms are that it is ahistorical and relegates to secondary status, indigenous knowledge systems and traditional education (Jansen, 1998). OBE sits uneasily with critical revisions in postapartheid curriculum that, Prinsloo and Janks (2002) discuss, focus on oral and aural skills as well as literacy skills. e.tv's *Backstage*,[14] a local 30-minute soap based on the American movie, *Fame*, found an ardent fan in Rabia—its music, dance, and its portrayal of a variety of issues such as teen conflicts, racism, sexism were highly relevant to her. She often enacted scenes in her room. She said it helped her learn:

> How young people cope with their school lives, balancing their school lives and their social lives, which is something I find a bit of a problem—because trying to integrate everything, when to go out with your friends, what is appropriate behavior—I am a Muslim girl so I have to bring my religious life in to the situation—certain things that they do might influence my life. ...

The rich variety of characters on *Backstage* helped Rabia cope with her multiple worlds. Like Natasha, an Afrikaner character from Bloemfontein who sought work in Johannesburg, Rabia learned how to adapt; she dreamed of making it big like the protagonist who had just started a modeling career. Kaybee, another character, was a talented musician; like her, Rabia wanted to be generous and ready to help at any time (F. Bulbulia, 2004).

Far away in Bangalore, with striking similarities in the ways in which Rabia talked about her dreams and competencies, was 14-year-old Anujoth. Although of a secure two-parent, upper-income home and indulged as an only child, Anujoth's conservative background, and lived religious experience carved an agency quite similar to Rabia's. Her father's heart attack and her nervous mother urged Anujoth to grow up quickly, standing shoulder-to-shoulder with her parents in household decisions. Anujoth professed a staunch loyalty to her family like all the other teens discussed so far, and believed the "world is literally at my feet!" A Sikh Punjabi, Anujoth was an all-round achiever in the 10th grade of National Public School (NPS), Bangalore. Her father was an aeronautic engineer and her mother a housewife. Anujoth's school is known for its rigorous standards and its brilliant students, who routinely secure the top ranks in the 10th grade national CBSE examinations. Anujoth's achievements in science merited her a Science Secretary badge (of the Science Association) in the 9th grade and her skill in writing (she regularly contributed literary, science, and math articles for the school newspaper) merited the Literary President badge (for the Literary Association). Although somewhat introverted, Anujoth quickly indicated this was because she thought carefully before she spoke, it was not because of a lack of confidence. She was focused on doing well in her 10th grade exams but wanted to stay away from the traditional fields of engineering or medicine that Indian youth are shepherded into. She aspired instead to a career in journalism. Anujoth's secure world was shattered in 2003 when her father suffered a heart attack on the last day of her 8th grade exam. Her father was rushed to the hospital at 5:30 in the morning. Anujoth went to school and excelled in the final paper, urged by her mother to see past the current situation into her future. Through that performance, she believed she anchored her mother and gave her the courage to endure a frightening experience. Speaking of the family's ordeal, Anujoth said:

> That's when I saw this real philosophical side of mine and I wrote this poem, Man and His Reality (about) how everyone, like we're just puppets in the hand of God and it's like staged. It's like this poem I was really inspired by when I read (Shakespeare's) Seven Ages (of Man), where it starts off with "All the world's a stage and all of us just its players," about how we just come play our parts and go, so it really got (to) the other (philosophical) side of me.

The experience transformed Anujoth into her mother's caretaker as well. The latter had become increasingly anxious and pessimistic, relying on her daughter to assure her that everything would be alright. Anujoth loved watching television. She was as cricket-crazed as her parents and other families in the neighborhood. Her crush was Irfan Pathan, a 19-year-old prodigy, and her journal entries and scrapbook were full of clippings and photographs of him. Like most of the teens in South Africa and India in this study, Anujoth preferred vernacular language serials and cricket matches. Her preferences were for the conservative Hindi language soap, *Kyunki Saas Bhi Kabhi Bahu Thi* that starred her favorite actress, Smriti Irani. She said:

> They are quite interesting (but) ultimately they make a muddle of your brains. ... It is a very *stupid* logic behind all those serials, *still* I sit and watch it. I don't know why ... *Kyunki Saas Bhi Kabhi Bahu Thi* is a huge family with 15,431 members and they just keep introducing new characters and then they just have to elaborate on everyone's life so the serial continues for 10 years. Secondly there are misunderstandings, which never get cleared. So these are two logics [sic] behind any such kind of a serial. Now because there are various characters like at one time they emphasize one couple or something of that sort. So because I like a particular couple, I watch that ... After the couple story is over, chuck it into the bin. I'm on to something else.

The logic of her own reasoning, where she understood the limitations of plot, yet followed it closely because it was so complex and ridiculous, provides an illustration of how consumption can sit quite compatibly with criticism. This seemingly contradictory position has been demonstrated time and again in various other audience explorations in Bangalore (McMillin 2003; 2008a). Young audiences could be quite vocal in their criticism of preposterous plots and in particular, sexist representations of women on television, yet were avid consumers of the same. Anujoth said her viewing choices mirrored what she believed was important in her life: variety. Her preference for soaps, news, talk shows, music, and fashion shows made her a heavy viewer of television. It also prompted her tastes. For example,

> ... when I watch a serial connected to the army or the air force, patriotism suddenly blooms yeah, okay, I have to do something for the country and then I want to be an air force pilot. The next day when I see a doctor serial, I want to be a doctor. So it's like that, I'm *very* influenced.

If Anujoth were to star in her own Hindi serial, she said she would choose to play the villain or a

> ... *vamp* in a serial who goes and butts her nose in every single thing and tries to create problems ... playing a *totally* negative role, something *totally* different, because as I said variety, *difference* in life, doing something *fun* ... is what I think is ... the essence of life.

Anujoth also watched religious Sikh programs because "it kind of instills in me (that) I should do little bit of *something* ... it kind of inspires me."

Similarly, 15-year-old Nina, a white South African, had everything she could need—a secure home, an upper-income lifestyle, and loving parents. She believed she had a sensibility and maturity that went far beyond the average teen because of the exclusionary politics she faced due to her club foot. The older of two children in a loving, two-parent home, Nina loved to debate and act. She said, "I love anything cultural, drama, anything to do with media, theatre, I debate and I do a lot of charity work, wherever I can, I'm not a really sporty person at all!" Physiotherapy had been a daily feature in her childhood, leading her, she said, to develop into a compassionate young woman.

Nina lived in the still predominantly white, upper-middle-class suburb of Parkview, a privileged segregated area under the 1950 Group Areas Act. Her all-girl school had been transformed into a Model C School that meant it was now open to all races, not just whites. Students of color now included very affluent blacks, or the children of black domestic help who lived nearby. Although her father worked from home, Nina complained that she had very little quality time with him. She had a more active and open relationship with her mother. Through her work with various charities, Nina understood what many black children went through, some raising siblings, and often, their own young ones. Her hope was for all children to have as loving and supportive a family as she did. She was interested in being an anchor on television, having enlisted in a children's media production team. Nina worried about her body image, especially having been teased and bullied by her peers because of her disability. She enjoyed sports vicariously through her brother. Nina aspired to become a news anchor on television and had already sent in an application to the SABC. Like Rabia, she was involved in producing programs for a children's news and current affairs program. She preferred reality shows on television, although she was critical that they sometimes went

> too far ... I mean choosing a wife or a husband for somebody—according to a moral basis you need to fall in love and find the right person—but in those programs they are saying ... oh, let me find a wife for you.

Too often such shows made money just by going against "moral codes," said Nina, conflating the "moral" with conventional practice. She enjoyed British comedies like *Kumars at No. 42*, *Blackadder*, and *My Family*, on SABC. Comedy served an important purpose in that it "mocks the issues of society as well as gives you something else to think about, it lets you escape—and you need that, you can't always be serious—humor is very important." Nina identified better with comedic than with dramatic characters, believing they had a tremendous amount of freedom in using their wit to get a point across. In particular, she appreciated Susan Harper in *My Family* because she kept the family together through a great sense of humor. Nina watched *Carte Blanche* on M-Net regularly to pick up tips on professional broadcasting. A highly reputed talk show, it was formerly targeted to white South Africans and was only just beginning to cater to a diverse community with the inclusion of Themba Bingwa (black South African) and Devi Sankaree Govender (East Indian). Although still predominantly white, the news show is gradually recruiting nonwhite staff.[15] Another talk show she watched frequently was *3-Talk* (SABC3), with anchor Noleen, who had crossed over from a successful radio talk show career. Noleen's show had high ratings among black and white South African viewers and her studio-based show dealt with a wide range of topics such as health, sports, arts and culture, and fashion. *3-Talk's* Web site describes the approach of the show as "one of realism: a presenter and expert guest in a television studio responding to live telephone calls and SMSs, providing an on-air talk platform, in the moment, as it happens." Nina admired Noleen's debating skills. *The Oprah Winfrey Show* was another relevant show for Nina for its direct lessons on "not to drink, take drugs, get too thin or too fat ... They (hosts such as Noleen and

Oprah) have opened my eyes to the real world and I have become more aware of what really goes on" (F. Bulbulia, 2004).

Perhaps 15-year-old African American Tia in New York, from a low-income household, would be able to relate to Anujoth and Nina. Tia said she was "the most popular girl" among her peers, who "are all true friends." She loved being a teenager, and she enjoyed Math and English. Like Anujoth, she was a member of the student government and was part of the national honor society. She wanted to become a lawyer; her education was very important. Tia too enjoyed sitcoms such as *Everybody Loves Raymond* (particularly the character of Marie) and *The Parkers* (UPN), particularly the character of Mo'Nique. Both depicted mothers who were brash, overprotective, and interfering. In *The Parkers*, Tia pointed out that Mo'Nique was a character she could relate to because the latter modeled what many young African American girls went through. The show followed the story of Mo'Nique who was now in school with her teenage daughter, having gotten pregnant herself when she was a teenager. *The Parkers* signaled to young African American girls like Tia that no matter what, you could still go back to school, get an education, and get ahead in life (Fisherkeller, 2004).

In the above narratives, we used as our stream of connectivity the role of teens in homes where fathers were absent. We drew on the experiences of Anujoth and Nina in that they also shared responsibility with parents in the time of need and connected with single-parent peers across the world in their strong allegiance to family. We detect another connecting fiber: all who cared for siblings and who articulated aspirations of being more in control of personal and professional lives than their mothers were young girls. For most teen boys with absent fathers, more emphasized were feelings of anger toward both parents. It is possible that the boys were more prone to discussing feelings of anger while the girls sought to articulate feelings of abandonment in socially appropriate ways, choosing shows that resonated with their socialized ideas of motherhood and femininity (see also Ex et al., 2002; Mayer, 2003).

Action and Comic Heroes

To avoid the risk of essentializing gender differences, we once again examine context to get closer to the realities from where the teen boys spoke. In their narrations, we see that ironically, the absent father was idolized in some cases, with the mother marked as the weak one, despite the latter being the primary breadwinner in the household. The boys coped with these feelings by developing their bodies, taking their anger out on their mothers or siblings, or by withdrawing completely. Their television choices revealed a fascinating pattern. They mostly discussed strong, stoic movie heroes like New York policeman John McLane (played by Bruce Willis) in *Die Hard* or Colonel O'Neill in *Stargate SG-1* (played by Richard Dean Anderson)—heroes who were pushed to violence and destruction for a noble cause. Yet, they talked most about television characters who actually subverted systems through their wit, humor, and even ignorance. For 14-year-old Mario in Munich, Bart Simpson could get away with practically anything. For 14-year-old Zohrab in Bangalore, Richard on *Caroline in the City* or Chandler on *Friends* (both sitcoms on Star World, had an enviable superior wit—they could make their point through humor and sarcasm and avoid the consequences that could accompany direct confrontation. These choices revealed the anxieties of young adolescents who felt the deep need to assert themselves, lash out at restrictions, and yet avoid the punishment that came from stating their needs. We see then, the very workings of a transformative agency and the ways in which television and film choices were a conscious extension of their exercises in assertion and structural manipulation.

We begin with Mario, a 14-year-old, white, middle-income teen from the *Isarvorstadt* suburb of Munich, who, Strohmaier and Lakhotia (2004) discuss, had been retained in the seventh grade and was bullied and even beaten by his schoolmates. The *Isarvorstadt* district is a relatively recent merger (in 1992) with the Louis suburb southwest of Munich's city center, and lies adjacent to the Isar river. It is home to a large Turkish immigrant population. Mario was often in the principal's office for bad behavior and used his baseball cap to hide his face. His parents' divorce caused his move, with his mother, stepfather, and 11-year-old sister, from Neu-Ulm (North Bavaria) where his father and relatives on both parents' sides lived. He was resentful of being away from his father, whom he considered a role model, and waited eagerly for alternate weekends and summer vacations when they would be reunited. Mario's mother, daughter of an Italian immigrant from Sardinia, was the sole breadwinner, working as a controller for the railroad. His stepfather was currently renovating his 100-year-old family house in which they all lived. Mario loved tinkering with model trains and had built a set in his room. His passion was trucks however, something he shared with his father, a truck driver. He was very clear and deliberate about his plans to become a truck driver:

When I am done with school (I'd like to be) a car mechanic, and then I will be trained in this profession and then sometime well, at the age of 21, I'll start with it (driving a truck) ... I will drive, I already know what company I will be working for ... there at the garage where I will be trained as a mechanic ... there in Neu-Ulm ... Every weekend I will drive home to Munich.

Mario exercised daily; he believed it was important to toughen up by working out. He said he beat people up if they disagreed with him.

... when someone attacks me then I beat him up ... when someone gets on my nerves then I get on his nerves, too, and then, well, then I beat him up. ... Honestly, fighting (is) crap, I think, but if someone attacks you, you *have* to fight back ... I almost never speak ... I'll smack his face.

His workouts included anywhere from 10 minutes to 2-hour sessions every day where he strapped books to his back and did push-ups. His favorite movies depicted his own ideals of strength and endurance; some examples were the 1995 action thriller *Desperado* (starring Antonio Banderas and Salma Hayek, and distributed by Columbia TriStar), the 2003 supernatural thriller *Final Destination II* (starring Ali Larter and A. J. Cook and distributed by New Line Cinema) and the 1995 historical action-drama *Braveheart* (starring Mel Gibson and distributed by Paramount Pictures and Twentieth-Century Fox).

Mario believed Bart Simpson of *The Simpsons* (telecast on ProSieben, a commercial channel available through cable, satellite, and DVB-T or Digital Video Broadcasting-Terrestrial), was "the coolest." He explained that Bart could do whatever he wanted and rarely cared or thought about consequences. His inability to think situations through awarded him an enviable freedom and flexibility. Bart was unapologetic and acted on impulse. Mario said,

Well when he beats up his father, he makes fun of him, I mean Bart puts his father on a hook, clothesline or so. Then he dumps him (in) ... first some glue, resin and stuff like that. And then feathers and then he falls into green color and well, and then after that into grass as well and something.

Bart's tarring and feathering of his father and hanging him up to dry on a clothesline may very well seem a useful thing to do for Mario whose interactions with his father, exciting and fulfilling as they may have been, were limited to occasional weekends. Mario stated laughingly that if he had a choice, he would play the younger Simpson and probably "break into a supermarket" or "make fun of my father" or "my friends." Mario went on to wrap up his descriptions of Bart by saying perhaps the character was a little too cheeky and irresponsible and that he himself would not really want to be Bart. This retraction signified Mario's sudden awareness of a teen hood where consequences existed, sanctions on transgressions against adult-authored lines of discipline were all too real.

In Johannesburg, Luke, a 15-year-old 10th grader, lived with his mother, stepfather, 11-year-old sister, and 1-year-old baby brother. Luke was deeply conflicted about his biological father whom he last saw when he was four years old. His parents, not married when he was born, separated soon after and built new lives with different spouses. Luke was very angry and resentful about his father, but loved and was proud of his mother. His mother tried to cajole him into discussing his feelings, but for the most part, Luke kept these suppressed, partly blaming his mother for his absent biological father. He said, "All my friends—they know me as an angry person because of my relationship with my dad. I really need to sit down and talk to him. But it won't happen—it will get very hostile." Luke craved a good relationship with his peers but was unsure of how to break through the angry persona he had created for himself. He enjoyed math and science and hoped for a career in aviation. He felt lucky to be in a school for high achievers who could not afford the more affluent schools. Fees were paid through the school bursary and students were expelled if their grades fell below a certain level. Just like his peers, he loved sports, especially soccer and cricket, in fact, "everything but rugby!"

Rugby is a sport associated with the oppressive apartheid regime and regarded as the game of white Afrikaners. Former President Nelson Mandela hosted the 1995 World Cup Rugby as a reconciliatory gesture, and supported the blended team named *Amabokaboka*, which reflected an African twist to the apartheid name of *The Springboks*. South Africa went on to win the World Cup, yet many remain skeptical of surface symbols of unity, giving rise to the phrase, "everything but rugby!" Luke was all too aware of discriminatory politics, worrying about whether he would really succeed when former Apartheid Education Minister Verwoed had declared the futility of educating blacks and encouraging them to be more than laborers. In the current climate, Luke could compete for a variety of scholarships that would support the education of a black child. He was quite diligent with homework and watched television only after he was done with his assignments. He argued with his younger sister about the choice of channels and usually watched comedies and variety shows such as the South African *Pure Monate Show* (on SABC1 and produced by 14 10th Street Productions) and *Theta Msawawa* (targeted to youth and filmed in Cape Town). *Pure Monate Show*'s editors Tongai Furusa and Neo "Snyman" Mayephu are known for their fast-paced productions; Neo in particular had worked on the SABC 1 youth soap, *Yizo Yizo* (14 10th Street, 2004).[16] Luke was a fan of the protagonist, a young girl who solved problems and currently was involved in helping a young boy fight his abusive father. He said, "I think she would be like me—she is also colored, about my age—we have some similarities" (F. Bulbulia, 2004).

Ronald, a 14-year-old, Native American boy of Cherokee descent from the affluent New York suburb of Suffern, was another teen who helped in the care of younger siblings. His parents were divorced and his mother remarried when he was 11. Ronald's family was far from affluent, but he lived in Suffern because his mother and stepfather were training to be pastors with a national charity organization that located its training quarters there. He respected his stepfather but resented it when the latter tried to parent him. Arguments were routine with his mother serving as peacemaker. He was frequently punished for indulging in other activities (playing basketball or his saxophone) instead of studying. Having been homeschooled, he said he was bored in school now because much of the material was a repetition. He wanted to be a computer scientist. He enjoyed hanging out with his friends and wasn't keen on getting into a relationship with a girl. He had friends all over the United States, from such places as California, Ohio, West Virginia, Pennsylvania, Maine, and New Jersey. This was because his parents, like Ronald's, were on assignment with the same national charity organization (Fisherkeller, 2004, personal communication). He had two close friends, a girl in whom he could confide, and the other, a boy, with whom he liked to get into trouble. Like Luke, he quarreled often with his friends and parents. Another "fighter" as labeled by his friends, was Ronald's friend Dennis, a 15-year-old, middle-income teen of Italian, Irish, German, and American heritage. Dennis prided his individuality from the American masses who he believed were slaves to the mass media. Yet he himself was drawn to media violence. Dennis commented,

> In the media, there is always some sort of gang thing, a kid got really depressed and started bringing a gun (to) school. The devil really influences people and I guess it's him feeding into my ear all the time.

Dennis discussed how he wanted to get off the "angry fighter" track and get on to the "right path." To change, he talked with the church pastors and his parents. Perhaps taking care of his younger siblings and kids at school would make him a kinder, gentler person, he believed. He liked diverse expression in himself and his friends.

> In school, I hang out with kids that dress in hip-hop kind of clothes, like baggy clothes, or people that are Goths, who wear black. ... I don't like to be stereotyped to someone that is in one kind of group.

Like Ronald, he was reluctant to get into a serious relationship with a girl because there was plenty of time for that in college. He was athletic, enjoyed basketball, and lifted weights. His dream was to be an NBA player. If that didn't materialize, Dennis hoped to become a teacher with a master's degree in Social Studies.

Action-oriented television shows were the favorites of both Dennis and Ronald. *Blind Justice* (ABC), *Numbers* (CBS), and *Alias* (ABC) were top choices, all depicting either the FBI or CIA in gripping tales of pursuit. *Alias'* Marshall J. Flinkman (played by Kevin Weisman), the computer scientist first working in the SD-6 cell of The Alliance of Twelve, an international crime organization and then for the CIA, was Ronald's hero. Marshall is a social misfit, given to ramblings in the middle of formal presentations. Ronald said that Marshall's offbeat character resonated with him and made him want to become a computer scientist. To him, Marshall was

> very smart when it comes to computers and stuff but he is pretty stupid when it comes to conversation. ... He is always putting things into perspective and he jokes about everything. His personality on the show is like mine in real life. I like to joke about everything.

Marshall also served as narrator in the serial, talking over action so that Ronald could understand the complex plots. The show was a way for Ronald to relate with his mother as well—they often watched the show together and discussed it.

In addition to action dramas such as *24* (Fox), *Law and Order* (NBC), and *House* (Fox), Dennis was a self-proclaimed "soap opera kid." He enjoyed the maudlin romance narratives in *Las Vegas* (NBC), the *OC* (Fox), and *Point Pleasant* (Fox). On the *OC*, the character Ryan Atwood (played by Benjamin McKenzie during Seasons 1–4) was most appealing to Dennis. Ryan was portrayed as a conflicted teenager who supposedly moved from the city Chino, an agricultural and farming community in San Bernadino County, California, to the affluent Newport Beach community, where he is taken in by a public defender, Sandy Cohen (played by Peter Gallagher). Ryan's character struck a chord in Dennis because he

> came from dead poor to being a rich kid ... he is interesting because he can adapt to a lot of things. He is the kind of person that stands up for people (who) are in trouble and doesn't fight unless it's necessary ... He always seems to do the right thing instead of going down the wrong path.

Dennis said he could relate to the character's short temper and from Ryan, he learned "when to take a fight or when to walk away ... He helped me realize that even people with (a) short-(temper) can pick and choose and just not follow what my instinct tells me to do." Dennis believed he could actually have a fruitful real-life conversation with Ryan who could advise him on how to control his impulses. Fisherkeller (2004) discussed that it was possible that Dennis' ties to the charity organization that provided social and educational benefits to families such as his, influenced his preference for negotiation and conflict avoidance.

Across the world, in South India, 14-year-old Zohrab would probably relate. He too felt deeply the frustration of having little control over his environment; he had a burning desire to drop formal schooling and follow his passion for the stage. Yet he was embedded in a middle-class Indian environment where higher education was a prime commodity. His mother set clear boundaries on what he could aspire to, which urged him to seek out ways to strike back that were socially acceptable. Zohrab's father died when he was just two; he talked more extensively about his feelings of displacement than anything else. Zohrab's mother is Goan and his father was a Parsi. He could relate to neither culture, hardly having had any contact with his Parsi relatives and rarely visiting Mumbai or Goa to meet his Goan relatives. His mother's job as a schoolteacher was erratic; she moved her children to the schools she taught in, to obtain tuition waivers. As a consequence, Zohrab had been to eight schools in eight years and often felt isolated in his interests and abilities. Because of his inability to speak the local language, Kannada, he could not connect with his school or neighborhood friends.

Zohrab primarily watched U.S. or UK-produced English language programs on Star World and preferred sitcoms such as *Full House*, *Friends*, *Caroline in the City*, and occasionally, *Will and Grace*. *Full House* was particularly appealing not just for the various comedic situations the daughters DJ, Stephanie, and

Michelle got themselves into, but for the way in which their father explained their mistakes to them. Zohrab admired Chandler's sharp wit on *Friends* because "he has a sense of ... a *real* good sense of humor. You know what, he actually makes most of the jokes. The others *being* stupid, make laughs—make people— laugh, but he *makes* the jokes." As an aspiring comedian, Zohrab was also a television critic, watching carefully how jokes were constructed and delivered and discerning between slapstick and intellectual comedy. In *Caroline in the City*, he admired the sarcastic wit of Caroline's love interest, Richard. Zohrab worked on perfecting his comedic delivery. He said, "I like him (Richard). I would like to *be* like him, but it would be hurting other people's feelings if you *are actually* like him." Sarcasm allowed Zohrab a freedom of expression that his conservative environment as an Indian teen didn't (e.g., where he had to respect his elders, and his peers from other religions and classes). His dream was to be able to produce quick comebacks that were intellectual and funny, yet were not hurtful where he could suffer a backlash. He said:

> I want to be funny, so most of them (TV characters) do (help), but ... uhm ... at the same time, *especially* in India, I have to keep conscious (of taboos): not religion. *No* religion, *no* culture. You can't bring that into *anything* now ... Actually abroad, you *can* say something and people (won't) take it seriously. Here you say something, they *act* as if they don't take it seriously and the next moment you see them crying somewhere else.

These narratives bring us closer to understanding how the complex make-up of television characters that included accent, wit, humor, clothes, automobiles, locales, and so on merge into avenues through which teen boys with absent fathers could cope with a seeming lack of agency in their own lives. In the next section, we follow a different connecting stream: teens with very strict fathers. These young people displayed a strong need to maintain a harmonious balance in their homes, often accepting blame and excusing violent behavior in others, just to keep the peace. Their television choices reflected a desire to lash back through aggression as depicted in wrestling shows, through slapstick violence as shown on cartoons, or through nonviolence and detachment as portrayed in the character Phoebe in *Friends*.

Taking the Fall

We step now into the living room of Teja's house, a middle-class apartment in Bangalore. Teja was tense about his 10th grade exam. He was in the same highly competitive school as Anujoth was, although he didn't know her. He considered himself to be in one of the best phases of his life:

> From my point of view it is enjoyable to be 14. If you have crossed your level, 18, you have to earn for yourself. At 14 you are allowed ... your mother and father, your parents give you shelter and clothing. So there is *no responsibility* as such.

Teja struggled academically but like millions of other middle-class Indian teenagers, he worked toward the engineering entrance exams so he could get into one of the seven branches of the prestigious Indian Institute of Technology. He said, "I fear my ambition. It's like a challenge to me. Plus the scary thing is you don't get it, you have lost your life's worth. It is a challenge which I *have* to take."

Teja's father was a scientist for a local branch of the national defense research center. Having moved with his family from the more conservative city of Hyderabad in the Telugu language state of Andhra Pradesh, Teja was a little overwhelmed with the fast pace of the cosmopolitan Bangalore city. He wrestled with low self-esteem brought on by his overweight body and his very dark skin. His parents were very protective of him and he trusted their wisdom explicitly. He rationalized even punishments as necessary for his own development as explained in one of his journal entries:

> Today (my father) was a bit short-tempered. Normally he never hit(s) me but today he slapped me twice continuously [*sic*]. After he slapped me I felt very angry and frustrated. But later I realized that I had made some mistake. I asked my father to excuse me and he excused (me).

His difficult relationship with his father emerged through lengthy conversations and detailed journal entries. He found that he could not predict his father's temper—at times he was loving, even jovial, but quite often he was tense and angry, striking Teja at the smallest provocation. Further entries demonstrated a tightly controlled schedule on weeknights with only time for homework and tuition and perhaps a few minutes of chatting with friends on the phone.

Teja felt marginalized at school. He worried excessively about whether he would be punished in class and believed his performance was directly related to how strict or lenient the teacher was. For example, he wrote about his social science teacher who "favors only those who are brilliant in studies. She thinks only the brilliant fellows can come up in life and she never tries to bring up the weak fellows, in my opinion." Teja thought his science teacher was very intelligent because she kept asking questions and urged students to think—he loved the stimulation. The Sanskrit teacher was the most boring—he knew his subject matter and taught well, but nobody understood his accent, wrote Teja. Lengthy comments about each teacher revealed a deep sense of obligation to the subject matter, school, teachers, and parents. How he performed in the class was not seen as an individual exercise, where he alone would bear the consequences of success or failure. Instead, there was a clear sense of obligation; to perform badly in the exam would mean to let down or disappoint multiple constituencies who had all invested in his progress.

Teja had a close circle of friends, but he was not the star. As with the punishments from his father, he excused any bullying from his friends telling himself that it was alright—they were his friends after all. His favorite activity was trading Pokemon cards. His need to keep his world balanced was so great that even when he was cheated out of valuable cards, he justified his friends' actions by saying they were his friends after all and he could not be angry with them. Teja's television favorites were *Pokemon* and *WWE* (World Wrestling Entertainment).[17] Of the WWE brands, Teja believed *WWE Raw* and *WWE SmackDown* were most aggressive. Yet he watched them with fascination, indicating from his comments that he was unaware that it was a choreographed show. He most frequently watched the sports channels: Ten Sports, Star Sports, and ESPN, and the cartoon channels such as Cartoon Network.

Journal entries were full of detailed synopses of *Pokemon* particularly with regard to how the protagonist, Ash, overcame obstacles to collect Pokemon creatures. Teja had to defend his preference for *Pokemon* with his classmates and neighborhood friends who ridiculed him for watching a show meant for younger children. Although he argued with them that he also watched more "adult" programs like cricket and wrestling, he was teased for these choices as well. His precocious friends, particularly teen girls, taunted him by saying he watched wrestling only to develop his muscles and make himself attractive to girls. Painfully self-conscious about his overweight body and extremely dark skin, Teja lashed back that girls were too vain anyway and that he didn't care about his body.

In 2004, Pokemon (owned by Nintendo) was a craze in India, with the pocket monster characters sold out as soon as they hit the stores, marketed by the toy giant, Funskool (India) Ltd. Verghese (2004) reports that despite each card priced at Rs. 30 (approximately $0.68) and each figurine at Rs. 50 (approximately $1.14), a relatively high price for the average middle-class consumer, stocks were cleaned out within days, perhaps because they were marketed in

November, at the beginning of the holiday season, just after the series was launched on television in August that year. The aggressive consumer focus of the show, as forcefully articulated in its catch phrase "Gotta catch 'em all!" has been critically discussed elsewhere (Buckingham & Sefton-Green, 2003).

Angel, a 14-year-old Puerto Rican from New York, could quite possibly be among Teja's friends, with his interest in the WWE shows and cartoons. Angel particularly enjoyed WWE Raw, which Teja critiqued for an excessive show of blood. For Angel, watching television also meant time with his father and sister; he watched wrestling with his father on Mondays, and the OC with his sister on Thursdays. However, like Teja, Angel loved the slapstick humor of cartoons. His favorite was Daffy Duck from the Looney Tunes. He said, "Daffy Duck is always the one that gets hurt when it comes down to him and Bugs Bunny. He is the one that always gets beat up and put down." No matter how many times Daffy Duck was defeated, he was happy. This taught Angel that "you can get hurt but still be happy. And that if someone is happy it does not mean that he is not hurt." The character also taught him to stay away from people who deliberately hurt others (Fisherkeller, 2004).

The need to maintain peace was articulated by 15-year-old Martina as well, in Neubiberg, a suburb of Munich. Her mother worked in the Personnel division of the local municipal office, while her father did odd jobs such as bartending or gardening. The family lived in a small apartment that Martina's father reno-vated; however, all furniture was paid for by her mother. As a rural community, Neubiberg did not have very many places for youth to gather; in fact, gangs were a problem. Martina stayed out of cliques and gangs. She preferred stay-ing at home. The family did not travel much, even during summer holidays. Because of her struggles with math and science, Martina spent much of her time studying. During the weekend, she biked with friends. She laughed that her father was too old (he was 54) to do anything much with, and her mother was too busy with her work. Money was always scarce so she tried to help out by buying things for her room with her own money. She also did not discuss her anxieties or worries with her parents, especially her mother, who she believed was very tired at the end of the day and had enough worries of her own. Even if she did argue with her parents, the overall peace of the household was very important to her:

> ... if I have an argument with my parents, I'll always come back after five minutes or so and apologize and, fortunately, we all make up soon in the end—because if there is a divide and no one is talking to each other that's terrible, I can't stand that at all.

At school as well, Martina was a negotiator, often solving conflicts among her friends. She dreamed of owning her own hotel and becoming the big boss, "a big name in the world and everybody knows the hotel, and that is just great." She longed for autonomy and called being a teenager "another Dark Age in which you have no rights at all." Like 14-year-old Verena, Martina loved the show *Berlin, Berlin* and the impulsive and chaotic protagonist Lolle. Lolle was laid back, had fun with her life, and laughed at herself when she messed up. Lolle was a freewheeler, without a family to temper her freedom; Martina could vicariously enjoy the autonomy Lolle exhibited over her environment.

Just as Martina's experience connected with Teja's need to maintain the peace, Teja's struggles with a very strict father, with maintaining good grades, and with low esteem about his physical appearance resonated strongly with the experience of Keenan, a 15-year-old, white South African in Johannesburg, and Nazan, a 14-year-old Turkish-German in Munich. By his own admission, Keenan was unpopular in school. He lived in an affluent suburb, in a nuclear family comprising of his parents and an older sister. Methodist and upper middle class, he said:

> I live in a really posh area—I (am) a rich person. (I have) a cell phone, running water. It means that I am privileged in many ways, I don't worry about many things ... I deal with emotions a lot, I am bigger than everyone else. They thought I was ugly. ...

He was frequently bullied at school for his size and felt marginalized by the politics of New South Africa where he believed he was now openly associated with the white oppressors.

Keenan was close to his mother. She was the "nicest person" he knew. His father, on the other hand, was very strict and slapped Keenan when he lost his temper. As the younger of two siblings, Keenan believed he had to fight for attention because his sister absorbed much of his parents' time and energy. Through their shared interest in aircraft, Keenan and his father spent time together in a flying club. Keenan had crashed his plane a few times, creating a big dent in his weekly allowance. His father pressured him to fly successfully and despite the stress to perform well, Keenan counted his weekend outings with his father as valuable bonding time. He had several aspirations—he wanted to be a science whiz, and to make the school cricket and rugby teams.

Unlike the perceptions of Themba, Shubha, and Ambika, Keenan, like Teja, displayed an almost childlike worldview. As the youngest in his family (his father had children from a previous marriage and was now a grandfather as well), he was protected in a variety of ways and given all the material comforts and luxuries he could need. His cell phone ("to SMS"), palatial home, private education—all these placed him above his peers, he believed. Keenan had a girlfriend who was "not the best, but not 100 percent, but I'm still working on that." Even an "imperfect" girlfriend was better than no girlfriend, according to Keenan. He had one best friend with whom he shared almost everything. As with the other upper-middle-class teens in this study, Keenan watched primarily North American and British sitcoms. In particular he mentioned American serials *Frasier* and *Days of Our Lives* (on e.tv) that he watched with his family. He enjoyed intrusive reality shows, and watched *Smallville* with great interest (the show features the growing years of Superman, who lived in Smallville, Kansas). Keenan said Clark Kent, played by Tom Welling, was his sister's favorite character. By studying the young Kent carefully, Keenan believed he could model behavior that was desirable to girls. The travel series on SABC3, *Going Nowhere Slowly*, was another television favorite for Keenan; it featured lead characters Vivienne Vermaak and Stuart Taylor who visited all sorts of places in South Africa in a 1970s Chevy Impala.

Like Keenan, Nazan, a 14-year-old, had failed a class and was retained in the 8th grade. Similar to Teja, she felt somewhat displaced from her native land. A second-generation Turkish immigrant, she lived in Gersthofen, a small town north of Augsburg. Nazan received private tuition at one point, but her parents gave up on that because her grades did not improve. She enjoyed being part of a clique and met Friday evenings with her friends at the youth center meant primarily for Turkish immigrants. Nazan spent her monthly allowance of €25 on magazines, clothes, and cigarettes. Her mother worked at the local post office while her father owned a small business. They often went to Turkey for holidays and at one point when she was a toddler, her parents had tried to make a living there, but returned to Germany for better prospects. Nazan's parents planned for their two daughters to settle down in Turkey once they finished their schooling. She clashed frequently with her very strict father; her mother, on the other hand, was more of a friend. She felt she straddled two disparate spheres: being Turkish and having to go to Turkey after graduation, yet living her childhood and adolescence in Germany. Nazan described herself as moody and irritable. She could not break her smoking habit:

> I have been smoking for two years now, that's very early but that's the way it is—that's common practice among my friends because they are all smokers and I thought if I do

not smoke they think I'm not cool enough and now I can't stop but I *could* but I don't want to stop it really ... I don't know, I can't explain it.

Nazan had a television set in her room until recently when her father took it away because of her poor grades. She called television her "side job" that she needed every day. Comedies such as *King of Queens*, *The Simpsons*, and the Turkish comedy *Europa Jakasin* were her favorites, with *Friends* topping the list. The fact that she was limited to *Friends* reruns was no hardship for Nazan who had watched every episode, several of them many times over. According to her, the show was funny, tragic, romantic, and silly. In particular, Nazan adored Phoebe who she believed was "absolutely funny" and "also very clever." Like Zohrab, she liked the way Phoebe protected herself through disarming humor and even simplicity. Nazan could relate to Phoebe's vegetarianism and love for animals. Her blonde hair and her slimness made her the ideal woman for Nazan. Despite Phoebe's age of around 25–30 years in Nazan's estimation, her simple-mindedness made her eminently relatable to 14–16-year-olds.

Nazan candidly discussed her friends' sexual experiences: one lost her virginity because she couldn't say no to her boyfriend, while another was in a "long-term" relationship, having stayed with the same boyfriend for almost 10 months. Nazan believed her first sexual encounter would be an eventuality without choice. Echoing much of the patriarchal discourse that limited her freedoms, she praised her friend for not flitting from boyfriend to boyfriend even though the boys in her social circle were rarely with the same girlfriend for more than a few months.

The seriousness of a teenager in a conservative household with a strict father was evident in 15-year-old Ashok as well. From a middle-class suburb in Bangalore, Ashok had just passed his 10th grade SSLC state examinations with an impressive average of 91%, second overall in his school. He was currently enrolled in an all-male, English language, private Catholic college in the heart of the city. The institution was known for its trend-setting fashions as well as its academic achievements. Ashok was nervous about college and unsure about what to wear every day. During his first few weeks, he was aware that his formal slacks and Oxford shirts were quite out of place in the sea of jeans and T-shirts. He didn't know how to transition to "cool" and was also nervous about being distracted from his goal: "(The) main ambition in my life is to be a doctor and find a cure for all the incurable diseases and establish many hospitals across India, in the slum areas, in villages, all sorts of rural areas." A deeply religious Christian, Ashok believed it was only the grace of God that produced his success. He loved football and, although part of the school team, did not qualify for the college team, so now only played the sport with his neighborhood friends. He was active with the church group, but was aware that he needed to devote much of his time to his studies. An avid television watcher, he preferred primarily English language shows on foreign networks such as Star World, CNN, ESPN, and CNBC, because "(from) all these news channels I get to know a lot of things abroad and all the international affairs." During most evenings, however, the family was limited to the GOD channel that his mother watched extensively. With only one television set in their two-roomed home, Ashok and his brother often had to succumb to their parents' choices. He and his brother argued regularly with their mother so they could watch action films. He particularly liked the call-in program *Reach Out* on the Sun TV channel where viewers phoned in their song requests. Reality game shows such as *Fear Factor* and *Amazing Race* on the AXN channel were family favorites. A particular favorite was *30 Seconds of Fame* on AXN:

> …where you expose your talent in 30 seconds. They select the best out of them and give them a cash award or something. And many people like, they come out with talent like, cracking glass with their mouth in 30 seconds, some dance very well in 30 seconds, and some are fire eaters in 30 seconds—they do all those things.

Ashok's favorite television character was a movie comedian named Vivek, who frequently appeared in the film-based programs on the Sun TV channel. Ashok liked the fact that Vivek didn't speak much, yet conveyed a lot through his body language. Similarly he liked Jim Carrey in such movies as the *Mask* (distributed by New Line Cinema) and *Ace Ventura Pet Detective* (distributed by Warner Brothers), because his actions conveyed much more than his words. Like Zohrab and Nazan, he thought *Friends* on Star World "shows how friends can get to know each other very well and how they can be one and ... how there can be unity." He watched cricket matches regularly on Star Sports and a medical talk show, *Doctor*, on the NDTV channel.

Finally we come to several teens for whom, quite simply, all was right with the world. These teens reflected very patriarchal views of their parents, reinforcing the value of the mother at home and the father at work.

It's Good to Be Me

Christian, a 14-year-old who lived with his 16-year-old sister and parents in the *Isarvorstadt* suburb of Munich, was an easygoing 7th grader who required private tutoring to keep his grades up. He expected to be an electrician when he graduated, unsure about whether he had the grades for higher education. Christian's father was hardly home, usually working late as a freelance contractor. Christian's mother, a part-time medical secretary, took care of the children. Real estate in the *Isarvorstadt* was on the rise at the time of fieldwork, and the community was diversifying significantly from its concentration of Turkish immigrants. The *Isar* river that the neighborhood bordered on offered Christian and his friends a pleasant and lively place to meet. The family spent most summers in Portugal where Christian's aunt ran a lodging business. Christian was not interested in school at all and preferred to spend time with his friends, playing soccer or computer games. Keenly interested in all things electric, Christian often tinkered with household appliances like the vacuum cleaner. An electric train set in his room, assembled on a platform that his father engineered so it could be raised up to the ceiling with a motor, was Christian's prized possession. He also spent quite a bit of time with his 14-year-old girlfriend of two months. All he wished for was that his easy life did not change. If things got too tough, Christian had a simple solution—he got out. As an illustration, Christian said he dropped out of soccer when training got too strenuous. He started walking when his bike broke down. Christian's father was his role model. While he talked about how his father taught him to drive and helped him set up his train set, his mother did "Well, cooking (laughs)—I don't know washing, frying."

Christian was an avid fan of *Stargate* on the RTL2 channel. Although he had little time for television, he tried not to miss even a single episode of the sci-fi drama. He thought it was "cool, because they, when they simply walk through the gate and then they are ... in different countries or worlds." The show features what is called a wormhole that facilitates teleportation between cosmic worlds. Produced by MGM, and first released as a movie under the same name in 1994, it was adapted for television under the *Stargate SG-1* series. The narrative follows United States Air Force Colonel Jack O'Neill, commander of SG-1 who leads the team in a variety of adventures. The ability to move across time and space and the straightforward good versus evil storyline was appealing to Christian. His hero, Teal'c (played by Christopher Judge) is a human-looking character, but posses an abdominal pouch that incubates Goa'uld larvae which enhanced his health, strength, and abilities. Teal'c is supposedly over a 100 years old, with a golden insignia tattooed on his forehead, indicating his First Prime, Jaffa rank with the System Lord Apophis. Christian also talked about the *Terminator* (starring Arnold Schwarzenegger and distributed by Orion Pictures and MGM) as an ideal hero because he was a robot, was from the future, and best of all, had the sole mission of protecting a young boy. Christian enjoyed educational programs such as *Welt der Wunder* and *Galileo* (on RTL II) that provided information about animals, humans, and technology in far more interesting ways than what was presented in school.

Pascal, a 15-year-old from Putzbrunn, a small village in Munich, was also an ardent fan of *Stargate SG-1*. From a secure, two-parent home, his concern revolved around his appearance and studies. From his carefully styled hair to brand name clothes bought with his allowance, he projected a self-contained, polite image. Pascal considered himself transitioning to adulthood, with the ability to be quite serious when he wanted to. He was self-conscious about pimples and his "too red nose." The walls of his room were filled with posters of women in bikinis posing provocatively. He thought girls were "sweet," but inscrutable:

> when you flirt with them and then they find out that you are 15 or 16 and although they are only 14 then they say something like "get away" because what they want are older ones, something like 18, 19, 20. Well, and, I mean well I can partly understand that because some guys my age are really that childish, but not all of them are like that.

Pascal struggled in school; he wished he had chosen economics instead of social science. He felt excluded from cliques—a stark contrast from his popular brother. He worked as a shop assistant in a mall two afternoons a week and was bored with the neighborhood populated by either farming families or by civil servants, like his parents. Pascal felt a certain sense of independence having moved into the cellar of the house, while his 17-year-old brother roomed in the attic. Family life was contentious with quarrels a daily feature. Conflicts invariably were between Pascal's brother and the parents, but recently marital troubles had cropped up. Despite all the squabbling, his parents had not seriously considered divorce because staying married was the condition under which they could live in the house as civil servants. Pascal longed for autonomy where he could experience something without his parents around. He believed he was ready to strike out on his own, yet his mother argued that he needed a lot of supervision. Like most teens his age, he enjoyed hanging out with his friends, going to parties, and meeting girls. He wished he had "Courage, well with girls, to do something with them. Well for example I would not mind crossing the graveyard or something no problem, but girls, not likely ... " This sort of crossing, out of local stresses to perhaps conquering another world, was possible through Teal'c in *Stargate SG-1*. Pascal maintained a scrapbook on the show and even had *Stargate SG-1* wallpaper on his desktop computer. Colonel O'Neill was his hero because of his complete control over his surroundings. He could approach anyone and engage in conversation without hesitation. For Pascal who wrestled with shyness and diffidence especially around girls, this was an astounding feat. Anderson the actor himself was a star in Pascal's eyes, for the way he tackled the role—perhaps he was the same in real life, Pascal believed. He was scornful of music programs, particularly the reality *Idol* type shows that, in his opinion, were just about making money without providing any real value for the viewer or participants (Strohmaier & Lakhotia, 2004).

Putting It All Together

This chapter has taken us through a variety of locales. We have avoided using location or identity position of the teens as a starting point for a discussion of their lives and television choices, to move away from the conventional theoretical stops that lead to dichotomic analyses. With *location* as the epistemological point, we could run into the risk of global-local analyses; with *identity* as the epistemological center, we could hurtle on down male–female, white–nonwhite tracks, to name a few. *Class*-based analyses prove unfruitful because how class is defined varies among nations and cultures. Yet these are all important in combination. What we have shown in this chapter is that each teen had multiple stories to tell, multiple spaces to journey through. Operating on the premise that identity positions are not extractable or isolatable but work in complex relationships depending on the interpellatory dynamic, the responses of teens were organized according to the most striking theme in each teen's story that structured her or his choice of television programs. R. W. Larson (2002) reminds us that

> Adolescents' lives are more directly shaped by their interactions with more proximal institutions and setting, including families, schools, occupational worlds, and community organizations. These settings include many important people such as parents, teachers, and employers, whose actions affect adolescents' experience and preparation for adulthood. (p. 25)

As media scholars, we want to understand the mediating presence of television in the teen's life. As critical researchers we want to show how context bears in on the experience and how together, they produce agency.

Quijada (2008) writes that "institutions whether familial or educational, organize ways of communicating that silence 'talking' as a form of everyday activism" (p. 215). Many of the teens had indeed experienced sanctions on their talking. Some, like Teja and Keenan, were slapped for defiance; others, like Shubha and Ambika, were not taken seriously because they were girls. Media anthropologists remind us that a *critical geography* is essential in the study of youth in differing locales (Hay, 1996; Massey, 1997). This chapter has attempted to provide some sense of the actual locales that the respondents resided in. Their television choices were then mapped, as far as possible, onto the local contexts such as family, neighborhood, work, and school.

We explored transformative possibilities with the understanding that the agent works, in fascinating ways, to fashion her or his environment so that it makes meaning for the resident within. That meaning has to be valued and used as the point of departure for any larger discussion of transformative politics. In the stories that unravelled from fieldwork, self-consciousness about the body, anxiety over bullying at school, obsession over grades, irritation with parental control or lack of it—were some of the issues that cropped up over and over again. Favorite television characters, be they from local, vernacular language soap operas, or from U.S. sitcoms and animations available globally, embodied a certain control over the environment. This control was demonstrated through the form of superpowers such as those of Teal'c in *Stargate SG-1*, brute force such as that of the *Terminator* or *WWE* wrestlers, stoicism such as seen in O'Neill in *Stargate SG-1*, a superior wit as in Richard in *Caroline in the City*, or even, as in the case of Bart Simpson in *The Simpsons* and Phoebe in *Friends*, a lack of awareness of complex happenings. For young girls in particular, free-wheeling characters like Lolle in *Berlin, Berlin* taught them to toss aside worries; heroines on *Mangalya* and *Mahabayi* taught them to navigate conflict through silent strength, an arguably problematic option in itself. Anchors like Noleen and Debora Patta provided lessons in leadership, pursuing the heart of a controversial story even in the midst of social pressure. Delineation of multiple choices linked with varied needs of each teen revealed patterns across disparate contexts. Among middle and upper-income teens, American sitcoms such as *Friends*, sci-fi dramas such as *Stargate SG-1* and movies such as *Terminator* were most often cited as examples of favorite shows. Interpellations to agency were most obviously provided by such media products, necessitating varying levels of transformation to acquire that level of agency. The transformative process and the inequities embedded within it are dealt with closely in Chapter Five, from the vantage point of Indian teens.

Perhaps a linear connection can easily be drawn between teen developmental needs and the gratifying shows they sought out. As has been demonstrated from the circuitous route through the theory that has gone before, such connections miss crucial topography that shapes how those choices are made. The detailed journal entries and lengthy conversations that sometimes meandered through several home visits, and took place across the dinner table, in the garden, at the teen's school—all produced fascinating and richly textured journeys through the mediating systems in each teen's life. It is through these lenses that choices of superhero television characters by a few teen boys must be seen; these choices were made by those who were not just critical about their own physical appearance, but who were also bullied at school, were angry at absent fathers, and felt helpless about supporting their mothers economically. Women-centered soap operas were watched faithfully by young girls in rural neighborhoods who were deriving important lessons on how to navigate sexual harassment and patriarchal constrictions within the household, through silence and carefully calculated outspokenness. Light-skinned characters with sharp, sarcastic wit were chosen by dark-complected teens who lived in environments that structured privilege according to caste and skin lightness. These characters demonstrated to them that battles could be won through intellect and physical strength. Skin lightness was a pre-condition for such mobility and victory, reinforcing the teens' sense of inadequacy while simultaneously offering them avenues to excel. The powerful influence of interlinked webs of relationships on the production of the subject is apparent here. Butler (2005) writes that the articulation of moments of experience brings into consciousness the *being* of the subject. Specifically,

> Moments of unknowingness about oneself tend to emerge in the context of relations to others, suggesting that these relations call upon primary forms of rationality that are not always available to explicit and reflective thematization. If we are formed in the context of relations that become partially irrecoverable to us, then that opacity seems built into our formation and follows from our status as beings who are formed in relations of dependency.

The relations of dependency that each teen was embedded in achieved clarity for them, in their enunciations. After fieldwork was completed, researchers discussed how several respondents thanked them for the opportunity to speak about their lives and interests. Deep distinctions in class and ethnic status, to name a few, differentiated the future trajectories of each participant, in terms of the cultural and social capital they would have access to as adults. However, their television choices can be seen as counterdiscursive practices whereby they could escape or resist their feelings and realities of disenfranchisement through *interpolation,* where they used the images provided to them, however limited in range due to their production by a few synergistic global conglomerates, to transform their immediate lived constraints.

Amidst all their existential challenges and victories, what also emerged was a widely varying sense of the teens' place in the world. *Where* the teens were located in the neocolonial world system played a crucial role in how they perceived their positions in a global structure. Chapter Four unravels striking differences in the ways in which teens talked about neighborhood, community, nation, and world. Keeping in mind variations in how time and "global" product was experienced, the teens' comments are placed in terms of the *lived fusion* (Serequeberhan, 2007, p. xix) brought about by colonialism. In the discussion of teen lives in globalization, we take into account the interconnectedness of diverse mediating systems that produce the agent that emerges. This agent is sometimes bold, sometimes petulant, sometimes reticent. At the end of the day, the global economic and political order defines how far the agent will go and what her or his possibilities are.

· 4 ·
SUBJECTS OF GLOBALIZATION

The interconnections of globalization lead to broad assumptions that urban individuals are linked to the same cultural experiences through a variety of media technologies (Featherstone, 1995). As stated in the introduction, many scholars of globalization contend that "Cultural proximity in the consumption of media texts is ... being articulated and made conscious under homogenizing forces of 'modernization' and 'globalization'" (see Iwabuchi, 2005, p. 28 for a critique). Chapter Three took us through a variety of experiences in Bangalore, Johannesburg, Munich, and New York. Teens talked about their desire to get out of impoverished neighborhoods, their dreams to become professionals, and their need to seek stability within their homes. Their television choices represented ongoing journeys toward selfhood. The programs they watched provided another avenue, apart from an integrated matrix of family, religion, and education systems, to understand themselves. How may we connect their contexts and stories to globalization? How do the interdependent, transnational media networks partner with interconnected market and government systems to create choices for the teen consumer? What conditions forge the teen's acceptance, subversion, or manipulation of these choices? In this chapter, we connect dynamic, flowing culture to structures of globalization by questioning the interpellatory power of such processes as urbanization and capitalist expansion.

While it is true that all teens could access such U.S.-produced programs as *Friends, Caroline in the City*, and *The Simpsons*, the synchronicity of experiences did not mean a collapse of the colonial time lag between developed center and developing periphery as some claim (Wilk, 1994), nor a homogenizing trend across the world (Herman & McChesney, 2003). In fact the simultaneous worldwide Hollywood movie release of, to use examples from the time of fieldwork, *Spiderman* (2002, Sony Pictures), *X2: X-Men United* (2003, Twentieth-Century Fox), *The Matrix Reloaded* (2003, Warner Brothers),

and *2 Fast 2 Furious* (2003, Universal Pictures) should be seen as an ingenious strategy to combat piracy ("Mutating: Hollywood Blockbusters," 2003),
a significant problem when postproduction is outsourced to countries such as
China and India. The depiction of conflict and regeneration within bustling
metropolises was a theme with a renewed sense of urgency in the aftermath of
September 11, 2001.[18]

The modern city as the site of romance and mystery was duplicated in
India, in Bollywood films. A couple of 2003 examples are *Kal Ho Naa Ho*
(2003, Yash Raj Films and Dharma Productions; filmed in New York and featuring Roy Orbison's *Pretty Woman)* and *The Hero: Love Story of a Spy* (2003,
Pathfinder Pictures and others; filmed in India, Canada, and Pakistan). The
co-option of media products successful in one market for circulation in another is well documented (Moran & Keane, 2004; D. H. Lee, 2004). Hollywood
films remade for Indian audiences should be seen simultaneously as marketing
strategy, but, perhaps more importantly, as a courting relationship between
Indian filmmakers and their fans. Ganti (2002) calls this process "Indianiza-
tion" and argues that

> From a Hindi filmmaker's point of view, identification is not dependent upon an aes-
> thetic of social realism or even a realistic mise-en scène ... but more dependent on
> whether the portrayal of the joys, sorrows, and dilemmas faced by the characters are
> able to resonate with—rather than replicate—audience's own experiences. (p. 285)

Bollywood films and the subsequent stream of films from other burgeoning
regional movie industries such as Nollywood (Nigeria), Lollywood (Lahore,
Pakistan), and Tollywood (Hyderabad, India) provide synchronous experiences
of fast-paced, technologically sophisticated, city life. In the films of the 2000s,
there were increasing similarities among the urban locales featured in blockbusters from such movie industries. Perhaps, as Sudhanva Deshpande (2005)
proposed through an analysis of the globalized hero in Hindi films, this was a
reflection of the heavy sponsorship of film production by diasporic communities
who want their contexts reflected on the big screen. Mechanics of production
aside, depictions of themes and locales are generally amalgamations of what is
glamorous in New York *and* Lahore or Mumbai, tailored to the needs of regional and diasporic audiences. These perpetuate the ideological temporal distance
between so-called core and periphery. Regional film industries, taken together
with extensive transnational underground piracy networks marketing inexpen-
sive camera copies of films from these industries, qualify how we understand the
concept of cultural proximity.

Cultural proximity may facilitate a sense of *synchronicity* whereby media technologies and transnational media networks allow non-Western consumers to "live" in the same temporality as their Western counterparts. However, the coincidence of timing is *not* actually directly translatable into coincidence of cultural experience. Hybrid products (see Bhabha, 1994; Kraidy, 2003), which combine elements of global and local, contribute to synchronicity while denying contemporaniety. As Iwabuchi (2005) explains, contemporaniety refers to the availability of hybrid products on the local marketplace, enabling the consumer to partake in a global experience within a locally relevant context. The remasking of a global product into something highly profitable locally also disallows a contemporary experience between the centers of production and the sites of consumption. To use the examples of programs watched by teens in the *TV Characters* project, local imitations of ABC's syndicated *Newlywed Game* such as the Kannada language *Adarsha Dampathigalu* program that rural Indian teens Shubha and Ambika talked about, or the *Ugly Betty* (ABC) adaptation—*Jassi Jaissi Koi Nahin* (Sony ET)—that urban Indian teen Anujoth loved, provided somewhat synchronous experiences with peers across the globe watching the original versions, but certainly not contemporaneous experiences.

Contemporaniety then, to put it succinctly, refers to the synchronous use of the similar global product but in locally specific avatars, also leading to *technoorientalization*. As explained by Kelly Hu (2005) in the case of the widespread success of VCD technology in Asia while the much superior DVD technology was taking over the Western world, *orientalism* is very much a part of *globalization*. The marketing of technologically inferior products in the so-called East and the development of support services and product outlets for these parallel technologies sustain the material and ideological divide between ex-colonizers and their former colonies. Also, it feeds the development of local, regional markets that create and distribute imitations of a globally revered product (as, for example, the sprawling ghetto markets in all the four cities that hawk imitations of Nike, Levis, and Tommy Hilfiger products, to name a few). The circulation of such so-called global products, or quite specifically, brand names that are recognized in urbanized areas across the world, obviously creates classes of consumption. Few can afford the originals, many more, their pirated versions. A vast majority could even partake of products without any knowledge that an "original" exists; the product is considered "real" in itself. All of these contribute to the discrepancies in how the global is experienced locally. As many number of scholars have argued for the local relevance of hybrid products, many more have identified the inherent asymmetrical configurations of power within, where the industrialized West or ex-colonial power is invariably privileged even while it is possibly caricatured (Donadey, 2001). Iwabuchi (2005, p. 27) comments:

> The development of global communication technologies and networks may further the denial of "contemporaniety" of the periphery through the facilitation of "synchronicity"....The disappearance of a time lag in the distribution of cultural products in many parts of the world has left wide political, economic, and cultural gaps intact, so much so that they facilitate the feeling in non-Western countries that "catching up" is never really possible.

This insightful critique has to be qualified by a few points. First, the intensification of nationalist conservative efforts to seal imaginations from foreign cultural intrusions through the media works to exacerbate the distance; these efforts must be seen to work in a parallel field, adding muscle to that distance. Second, with the interconnections of globalization comes the awareness of the consequences of bridging that distance as well; at a simple level, it could be mere ridicule and outcasting as many immigrant communities have experienced, or at a more fundamental level, a psychic and perhaps even physical violence, on those who dare to bridge the distance.

The "expert" respondent narrating locality and moment for analysis should then be viewed as situated among synchronous, contemporaneous, and techno-orientalist products, using "alien and imperialistic images (naturalized) into authentic representations" (Juluri, 2003, p. 179) for a variety of identity projects. In some of the comments, we see awareness of bridging the ideological gap between "core" and "periphery."

When teens in Bangalore, Johannesburg, Munich, and New York were asked to talk about their hobbies and activities, very few talked about consumerism in specific terms. They loved to shop with friends as an extension of their time together. Rather than explore to any depth their consumer habits and link those to globalizing processes, we focus here on their responses to questions about their position in locality. That is, we wanted to hear about their feelings and ideas about neighborhood, community, nation, and world. For most, discussion of global citizenship or even national identity was very difficult. They were puzzled with such questions, and talked about national identity in terms of watching events on television such as cricket (Anujoth, Ashok, and Teja in Bangalore, for example) and rugby (Keenan and Luke in Johannesburg, for example). They preferred, instead, to talk about their lived ethnic and religious experiences; these, whether involving churchgoing or harvest festivals, were immediate, relevant, and real.

Yet there was a key difference between all the urban respondents and the two rural teens in India, Shubha and Ambika. These two girls spoke most passionately about how their land was changing and how the green fields of their village were being transformed into paved compounds of multinational headquarters. Defending their village and farming culture, they talked in very strong terms, about the predatory nature of the "foreigner." Their narrative provides the link to Chapter Five in which we explore the urgent demands of a changing world foisted upon Indian youth in particular. In this chapter, we get a deeper view into the "production of locality" (Appadurai, 1996) and learn that for all the theorization of globalization, life is still experienced in very local terms. We enter this production through the ground of the city itself.

The Restless Ground

Anthropologists Wong and McDonogh (2001) discuss the critical importance of the media landscape of a city: its billboards, cinema, murals, and architecture provide the citizen with the sense of an always moving, always alive city. Movies, television, and advertising play a crucial role in establishing how the city should look and what commodities its citizens should posses. Each urban center, Bangalore, Johannesburg, Munich, and New York, was also an ongoing modernity project of the nation-state. Each represented for the nation, its future self, and its possibilities for progress.

The Hollywood and Bollywood blockbusters of 2003 certainly served as reservoirs of cityscapes, deploying images of the futuristic, restless city with anxious, fear-ridden citizens awaiting salvation from a superior being or technology. Depictions of big city life were not limited to movie screens, of course. Local television programs used the city backdrop to provide important anchors of locality. To recount a few examples of city-based programs that were avidly watched by the teen respondents, *Berlin, Berlin* portrayed the freewheeling Lolle in the city, *Jozi Street* revolved around cops-and-robbers skirmishes in Johannesburg, *NYPD Blue* obviously centered on the workings of the New York Police Department, and reality shows in Bangalore such as *Adarsha Dampathigalu* and *Demandappa Demandu* (on Udaya TV) featured wandering anchors and camerapersons in various parts of the city, talking to viewers about relationship issues and program preferences, respectively. Combined with the other visual culture such as billboards hawking Levis and Reeboks or local brand names, such products

> become interwoven with the production and reproduction of urban community and conflict. More than cultural proximity, then, we deal with cultural production, within a framework that recognizes the styles, themes, and even prejudices of mass media depictions of the city and grows from that knowledge in new visual media and cultural interpretations. (Wong & McDonogh, 2001, p. 108).

"Locality" intersects with representations of diverse and remote locales. Respondents become expert informants and many studies re-present informant comments as closed authoritative systems of the lived culture itself. How the teen imagines herself or himself as part of a locale becomes a fascinating line of inquiry in youth and global media studies. The filling up of public spaces by corporate and government initiatives to represent a modern ideal illustrates Butler's (2000) point that ultimately, it is inevitable they will fail in this mission. The inherent incompleteness of identity is precisely because "no particular identity can emerge without presuming and enacting the exclusion of others, and this constitutive exclusion or antagonism is the shared and equal condition of all identity-constitution" (p. 31). While Butler is referring to the individual subject, in this chapter we see the teen subjects as embedded within a city, *subject itself* to large-scale identity projects. Teens' incomplete and ongoing identity projects should be seen as intertwined with the incomplete city as well. Their responses to perceptions of local and global identities are therefore digested as informed by and integrated with their membership within the city.

The Rainbow Nation and Global Culture

If the heart of the city is represented in cinema and television as "modern" (Le Marcis, 2004), its ghettos, slums, and townships represent the "premodern," often the childlike primitive, simplistic in worldview and awaiting modernization. Where the teens were located—in developed or underdeveloped parts of the city, and in Western or non-Western nation, to put it simplistically—textured how they assessed their citizenship and belonging to locality.

We begin with the anxieties and ambiguities expressed by teens in Johannesburg, as they discussed the changing character of their nation. Chapter Three provided a brief description of the informal settlements and townships that were established by the apartheid government under the 1950 Group Areas

Act and the 1956 Native Resettlement Act. These separatist policies also produced the "pass laws" where blacks had to carry a "pass," valid for 72 hours, to
work in a white neighborhood. After 1952, the law was revised so that blacks
had to carry a "reference book" that was, in essence, an identification book
carrying the holder's fingerprint. Without the book, a black person in a white
neighborhood could be apprehended and jailed.[19]

Township spaces in South African cities may be considered hybrid and
ambivalent spaces between modernity (the urban white neighborhoods) and
premodernity (rural areas). Ellapen (2007) argues that although cinematic
representations treat urban and rural as fixed spaces and dichotomic ends of
the development scale, township spaces must be seen as protean and dynamic, consisting of the "rural within the urban" (p. 117). The very movement
of blacks between urban and township neighborhoods (necessary during and
after apartheid because of the dependence of white Afrikaners on black labor)
resulted in white anxieties about the black predatory body, and tragically, devastating violence on blacks. Nuttall (2008) discusses how in the postapartheid
period in South Africa, the visual culture of the city plays a crucial role in revis-
ing the past and pointing to future possibilities. The history of apartheid and
the momentous overturn of the racist regime in 1994 were deeply ingrained in
all teens from Johannesburg. Their historical knowledge may have been from
a shared educational experience; their internalization and descriptions of its
meanings were qualified by their location in terms of neighborhood, ethnicity,
and social class.

For example, Nina, a white South African of European descent, talked
about the importance of living and working in harmony. She believed she was
growing up in a nonracist society. She said, "Being a South African is easy
because it is something we have in our blood. We are born to love our country!" At the same time, she was apprehensive of "reverse-apartheid" and the
possibilities of being harassed for being white. For Keenan, a white South African as well, ethnicity was an empty or "colorless" category, because it did not
threaten, but worked *for* his privileged life. He too was apprehensive about the
changing cultural climate. In this context, we understand Keenan's cautious
response to what he felt about his country. He said he was proud to be South
African (a catch phrase duplicated infinitely across a variety of media and products), yet was worried about his future. He discussed the increase in crime and
talked about the high incidence of black on white crime. Homes in affluent,
historically white neighborhoods were frequently burglarized; carjacking was
a common occurrence. So common in fact that a special police force—the

Scorpions—had been launched to combat crime and a troubling increase in child rape based on the faulty premise that sex with a virgin would cure HIV-AIDS. Keenan discussed the art and cultural heritage of South Africa and said that the beauty and vibrance of the nation was apparent even on the street corners.

Nina and Keenan were experiencing a changing political environment in very visual and graphic ways. Television news shows typically targeted to white Afrikaners were now including black anchors. Various corporations were instituting the changing ethos in their advertisements. For example, the fashion label *Loxion Kulcha* (for location culture) launched an innovative campaign pulling together African American styles and local black township culture in what Nuttall (2008) terms "ironic deformation" (p. 155). The objective was to represent neither a fractured self between apartheid and postapartheid eras nor a hybrid image of both. Rather it was to showcase a deliberate self-consciousness and manipulation of identity as an art process. Other brand names that use indigenous designs to develop contemporary ones are Black Coffee, Craig Native, Stoned Cherrie, and Sun Goddess (Rogerson, 2006). Contemporary teen culture in Johannesburg, labeled *Y Culture*, does not swirl around so-called hybrid products celebrated in globalization theory. Instead, writes Nuttall (2008), we see ingenious campaigns that own up to the past while signaling the future. The K-Swiss 2004 shoe advertising campaign running at the time of the *TV Characters* project is an illustration of a subversion of apartheid hierarchies. Nuttall (2008) explains that the campaign consisted of a series of billboards depicting black and white South Africans engaged in activities that clearly transposed the apartheid power structure. In one billboard, for example, blacks wearing the K-Swiss shoe urinated in "White's Only" stalls cleaned by a white South African. While certainly signaling a new phase with a white South African mopping the floor, the advertisement's message was about subversive possibilities created through the purchase of the K-Swiss shoe. Those who possessed the shoe used the urinal. Those who didn't, cleaned it. The billboards captured the essence of the antiapartheid movement: one does not have to be white to avail of a desired membership. Yet, we might add, it neatly slipped into place a different "pass law": one needs the K-Swiss shoe to enjoy the privileges of the system. The phrase "Proud to Be South African" used in the campaign and by citizens of the nation becomes a sign for consumerism, patriotism, and even teen identity.

Luke reiterated this sentiment, and added, "I am a *colored*—I am *proud* to be a colored." He inhabited an ambiguous territory. Whites and blacks had their places and roles after apartheid. As colored, he existed in a netherworld, yet was clear that he was unique and special. In historian Mohamed Adhikari's words (2005, p. 2),

> The coloured people were descended largely from Cape slaves, the indigenous Khoisan population, and other black people who had been assimilated to Cape colonial society by the late nineteenth century. Since they are also partly descended from European settlers, Coloureds are popularly regarded as being of "mixed race" and have held an intermediate status in the South African racial hierarchy, distinct from the historically dominant white minority and the numerically preponderant African population.

The apartheid regime worked through the sustenance of this "mixed" status whose markers were lower socioeconomic class, Afrikaans language, and higher cultural status than the African majority. Coloreds, especially women, were historically a main source of low-wage labor (Alegi, 2008).

Luke's responses were often clichéd, echoing the catch phrases of the new South Africa that it was one nation and he was proud to be part of its revival. At times however, his frustrations broke through the political correctness and he expressed pessimism that racism would ever be eradicated. According to Luke, many people were still stuck in their religious cocoons and cultures and were unable to see the larger picture of the diverse nation. Rabia, who as we recall from the previous chapter is of Indian heritage, also talked about the continued relevance of racial identification:

> it is still something very important, it is a way of identifying people. He (Nelson Mandela) was the red dot amongst the black—Nelson Mandela is one of my biggest role models—he needed courage to stand out and say what it was that he really felt.

We see an interesting trend here: Nina and Keenan could talk about a changing ethos in the political realm conveyed to them through television and advertisements. They expressed a certain anxiety about what this would mean for their prospects. Luke and Rabia were hopeful for the future, yet believed the nation could not escape the violence of its racist past. Their ethnicity continued to act as visible markers of separation between them and their white school friends. For residents of the informal settlement in Zevenfontein, Themba and Kgomotso, the actual mechanisms of postapartheid were experienced in a very real sense. These teens were witnessing crime in their neighborhoods, crowded living arrangements, and had to care for siblings while their mothers still traveled to urban white neighborhoods to work as housemaids. The Rainbow Nation was glorious in rhetoric, but not many of its benefits had trickled down to them as yet. Themba and Kgomotso's opportunities for education and advancement had expanded tremendously; discrimination based on color was illegal in policy. Both had found outlets in the media projects and the *Survivours* group they were members of. For Themba, church was another welcoming space. He said it was a sanctuary for him to reflect on his life, a place to be with his friends, and the meeting place for the *Survivours* group that attended the free Sunday school.

In her notes explaining the contexts of South African teens, F. Bulbulia (2004) echoed these points. Many young South Africans were conflicted about the changes brought about by apartheid. For white youth, the enormous privileges awarded to their parents under the apartheid government were significantly diminished. Those white youth whose parents supported the transition were possibly more aware of the benefits of the new South Africa. For those whose parents didn't, the changes could be scary; it is possible they were experiencing very real fears about their safety and prospects. Although they still lived in largely segregated neighborhoods based on color, South African teens could discuss, at least on a theoretical level, the inequities in their history. The media environment had changed significantly to reflect political changes. There was an increase in the number of faces of color on predominantly white South African news shows as discussed earlier; there were more women anchoring programs; there was greater impetus for entertainment-education programs like *Soul City* and *Soul Buddyz*. Billboard advertisements depicted subverted racial hierarchies; fashion labels were asserting that South African urban culture was its own blend of traditional and Western (primarily African American) hip-hop styles.

Producing Locality

In India, the insecurities of a rapidly changing environment were most poignantly expressed by rural teens, Shubha and Ambika. As students of a Kannada language school at the outskirts of Bangalore city, and with a dynamic principal who emphasized pride in language, region, culture, and history, they had a very strong sense of local heritage. They were proud to be Indians, yet talked most specifically about their pride in their native state, Karnataka. Referring to ongoing battles with the neighboring state of Tamil Nadu, over ownership of water from the Cauvery River, the two declared that Karnataka had not been given the importance it deserved. They talked passionately about the lush green fields of their village, and of a variety of Kannadiga poets, writers, and singers. They described the dignity of the farming community and the annual harvest festival that was a time of celebration, friendship, and sharing. In simplistic binary terms, they upheld local cultures as pure and sacred, while foreign intrusions in the form of global television or even the multinational corporations in the city were criticized as neocolonial culprits. Although a world apart from the upper-income privilege of Keenan and Nina in Johannesburg, Ambika was feeling the backlash of affirmative action policies. She was a Gowda, a higher caste;[20] yet India's affirmative action policy for education had provided great benefits for those of lower castes, such as all-expense paid schooling, reservations of seats in higher education, lower grade point average requirements for entrance exams, and so on. She said:

> There shouldn't be such thing as caste. When I think of caste I think in terms of animals, birds, humans. That's *it*. In terms of caste, some eat meat, some don't trouble animals. But caste is all manmade. The Jains came and made Jainism, the Buddhists came and made Buddhism. Just as there are many opinions (*abhipraya*) these (men) have made that many castes. We shouldn't give castes too much value. Now everyone gives SCST (scheduled class and scheduled tribe) children food and clothes. But SCST children are coming ahead but our caste is still poor. Why can't they give our caste also? As if our caste is always rich! Even we are poor aren't we?

Politics of class and caste, where one could be of a higher caste and lower class simultaneously, put Ambika outside of many benefits accruing from a decreasingly welfare state. Ambika talked at length about the importance of the farming community and the richness of the Kannada language. She believed neither had been given much significance in the nation. In fact the nation had failed her community, allowing green fields to be paved over for urban development. She clung to what was left of her neighborhood.

> We are farmers and now we have that pride of ownership. This is our land, these are our crops. If we lived in Bangalore (city) and faced all that pollution, that would be bad. Now if we stay here we have good air, good environment. But in the town we don't have all that. Here once a year we have a festival and all the ceremonies with it. There in the city we cannot do all these community festivities. Everyone sits in their jobs or their own homes.

Shubha and Ambika discussed the irony in the authorship of the first Kannada language dictionary by the British priest Reverend Ferdinand Kittel. The cultural residue of British colonialism lingered in the dominance of English language films over regional language films, they believed. Kannada films frequently either cloned formats and storylines from other regional language films or merely dubbed them over in Kannada. In a blanket statement equating English language cinema with the only Western dominant entity she was aware about, that is, the British colonial empire, Ambika said:

> We have stopped seeing Kannada films. The men go to the cinema and say, "Oh there is nothing of value in the Kannada cinema. Let's go and see an English film." English, English, *everything* is English. These Britishers have brought so many things and what they have brought is their culture and language and left it here. ... They may have left the country but their culture has been left behind.

Such a statement is a telling commentary on the postcolonial awareness these rural teens shared. They were staunchly protective of their native language; they were aware of increasing forays into their local culture with the very visible presence of multinational corporations cropping up in their neighborhoods, which not too long ago were filled with rice and paddy fields. They chose Kannada language programs on Udaya TV. They watched such serials as *Mangalya* (Marriage) and *Mahabayi* (Great Woman), which portrayed loyal female characters who silently yet stridently negotiated through various crises in their lives. These characters were able to effect change in their circumstances without disrespecting traditions and cultural norms. Their appreciation of Kannada serials did not extend to film and music-based programs, however. They believed Telugu language programs were far more innovative than the mundane fare on Kannada language networks. Despite the fact that regional language networks indulged in large-scale cloning and copying, Shubha and Ambika wished Udaya TV borrowed more from its other vernacular counterparts. For example, Ambika said:

> In Telugu, in (Eenadu) TV they have the *Dance Baby Dance* (competition) program. Now if they only had that on our Udaya TV or our Ushe TV—in all our Kannada TV networks—that would be great. They think these Kannada people have no brains and they cannot dance properly. That's what the Telugu people say. But the Kannada people are in no way less than the Telugu people. If only we had the same program on Udaya TV, we would get fame and importance.

It is ironic that Ambika is referring to a reality dance competition that draws from Western dance styles and is naturalized as the "Indian urban" in Telugu films. The popularity of the dance program has provided a spotlight on Telugu language and culture and it is that popularity that she desired for her own language. Similarly, Shubha discussed other Telugu programs such as *Once More Please*, a reality show where competitors imitate film actors, cricket players, and so on. In the *Demandappa Demandu* program, viewers' mail and phone calls were answered. Shubha wished these popular programs were cloned on the Kannada networks.

All of these comments indicate the fierce pride both girls had in their state, village, neighborhood, and school, which had recently added buildings so students didn't have to sit under trees for classes. Their lives, which depended on the vagaries of nature, gave them a keen sense of their immediate surroundings. They were reminded every day to be respectful of nature and personified its manifestations. The rain fed their crops, the crops kept them alive. Although suspicious of the "modernity" brought about by the obvious multinational intruders in their neighborhoods, they desired the "modernity" depicted on private, regional television networks. They talked about foreign cultures and television programs in disparaging terms and reconstructed mythical pasts and landscapes even as they recognized the value of their education in joining the nation's journey to globalized modernity.

The words of Shubha and Ambika reflect the systematic process of political forgetting where, Fernandes (2004) writes, rural populations and marginalized groups are rendered invisible in the nation-state's strategic efforts to advance the interests of the middle class. Such a "forgetting" is not the inadvertent offshoot of economic globalization, but is a political process "in which dominant social groups and political actors attempt to naturalise these processes of exclusion by producing a middle-class-based definition of citizenship" (p. 2416). The success of India's new middle class (NMC) is vital for the progress of the nation. These teens demonstrated an increasing awareness of the disappearance of their neighborhoods, demanded recognition through essentialized notions of their communities (as farmers, for example), and sought avenues of representation through the synthetic constructions of "modernity" on television. The irony is apparent: they sought visibility through the same channels that rendered them invisible, arguing for a more "modern" representation of their native state, even though those very representations would further wipe their faces off the screen.

This fascinating accommodation of certain types of modernity based on familiarity with language, style, and region, to name a few identity markers, will lead to a discussion of the intricate ideological workings of translation, at the end of this chapter. We now examine a connecting narrative to Shubha and Ambika's tales of local pride—Anujoth's description of Sikh Punjabi life.

Highlighting the various festivals in her Sikh religion, Anujoth said they symbolized a time for cooking together, running around with friends, and dressing up in vibrantly colored clothes. The practice of Sikhism involves daily recitals from memory of the teachings of Guru Granth Sahib. Followers revere 11 *gurus* or teachers, beginning with Guru Nanak who lived in the fifteenth century. Commemorations of either the birth or martyrdom of each of the *gurus* include attending the *gurudwara* or place of worship where passages from the scripture are read. Communal cooking and eating take place before and after worship, respectively. Growing up in a Sikh household, Anujoth had a deep sense of secularism and social justice. Sikhs generally regard child marriage as taboo, are welcoming of anyone who wishes to enter the *gurudwara*, and are taught not to discriminate against caste and class, even in marriage. Anujoth glowed with pride when she talked about her culture:

> I think it is a *very* vibrant culture, full of energy, and it is really nice, we celebrate our festivals. As Sikhs, we go to the gurudwara. And we are supposed to do these five *kaurs* (conditions) among which are to have long hair, wear this *kesh* (bangle), *kada* (comb) and a *kirpan* (sword) which many men carry [*sic*].

Anujoth joined her family and elders in preparing a variety of foods at the gurudwara for a Sunday community dinner (*langar*) after prayers. She talked animatedly about festive street processions (*julus*) to commemorate the birth of a saint or *guru*. While men and women walk in the procession, children are taken in trucks that proceed slowly through the streets amidst cheers from their occupants and passersby. The processions usually end with fireworks and food. Reflecting on her friends, she was amused to find that each represented a certain region of the nation:

> I am a Punjabi, then there's a Gujarati, then there's a Marathi, there's a Kannadiga, there is a Malayali, so we're all over the country, and we are all so different in every way but we blend together really well. So it's like having a variety; all of us have different traits, different characteristics, our outlook towards life is different.

The Sikh community is a minority in India; national and private Indian television on the other hand cater to the Hindu upper middle class (Rajagopal, 2001; Mankekar, 1999; McMillin, 2002). Anujoth was an avid viewer of Hindi language soap operas and sitcoms and did not choose to watch religious Sikh programs on the rare occasion that it was broadcast.

As quite a stark contrast, other Indian teens were not so enthusiastic about culture, nation, or religion. Ashok (a 15-year-old, middle-income Christian boy) and Teja (a 14-year-old, upper-income Hindu boy) for example, talked about Hinduism as a detriment to progress because of its high value on mythology and rituals. These teens also talked about fluency in English as being a key factor to upward mobility. They discussed education as most significantly influencing their positions in city and nation. In fact, India was an embarrassment for its poverty and bureaucracy. Having lived in the heart of the city most of their lives, their attachment to ancestral villages or towns was not a tangible concept. Their membership in the cosmopolitan, technology-rich, and fast-paced Bangalore city was more concrete. Reminiscent of Luke's comments in Johannesburg, Ashok said the nation's tremendous diversity in religions, traditions, and customs kept the nation "backward." Luke said this would result in cultural "cocoons" in South Africa; Ashok said this would insulate people from one another in India. India's multiculturalism and development status meant that opportunities were severely limited for its youth. Ashok perceived there to be a very real "obstacle to knowledge and the pursuit of knowledge." Although Indians were pious and patriotic, their beliefs and traditions held them back in a globalizing world. He himself was poised for more active participation because of his religion: Christianity. This "modern" and rational faith set Ashok apart from the myth and magic of Hinduism; he believed:

> What I have heard about different gods is that when a person commits sin, he is punished. He is slaughtered and killed, but what I have experienced in Christianity is there is forgiveness and that's the advantage here. Whatever sin you have done you can confess it to the Lord and He forgives. He died for us, we have got the free gift of it.

Ashok was forceful in his assertion that he would primarily identify himself as Christian, not Indian, not a Tamil speaker, not even a resident of Bangalore: "Not just for the namesake but as really a follower of Christ." His involvement with the church youth group made him "feel it is easy to read the Bible and know about God and what are all His plans for me." His primary purpose, he said, was to live according to God's will: "I have to lead a righteous life. That is the main thing (that) is now in my mind. Like this is the age of getting distracted too much, towards evil things and many other evil oppressions." When asked what he meant by "righteous" and "evil oppressions," Ashok responded that righteous meant "keeping all commandments of what our God has listed out in our Bible," while evil oppressions meant sex. He struggled with the practice of being a Christian, however. His friends taunted him about proving that his God was "the one true God. ... These go exactly opposite to what we follow in Christianity, exactly the opposite goes. So it is difficult to be a Christian." He was radical about his faith yet was aware that he had to be tolerant toward other religions and cultures.

Teja believed that Indian teens' singular focus on education coupled with social conservatism prevented them from having fun like the teenagers on American television. As he put it, "A teenager should be more like what they show on TV. Teenagers who are in India, they are pretty much concerned about their educational qualification and about their ambition." He continued that "In India it is different you know, you go to foreign countries, you ask, every damn fellow will have a girlfriend. It is not (the case) here." He said Indian teens should relax and enjoy life more; they needed to ease up on their worries to get ahead academically. Teja's comments demonstrated a perceived freedom among peers in the West, a common trait among youth in disparate regions of the world. Images of freedom and of the "good life" may not actually be accessible even to those whose lives seem to be mirrored on television. Yet the very idea that such possibilities exist in the face of very real parental controls can lead to despair and frustration. Appadurai (2000) calls such occurrences "relations of disjuncture" (p. 5), where the consumer comes to believe she or he is watching a wonderful world unfolding, only from the outside.

For Zohrab, ethnic or regional identity did not carry much relevance. Relatives on both Parsi and Goan sides of his family primarily resided in Mumbai. What was more real to him was not a rootedness but a continual uprooting; he naturally saw himself as a voyager, an outsider. Speaking of his exclusion from school and neighborhood peers because of his unfamiliarity with Kannada, the local language, he said:

> I always feel like, I don't know, I feel like I am *acting* (with) them. Like I am acting as if I know everything and I am better than them and everything, and I *feel* that I don't mix in with the crowd well. I don't know, like they would be talking about their Kannada films and whatever, and I would (miss) out on that.

He was beginning to understand the Kannada language which sometimes made it harder for him because he could understand bits and pieces when other students talked about him: "They (other students) always think, 'Oh *he* won't understand what we are saying, let's say something in Kannada,' but I can understand it." Zohrab's awkwardness at not speaking Kannada also translated into a sense of superiority that he was not local or native to the state. Like Ashok, he placed himself above his peers because of his fluency in English, his lighter skin (although not light enough, he believed), his somewhat Western lifestyle, and his Christian religion. Zohrab had been raised Catholic and regularly attended the Catholic church in the neighborhood, about a 20-minute walk from his house. He also attended a Protestant church, half the distance away. He was active in the latter's youth group and enjoyed playing the lead role in its many plays. He shared the strong faith of Ashok and Themba: "I know there's a *God*, I know His son Jesus Christ, I believe in Him, and that's it." He preferred the Protestant church for its simple lessons on faith, he said, but recognized the material benefits of identifying himself as a Roman Catholic: first preference for enrollment in the prestigious English-language Catholic schools and colleges in the city, regardless of grade point average. In the context of the highly competitive, high-stress environment of college admissions, Catholics had a distinct advantage in the premier educational institutions in the city. Although Zohrab was an outsider in terms of language and ethnicity among his Kannada-speaking, Hindu classmates and schoolmates, he believed his religion was his anchor. He could worship one God while his Hindu friends worshipped many gods and his Muslim friends had to adhere to a very strict and complex religion, he said. Religion awarded him simplicity whereas everything else in his life was anything but simple. Unlike Ashok, however, Zohrab expressed a great amount of latitude:

> Actually I feel the purpose of religion is actually not like "Oh you are Allah and you are Christian and Jesus and you are some whatever God you are,"...uhm ... it's actually for a person to go on the right track. If there was no religion, people wouldn't go to church, they wouldn't bother about confessing their sins, they wouldn't bother about what they're doing, whether it is wrong or not, and ... uhm ... almost all the religions say the same thing. No religion is going to say go and steal somebody else's thing and ... all the religions have the same thing, don't steal don't kill don't ... whatever.

Zohrab was the only teen of all respondents in the *TV Characters* project who talked about himself as a global citizen:

> Just a few weeks ago, I used to throw plastic anywhere. ... Now I have plans of making plastic into something else like ... like (take) any plastic, strip it into a piece, just one strip, okay, then when the plastic gets over, then attach it to another one and then plait it. It becomes a thick plait or even a thin plait and you can make mats.

Zohrab excitedly discussed various ways to protect the environment. He was discouraged by how little Indians did to maintain clean surroundings. He believed it was a monumental effort to get fellow Indians to recycle, throw trash into garbage bins around the city, and to conserve energy. Unable to relate to his Kannada-speaking classmates and unable to speak any of the regional languages, Zohrab stuck to English television and films, further isolating himself from his peers.

Interviews and observations revealed a strong egocentrism within a majority of these teens. National or even global memberships were nebulous and abstract. More concrete were their connections to local and familial communities of religion, language, village, and culture. Television, rather than *creating* a space for expression of identity, provided an *extension* of an already evolving teen identity. The complex packaging of historical memory and current global possibility has stark relevance for Johannesburg and Bangalore that are witnessing significant changes in political and geographical landscapes. Indian rural teens in particular were living in the midst of transformations where within their own neighborhoods, ramshackle tenements were suddenly being smartened up with bright paint and wrought iron railings across terraces, to signal to new immigrant technical workers in the multinational corporations, that paying guest accommodations were available. These teens were keenly aware that their villages and localities were current hot spots of outsourced production venues. Their discussions of land, religion, customs, and television reflected this sensibility. Feelings of patriotism were intermingled with frustration at national bureaucracy; praise for local television programs were delivered with denunciations of amateurish productions that marked the divide between local and global media products.

In the comments of the teens in Bangalore we get a sense of India as what Ahmad (1992) calls "an unfinished bourgeois project." These include "certain notions of canonicity in tandem with the bourgeois, upper-caste dominance of the nation-state; a notion of classicism part Brahmanical, part borrowed from Europe, (and) the ongoing subsumption of literary utterances and cultures by print capitalism" (p. 15).

Hierarchies of class, ethnicity, language, religion, and so on receive strange assimilationist and segregationist treatment simultaneously. Ashok, Teja, and Zohrab could relegate the Indian nation to premodern status, in their ordering of a world that progressed through rationality and universality. They internalized Enlightenment ideals circulated in various residual colonial and contemporary neocolonial processes that were integrated into their educational and urban lived experiences. We see here at work Fanon's (1965/1961) conceit of the split subject that locates the colonized within a torture chamber of identity where the individual wrestles with a self as traditional and as a loss of self within the modern. What exactly makes a nation postcolonial is difficult to define, particularly when such a condition is complicated by surges of neocolonialism in globalization. What *is* apparent is the continuation of the internalization of the colonizer's loathing within the postcolonial subject, an ambiguous self-criticism within the struggle to express the urban or modernized self. As Venn (2006) writes:

> The recognition of the co-existing "multiple temporalities"—the linear, fast time of modernity and the slower recurrent time of "tradition," and the home or the domus in which real subjects find themselves in concrete situations everywhere is a lesson that postcolonial theory must keep on its agenda. (p. 3)

The urban teens' valuation of the perceived mobility, fast pace, freedom, and clean environments that teens in Western cities enjoyed also cultivated within them a sense of opportunity. The ticket to upward mobility was apparent: "unaccented" fluency or rather, middle-America-accented fluency in the English language, and a professional education. On the other hand, rural teens Shubha and Ambika derided identifiable "foreign" products on the marketplace and English language movies and television programs. They were unaware of the cultural translations in the format transfer of countdown dance and singing reality shows or high-ticket game shows. Butler (2000, pp. 35–36) cautions that

> Of course, translation by itself can also work in full complicity with the logic of colonial expansion, when translation becomes the instrument through which dominant values are transposed into the language of the subordinated, and the subordinated run the risk of coming to know and understand them as tokens of their "liberation." But this is a limited view of colonialism, one which assumes that the colonized emerges as a subject according to norms that are recognizably Eurocentric.

Here we see that the subjects that emerged were hardly recognizable as images of a neocolonial power (in this case, at the very least, as the implied consumers of local imitations of global reality game shows). Yet their appreciation of what they considered an "authentic" local product and their unawareness of its derivative nature speaks about the internalization of a circulation of social and cultural capital, where definitions of modernity and urbanity continue to privilege the industrialized core of the old order world system. The opportunism in hybrid programming that combines elements of global and local only inasmuch as such combinations are profitable (which means they rarely step outside of entrenched stereotypes, colonial or otherwise), means that the subjects of consumption of these products can never really be sure which guise they are operating from, trained in themselves to such opportunism. The recognition of the opportunism inherent in unequal relations of power, for both sides of that relation, is where transformative possibilities can also occur (Ashcroft, 2001), a theme we address at the end of this book.

Neighborhood as World

In urban locales in Munich and New York, we encountered a bewilderment, even disinterest, in questions of global citizenship. For example, Strohmaier and Lakhotia (2004) reported that 14-year-old teens in Munich, Pascal, Verena, and Mario, responded in literal terms when asked to comment on how they would describe themselves in terms of national and community identity: they said they were residents of Munich. It was as simple as that. The comments of teens in Germany have to be placed within the context of the political and media structure they were situated in. As briefly presented in Chapter Three, the teens were exposed to an integrated broadcasting environment developed by European Union (EU) to support the integrity of the region as a whole.[21] The Broadcasting Directive of the EU "is an effort to use television and radio to undergird a European culture and identity" (Price, 1995, p. 19). Ever since its establishment in 1957 after the Second World War, the European Economic Community (EEC) has worked its way toward achieving a common currency and an Internal Market (IM) or Single European Market (SEM) among its member countries. The European Union (EU) perceived as its immediate goal a free common market among its members. By the early 1980s, it was clear that for Europe to compete effectively with Japan and the United States, economic barriers that hindered the flow of people, goods, and services between European nations had to be removed. This, it was hoped, would achieve an economy of scale that would step up productivity, lower prices, entice foreign investment, and create the biggest and most powerful market of consumers in the world. While dominant political processes determined the economic and political integration of the members of the EU, these processes meant the social and cultural identities of each member nation underwent significant redefinition as well.[22] The activities and goals of the EU and the resistance and compliance from its member states have been brought to viewers through a barrage of media images.[23] Writing at a time when the EU was as yet nascent having been implemented in January 1993, Wilson (1993) commented,

> a war of images about the E(U) has been increasingly waged in the communication media of the member states. This media blitz—it is impossible to pick up any major

newspaper in any of the capitals of the E(U) 12 and avoid reading about "the E(U), the government, the nation, and you"—reflects both the importance of the events taking place and the need for individuals and groups to recognize their material interests in the process. (p. 8)[24]

The role of the mass media in facilitating a pan-European identity was of great interest to policymakers and media scholars alike. The year 1992 was defined as a landmark for the lifting of all trade and regulatory barriers between European nations. The "1992" moment was postponed to January 1, 1993, and has

> become a symbol for all social and cultural change, a potent new myth of identity which is tantalizing and troubling at the same time. For all members of the Europe-an Community (EC), the idea of Europe after 1992 raises significant questions about the future of national identity and about the nature of future economic and cultural relationships. (Jaffe, 1993, p. 61)

Morley and Robins (1995) argued that the public service mission of media corporations shifted to an aggressive commercial mission. Their imperatives were to break down old nationalist boundaries and to reorganize business strategies so that citizens across Europe could subscribe to "universal" principles of consumerism.

The German teens in the *TV Characters* project had grown up within an integrated EU and an aggressively commercialized media environment. The birthing anxieties and struggles for definitions of national and regional identity were features of the landscape of their childhood and burgeoning adulthood. The character of the Munich suburbs they lived in had seen rapid change in recent years. While in earlier decades suburbs were quite segregated ethni-cally, in the late 1990s and early 2000s, there were shifts in real estate where neighborhoods were getting more diverse in response to employment patterns. R. W. Larson (2002) discusses that congested urban neighborhoods create a variety of issues for young people. It

> bring(s) groups in closer contact throughout the world, making issues of ethnic coex-istence for adolescents paramount. In dense urban environments, where people live in look-alike high-rise apartments or blighted slums, one can imagine scenarios in which competition for identity and respect will fuel new levels of interethnic gang violence. (p. 11)

Some of these tensions were expressed by the teens in Munich. They wanted to be politically correct in their comments about diverse neighbors, but related an acute sense of discomfort at having to interact or negotiate with people of a different ethnicity than themselves. Mario, for example, stressed that he was German, despite his mother's Italian heritage and the fact that both parents' families lived in southwest Bavaria. When asked why he didn't include his multiethnic background in his response, he was clear, "I don't like *Kanaks*," a derogatory term for foreigner. Rather than attach himself to a particular locale, Mario wanted to be known as a "Schwab," identifying himself with the Schwaben, a people historically from Northern Bavaria from where Karl the Great (or Charlemagne) is believed to be from. He claimed kinship with his relatives living in the area without addressing their actual lineage from Italy. He emphasized that his mother was only part Italian, hardly knew the language, and was born in Germany. As for his maternal relatives, "Some are stupid but some are totally okay."

Other teens from ethnically diverse Munich suburbs preferred to be associated with the city of Munich itself. Martina, for example, who lived and went to school in the rural suburb of Neubiberg, said she would refer to herself as a native of Munich because "Neubiberg ... well nobody would really know it ... that is why I would say Munich." Her favorite television channel, ProSieben, depicted Munich as the backdrop for many of its programs and films. Christian, like Martina, said he should be called a "well, *Münchner* ... because ... this is my *heimat*, I was born here, here I know my way around. And that's it, and all my friends live here." Christian was a resident of the blue-collar town of *Isarvorstadt*, which had a high population of Turkish immigrants. He was quite clear that even when he grew up, he would move within 100 kilometers of the city, perhaps thinking of the village in Bavaria that his mother came from, at that distance from the city center. Verena as well identified herself as a resident of the city, even though she lived in the eastern rural district of Waldtrudering. She also called herself a *Münchnerin* because,

> I love this city. Well I have already been in very many cities because all my relatives live in other places, and so far I find Munich the most beautiful place. ... In Munich you can get anything, you have it all, also quiet places, well I mean it is not that hectic and big as for example a big city like Berlin which is really huge but here you can also find your privacy. ... I have grown up here ... and I have lived in this house ever since I was born.

Unlike her peers who wanted to be associated with the vibrant and picturesque city of Munich, Nazan called Turkey home. Her comments on her Turkish "homeland," even though she was born and raised in Germany, reflected ideologies of development. She described Turkey as a "lesser self" of Germany. It was a country of stray animals and sunny weather, according to Nazan. Yet she felt a strong sense of belonging through her participation in youth events at the local Turkish center. While she was ostracized at school and in her neighborhood as an immigrant, at the youth center, people would say, "Hey cool! You are—you come from our country. You are cool." Her daily experience of being an outsider in her Gersthofen neighborhood, where she was taunted with "you are all stupid' and "you want to have our country" by German teens, made her Turkish "coolness" at the youth center particularly appealing and empowering. Nazan's experience and its difference from that of her peers convey a sense of the global ordering of nations and peoples that withstands fluxes in political and economic processes. Ideological positioning of modern and traditional, progressive and backward have remarkable endurance, internalized as "just the way things are" by newer and newer generations.

The responses of these teens resonate with some of the observations made by Grixti (2006) in his study of how Maltese youth accommodated the relatively sudden influx of foreign programs as the nation became part of the European Union. Among teens in Malta, there was a tendency to prefer the foreign over local programs, and to dismiss current mundane practices for the freedom of choice enjoyed by the wide range of characters on foreign programs. As with their discussions of gender, the Maltese participants essentialized how they talked about global and local, similar to the young people discussed here.

We see the continued articulations of these relations among the teens in New York. Fisherkeller and Freud (2006) discussed that few of these teens talked about being American, and from the biggest economic and political power in the world. Perhaps because none of them was Caucasian, and all were either African American or second- or third-generation immigrants, they talked most about their ethnic heritage. Angel, born in Puerto Rico, called himself New Yorican. This was an ingenious way to flag Puerto Rico as his birthplace, Spanish as the language he spoke at home, and America, as the country of his residence. Angel had moved among a variety of neighborhoods with his family. His wide circle of friends included a variety of cultural backgrounds. He said:

in all the schools I went to there were a lot of different people. Usually my friends in Philadelphia were black and white because I went to a black and white school. When I moved here there were a lot of Spanish [sic].

Tia, a 14-year-old, was proud to be an American, because in America, "you are allowed to learn from mistakes." Like Themba and Kgomotso in Johannesburg, she faced the stark realities of police brutality, racism, and poverty in her Brooklyn neighborhood.

Claims of Authenticity

For many of the teens, the distance between their world and that of the adults in their lives was vast; their sense of authoritative subjectivity (Demerath & Lynch, 2008) gained momentum in their discussions of self and interests particularly with adults (McMillin & Fisherkeller, 2008). The depth with which teens responded to questions about their neighborhoods, communities, nations, and selves varied with the access researchers had with the teens. In Johannesburg and Bangalore, researchers were quite often invited into respondents' homes and lengthy conversations took place over meals. In Munich as well, researchers were invited into respondents' bedrooms—questions were discussed in depth with ample time for clarification. In New York, however, interviews could be conducted only at the community center that the teens attended after school hours. Time was limited to develop rapport with the teens and responses were consequently limited. Nevertheless, the comments from the New York teens could be placed in context and brief as they were, provided important connections with those of the other teens in the study.

Overall, based on their class backgrounds and the extent to which they felt supported within their families, the teens expressed varying degrees of agentic beliefs (Demerath & Lynch, 2008). All recognized the supremacy of television programs from North American or British networks; aesthetics of production of locally originated programs in Bangalore and Johannesburg, although in many cases preferred by their viewers, were discussed in comparison to their global counterparts. For example, Rabia and Nina in Johannesburg critiqued the amateurish anchored variety shows on the SABC and wished they were more polished in production. In Bangalore, Teja, Ashok, and Zohrab were quite vocal in their preferences for American sitcoms, dramas, and reality shows, deriding the slow-paced melodramas on the Indian networks. What is evident here is the robustness of development ideologies not just in perceptions of program production quality, but in content as well. The processes by which hybrid products come to be profitable, affordable, and by which they are heralded as representatives of a new global democracy do not signify an easy comradeship between global and local; the alliance is hardly an equitable one. It is caustic, it is maddening in its power plays, and it packs in the trauma of colonial practices (Donadey, 2001). Simultaneous global releases, powerful transnational distribution systems, and hybrid products resulting from licensed and unlicensed copying (Moran & Keane, 2004) may certainly be facilitated through globalization. Global franchises such as *Idol* and *Big Brother* could quite possibly reconfigure the relationship between parents and children, and between citizen and state. At a very fundamental level, viewers may be pledging allegiance to a modern nation-state (Dolby, 2006). Yet the equation of the simultaneity of television time with the contemporaneity of cultural experiences (Wilk, 1994) results in a partial picture. Such a theoretical stance is a common trend in studies of consumption, and misses the important nuances in how so-called global media products are *received*. There is no unifying clock-binding experiences; the linking of globally disparate experiences through simultaneity of time is misleading. Instead what could also be occurring is a reinforcement of the gap between lives unravelling on television and those watching it, particularly in non western locales. Just when we see myriad market choices open up, we see a cooling off in theoretical fervor with regard to tackling agency and its limitations. In fact, we see a continued celebration of globalization with the deterritorialization of people, goods, and services in response to the call of transnational corporations who promise better standards of living than those offered by state-based institutions (Friedman, 2005). Many have cautioned against this "flat world" hypothesis, contending instead, that globalization, while providing liberatory interconnections, also exacerbates colonial hierarchies and creates new zones of inequality (Appadurai, 1996; McMillin, 2007).

What is argued here is not that we need to celebrate or romanticize difference as is the trend in corporate approaches to consumption. The neoliberal market logic thrives on articulations of "uniqueness," whether it is in the promotion of different cell phone covers for each day of the week, or custom Facebook applications. Shome (2006, p. 13) writes, "If the cultural logic of imperialism before the Second World War days was the suppression of difference, the cultural logic of neoliberalism (as the new face of imperialism in the 21st century) is the encouragement and production of difference." Cultural difference, then, cannot be the primary analytical category through which we examine teen choices, but the ideological distances between those differences.

The choice of English as the primary language of most of the interviews also played into its unquestioned global relevance. Rural Indian teens, 15-year-old Shubha and 14-year-old Ambika, as we may recall, were notable exceptions.

Shubha, in fact, prefaced her responses in the interview by saying that if anyone wanted to speak to her, the conversation would have to be conducted in her native language, Kannada. She said she was

> first a Kannadiga. Then *only* (will I think of) the nation. Now the Hindi language, they (North Indian nationalists) have worked so hard and made it the national language. In the same way, we should work hard and make (Kannada) the national language, even the global language. It should be the language of the world. *That* is my *dream.*

Ambika followed in the same vein:

> I am a Kannadiga. Not so much Indian (from) Karnataka (or) Immadehalli ... not so much ... We should give the Kannada language prominence. What is there to uphold in the nation? The *language* is most important and we should give utmost importance to the language.

For the other teens in this first phase of the *TV Characters* project, English, whether spoken natively or not, was the language of currency particularly in Bangalore, Johannesburg and New York. English awards a global mobility especially to young viewers across the globe. We are reminded of Ahmad's (1992) delineation of the ideological power brought about by the imposition of the English language on the colonies:

> The claim of English to be a unifying force ... has not been diminished but enlarged. These enlarged uses of English in India, and of the metropolitan languages in virtually all the ex-colonial countries of Asia and Africa, are connected, further-more, with the consolidation, expansion, increased self-confidence, increased leisure, increased sophistication of the bourgeoisie classes in these countries, including its middle strata, especially the modern petty bourgeoisie located in the professions and in the state apparatuses. ... (English is) *the* language of national integration and bourgeois civility. (p. 75)

Preferences for English-language programming by even non-native speakers of English must be viewed in this gentrification context. Their selections came easily, a logical outcome of their "naturalized" education and urban home environments.

To explore further how the ground provides, oftentimes, a markedly different picture than what makes it up into grand theory, we reiterate some observations about the Indian teens that set them apart from the other teens in this study. This is not because of any special ability, but precisely because they were located in a context that was and continues to be the hot spot to watch, globally. They conveyed an anxiety to succeed academically, and an awareness of material positioning that was different from that of the other teens in this project. Perhaps this was because their lives were unraveling through the cultural production of a postcolonial modernity that provided varying degrees to which they could articulate agency. Such agency was textured by what Lukose (2005, p. 931) calls "post-colonial preoccupations about tradition and modernity" deployed by elders in their circles of interaction. The *TV Characters* study indicated that in Bangalore, in the midst of larger-than-life reminders of unchecked capitalism in the towering billboards of Gap and Levis jeans, and the multistoried offices of IBM and Hewlett Packard, assertions of native pride were all the more vehement, especially by rural teens. These believed big city development was a real threat to their way of living and to their cultures and traditions. The "nation" as a community of belonging, didn't carry much significance for them. More tangible was their membership in communities of religion or culture. Television facilitated a certain subjective agency in its consumers where they were exposed to a range of responses that conveyed a sense of freedom and autonomy despite the fact that they were bound within the very systems that produced such responses.

Fernandes' (2004) discussion of the reorganization of urban spaces into areas of exclusion and marginalization in Mumbai are highly relevant for the transformations of Bangalore. High-priced multiplexes bring the latest Bollywood, Tollywood, and Hollywood films to the middle class, effectively keeping the lower class out of the air-conditioned, plush-seated theaters. Upscale clubs and restaurants provide venues for the NMC to pour its money, easily slipping into place segregatory membership structures set up by British colonial social clubs. Unlike patterns of workplace-residence separation in industrialized countries, disturbances in urban upper-income neighborhoods by slum dwellers and squatters is common, with some of these populations providing essential services such as house cleaning and *dhobi* or laundry service, and delivering vegetables and milk to doorsteps. In such a mix, neighborhood beautification programs and state-run efforts to weed out illegal immigrants must be seen as a larger national effort to sanitize the city by driving out its poor.

Shubha and Ambika were children of farmers in a country that was hurtling toward more and more aggressive capitalism, limiting even more than it did in its socialist past, its remunerations to the agricultural community. Yet through their television choices, they spoke with great agency on how they should have the same variety of programs depicted on Telugu television. They too could call in or mail in their requests for programs. Or they could participate in the endless reality shows and become big winners. Their sense of autonomy and empowerment was real. As is starkly obvious, however, such "breaks" are scarce. Viewers and on-screen participants contribute to television's success and the revitalization of the capitalist environment rather than any true individual betterment. For Ashok, Teja, Anujoth, and Zohrab, television offered tantalizing distractions from their serious pursuit of higher studies. It gave them a choice in how to live their lives; it told them they could sit back and laugh once in a while—perhaps even date. They were ambiguous about this distraction, however. Although television could draw them into a more carefree lifestyle than they were accustomed to, coming from conservative families, they knew there were no compromises on diligent academic work. Their sense of agency in choosing the lifestyle of the global teen was tempered by their keen sense of subjectivity in an environment that still rewarded education over enterprise. Obviously then, their loyalties were to the local, be it language, land, culture, education, or religion. The global was provocative, but the local came with familiar, secure, and time-tested structures to keep them in their places. India has, in the recent past, been touted as an emerging giant. With the economic crisis in the United States, predictions of India gradually holding the upper hand in information technologies in both service provision *and* research and development seem a possibility. The *TV Characters* study was conducted when the outsourcing industry was booming in urban Indian locales.

The conditions of globalization bring back into focus postcolonial identity. Postcolonial societies intimately engage in imperial culture, finding themselves at a competitive advantage with even the proletariat in the imperial center. The competitive advantage comes not just from the legacy of the English language or the manner of transactions left behind by colonialism; it also comes from knowing one's place, the ingrained internalized slave mentality or, to put it more elegantly, the role of the service provider. The long-term disadvantage of the momentary advantage becomes obvious. As Serequeberhan (2007) writes, "For in being malleable step children hiding behind timid and compliant smiles, in having endured the harder and stifling control of a 'mère coloniale,' is it not possible that *we see*, if not more, then *differently*, than those to whose humanity this heritage has always been partial?" (p. xx, emphases in original). To explore more closely, this *seeing*, and anxiety to be a super class, we examine in Chapter Five, fieldwork among teens in Bangalore.

· 5 ·
YOUTH IN A HOT SPOT

Slummin' It *Millionaire* Style

Slumdog Millionaire, grossing $160 million worldwide at the time of its clean sweep of the Oscars, winning 8 Academy Awards from 10 nominations on February 22, 2009, serves as a complex metaphor for the Indian nation as it becomes a key player in global economics. The frenetic pace of *Slumdog*, and the anxieties of the protagonist Jamal, produce the young Indian nation, relatively speaking, as a bewildered adolescent, imbued with a sense of romance and mystery, constricted by poverty and social structure, yet offered a lifeline and chance at love, through global television. The refreshing "underdog makes it" story resonated with viewers across the globe, perhaps most keenly with audiences in the United States who were receiving dismal and more dismal news about the economy every day. In a globalized landscape, *Slumdog* must be viewed as a success not just for its rags-to-riches story, but for its transnational relevance, its production and distribution pedigree, and for the "new" modes in which it presents India for global consumption. That is, we have to evaluate how the movie makes available the realities of slum youth in India, and simultaneously, renders unavailable realities of Indians who may sit shoulder-to-shoulder with audiences viewing the movie in the West.

In the months since it debuted in August 2008, a variety of commentaries, both scholarly and popular, pointed out that *Slumdog* is quite conventional in its storyline. The stark poverty and violence that urban Indian poor face every day are common themes in Bollywood and regional films, as in the Hindi language *Chakra* (1981) or the Tamil language *Nayakan* (1987), for example. Mira Nair's *Salaam Bombay* (1988) was, in many ways, a tribute to Mumbai street children. The dramatic portrayal of the exploitation of youth in *Slumdog*, and the inclusion of catchy song-and-dance numbers, seemed to many, to follow the routine formula of Bollywood films. What then could explain the global success of the movie adapted from Indian diplomat Vikas Swarup's novel *Q&A*, directed by Danny Boyle, and scripted by Simon Beaufoyle? Perhaps, as film theorist David Bordwell blogged (February 1, 2009), it is the very fact that it *is* so formulaic, following forms across film history in the flashback, chronological narrative of how the slum boy comes to win the Indian franchised game show of *Who Wants to Be a Millionaire (Kaun Banega Crorepathi or KBC)*, and how his life intertwines with others, including his lost love, who shared his childhood. Perhaps, as the real-life host of *KBC*, Bollywood megastar Amitabh Bachchan (played by Anil Kapoor in the film) blogged (January 13, 2009), it provides a morbid voyeuristic opportunity for the world to peek into "India as (a) Third World dirty under belly developing nation." Or perhaps it is because, as various Bollywood filmmakers countered Bachchan's scathing comments, the storyline transcends nationalities and particularities ("India no slumdog ...," 2009) and audiences can truly relate to the struggles of Jamal. The theme of youth, hope, and agency is universal; British director Boyle was able to convey that through locale, people, and A. R. Rahman's original music compositions, that are essentially Indian, they said.

A key element is missing in all the commentary and analyses from critics and filmmakers: the economic structures that made the movie a hit. Produced by Celador, the British production company most famous for *Who Wants to Be a Millionaire* and distributed under initial agreement with Warner Independent Pictures and in subsequent partnership with Fox Searchlight Pictures, *Slumdog* could be moshed over ecstatic shoulders across the world because of its transnational distribution networks. The movie also portrayed actors who, although unknowns in the film circuit, were as far removed from the realities of Mumbai slums as their viewers in say, North America or Great Britain. Dev Patel, a British actor from Harrow, London, and Freida Pinto, a Mumbai-based fashion model, were duly wide-eyed and fresh-faced on the talk show circuit, appearing on *Ellen Degeneres* and *Late Night With David Letterman* to talk about the movie. Both actors had a transnational currency and fluency in English that facilitated their attendance at a variety of publicity-generating venues. With the director and producers, each claimed resonance between the movie's plot and her or his own life. The other primary actors in the movie, real-life slum residents Ayush Mahesh Khedekar and Tanay Chheda (playing the younger and middle Jamal, respectively) and Rubina Ali and Tanvi Ganesh Lonkar (playing the younger and middle Latika, respectively) certainly did not go on talk shows nor were they identified by name. They served as backdrop publicity in the form of photographs from production.

The movie therefore portrays a winning combination: a television-formula-within-movie-formula plot. In doing so, it provides currency and popularity for the ongoing *Millionaire* franchise on the small screen. It also taps into audience dreams and desires. It revives the colonial stereotype that India's poor *is* its urban landscape. It builds on India's *post*colonial stereotype that the country's own class and caste system and its corrupt bureaucracy are the cause of its downfall. It trains the global spotlight to ongoing systems of exploitation of the country's poverty-stricken youth. And it suggests, in a technique compatible with the economic logic of all reality shows (whether franchised or plagiarized, cloned or copied), such as *Millionaire*, *Idol*, and *Survivor*, that *any*one can make it. During a time in the United States where most people can identify with the kicked-in-the-groin breathlessness of Jamal, the victory of a nonmaterialistic slum dog can be deeply felt and rejoiced.

That victory can also be feared and caricatured, a phenomenon that has tragically repeated itself in colonial and imperialist histories around the world. Film and television serve as hegemonic structures that, as Butler (2000, p. 13) delineates, outlines the range of possibilities within a particular historical and political moment. *Slumdog*, quite predictably, in a hierarchical world that is witnessing the not-so-endearing rise of the periphery and the continued destabilization of the center, has deployed another round of essentialist interpellations for young Indians everywhere. One notable example is in the caricature of Indian American Bobby Jindal, Governor of Louisiana, that followed on the heels of *Slumdog*'s victory. Gov. Jindal's February 24, 2009 televised response to President Obama's economic stimulus package was widely criticized for its stiltedness and uninformed opinions. Speaking March 1, 2009, on his *D. L. Hughley Breaks the News* show on CNN, Hughley deadpanned in Jindal's monotone that the latter was *not* Jamal in *Slumdog Millionaire*. Conservative author and political commentator Ann Coulter wrote on HumanEvents. com: Headquarters of the Conservative Underground, "Wasn't Bobby Great in *Slumdog Millionaire*?" (Coulter, 2009). Jindal's own conservative policies aside, these flippant comments strategically reduce all "Indians" (regardless of whether their immigrant history is in fact more similar to the interpellator than the "native" they are identified with) to one unitary slum dweller. They also reflect a changing center-periphery dynamic. The periphery performs an important intimate function for the center as we see in the very obvious example of Indian urban labor servicing U.S. information industries. The periphery may no longer suffer as dramatically as the spill offs from center capitalist policies, but is a contentious presence at the table, demanding its share of the pie. With the rise in skepticism in the government's role in effecting any substantial solution for the U.S. economy, the anxieties of the popular are picked up by its scribes, reaffirming center-periphery divides, at least in discourse.

Our task in Chapter Five is significant. Not only do we unearth global interpellatory forces that call the young Indian to take on more and more jobs crafting for her or him the immediate rewards in the system, but we also draw in the inherent violence in such interpellation, where the slum dog *can be* a millionaire, but remains a slum dog, nevertheless. Once again we draw on Butler (2000) to remind us that "in this sense, the task of the postcolonial translator, we might say, is precisely to bring into relief the non-convergence of discourses so that one might know through the very ruptures of narrativity the founding violences of an episteme" (p. 37).

What we study in this chapter is the variety of contextual factors that prepare Indian teens for the globalized marketplace. These youth are frequently written about in *Time and Newsweek*, as the new labor currency in global politics (see, for example, Zakaria, 2006; Paley, 2006). During their early to mid teen years (13–16 years), they are still in high school, just getting oriented not just to the academic and employment pressures awaiting them after they graduate, but to notions of romance, upward mobility, and global agency. How they negotiate between the strong local, familial influences channeled through culture, religion, and so on, and the somewhat ethereal global media environment becomes an interesting process to examine. We discuss here, in depth, ethnographic fieldwork conducted in 2005[25] among 30 teenagers in Bangalore, from various ethnic, religious, socioeconomic, and regional backgrounds. A central question that informed fieldwork from February through May 2005 was how do family and social structures influence Indian teen identity and choice of television? How do these television choices work with the teen's local contexts to produce a sense of agency, that is, a sense of direction in *who* the teen is and desires to become?

The elaborate research schedule included individual interviews, focus group discussions, active immersion in the teens' social lives, and participant observation. To approach as close and varied an understanding of the community as possible, participants' homes were visited multiple times. Neighbors and relatives were included in discussions. Of the 30 teens chosen for the study, 4 dropped out for various reasons, some of which were family pressures, exam schedules, and lack of time. To include a broad socioeconomic and religious spectrum, the teens were interviewed in various parts of Bangalore city. Some were from the middle and lower-income Nagavarpalya neighborhood, particularly where families of Air Force and Army personnel lived. Most of the children in this neighborhood went to the nearby Kendriya Vidyalaya School that trained students for the All-India 10th grade CBSE examinations. Further interviews were conducted in the Whitefield, Indiranagar, and Koramangala neighborhoods populated by families of businessmen and professionals. Respondents from these neighborhoods went to the private, elite Bishop Cotton's High School, St. Joseph's European Boy's School, or the Indus International School. Fieldwork resulted in a rich variety of materials: transcribed interviews, photographs, journal and scrapbook collections, and personal observations. The complexities of the lived realities of the teens provided some insight into the latitude available to them in expressing and acting on their preferences. Differences in the value placed on education were strongest along lines of gender, giving substance to widely documented cases of gendered schooling where boys' education is valued over girls' education and where boys face greater familial demands to find paid employment than girls (see Ul Haq, 2003; Demerath, 1999, for example). Before we discuss grooming forces in these teens' lives, we examine theory on the interpellated subject, that is, the ways in which an individual enters into being. Elements of the interpellatory process were introduced in previous chapters.

Sticks and Stones

From our *Slumdog* example and the Jindal caricatures that followed, we understand that words can embody violence. Frantz Fanon's (1925–1961) exquisite delineation of the psychological effects of colonialism and systematic subordination that follows informs how we approach the role of television and film in India. Fanon's *Black Skin, White Masks* (1986/1952) and *The Wretched of the Earth* (1965/1961), although criticized for their reductive positioning of white oppressor and black oppressed, provide important insights into how colonialism is systematically internalized within the colonized subject. The subject often comes to see herself or himself as backward and helpless, through the terms of the colonizer. The process of subordination then becomes co-opted within the subject's own identity. This conceptualization builds on Althusser's (1971) explanation of rites of interpellation. How a person is called becomes the very label through which the subject comes to see herself or himself; therefore the response of the subject to the power structure that constrains her or him is the process through which identity is formed. Ideological state apparatuses, of which media are a part, circulate frames through which individuals under-stand their place and limitations within a society. While Fanon and Althusser were concerned with the macro structures that defined subjectivity, Foucault (1980) and Butler (2000) locate such influences at the level of micro discourse. Everyday mundane interactions provide powerful interpellatory instances as well, shaping the subject in intimate relations as much as external interactions. These provide useful ways to understand the mechanisms by which subjects attach themselves to specific positions. We also have to consider factors that uniquely constitute the postcolonial subject. In other words, we have to glean the robust structures and cultures that carry on the mission of the hegemonic system. This brings us to the basic existential "problems of being" (Venn, 2006, p. 89) in postcolonial environments.

In Venn's (2006) intricate analysis of identity and subjectivity, we see that colonial reformations demanded that modernity and progress were under col-onizer terms, acceptance of them by the natives meant a support for moder-nity and a validation of the colonizer's superiority. This was accomplished through a process of socialization where something external, on the outside, became internalized as part of the self. While a trend in the scholarship on this socializing process is to examine them in terms of slippage between the extreme traditional and modern positions, what is more efficient and accu-rate is to "focus on those theories that propose that identity is an entity that emerges in relation to an *other* or others; it is a plural self who is constituted by socio-cultural, corporeal and techno-material mechanisms of formation" (p. 90). This requires us to understand the individual as an ideological sub-ject, which explains why occidental values are so easily internalized. It also demands that we recognize the endurance of mechanisms of discipline and normalization that facilitate governance in postcolonial contexts. We then evaluate the ethical ramifications of how avenues are constructed to urge the subject along the process of becoming. In doing so, we acknowledge the powerful interpellatory influences of the "gaze" and the "the work of mimics" (p. 90). Applying it to the layered television environment that urban Indian teens have access to, we regard such reality shows as *Idol, Millionaire,* and *Survivor;* sitcoms such as *Friends* and *The Simpsons,* and drama-comedies such as *Sex and the City* and *Desperate Housewives* as providing the agentic subject rooted in an urban, somewhat Westernized environment with some degree of control. It invites mimicry from local, regional networks as well as from its audiences. The extent of their mimicry is contingent upon their internaliza-tions of limitations and the external imposition of sanctions.

In the interactions among media, market, and citizen in urban India, the first two confer upon the subject powerful avenues for "self" realization. The citizen herself or himself is part of a complex, interwoven culture that is compatible with the hierarchies through which media and market operate. Despite the seemingly endless choices available to the young urban Indian, the firm grasp of norms of propriety temper how far and to what extent the individual can avail of those choices.

Called to Labor, Called to Consume

Indian youth, generally defined as under 25 years of age, represent over 50% of the Indian population. Their desirability in the global marketplace is well documented for a variety of reasons: their technical qualifications, English-speaking ability, and socialization to a strong work ethic, to name a few (Zakaria, 2006). Former British cantonment areas in the country (Bangalore is an example) offer amenities in addition to skilled labor: electricity and water supply and a fairly reliable public transport system. Conditions in such venues are chaotic, to put it mildly. Ring roads around the city connecting neighborhoods and shopping areas are chronically congested. With outlying fields a premium for multinational development, farmers are compelled to sell their land and invest in informal taxi systems transporting immigrant labor back and forth from the city.

Zakaria (2006) reports that India is projected by Goldman Sachs to have the world's third largest economy by the year 2040. Call centers attract young, urban teens and adults. With this population earning higher incomes than parents, Zakaria speculates that family traditions and hierarchies may very well be in crisis. Cable and satellite television reach around 66 million of India's over 1 billion population. The national network Doordarshan reaches almost 90% of the population. All carry a hefty commercial and entertainment-oriented diet, complicating and reinforcing patriarchal hierarchies simultaneously.

Interconnected market and media systems give rise to what Kenway and Bullen (2008) call a "libidinal economy" that "consists of social and market structures and dispositions that release, channel and exploit desires and feelings (intensities), although never fully controlling them. ... Satisfaction is anathema to the libidinal economy" (pp. 19–20). Such an economy promotes a corporate curriculum that offers young people consumption as the primary mode through which to construct identity. As summarized in Chapter Two, the trend in scholarship on youth and consumerism is to equate agency with the autonomy one has to make marketing decisions. The myopic focus on the fluidity of identities and the declining significance of class in scholarship on youth and globalization shortchanges youth in the global south (Jeffrey, 2008). Certainly there is evidence that the emergence of flexible, albeit unstable labor markets have led to the decline of class distinctions in capitalist societies in the Western hemisphere. The focus on individual skill and labor may very well have diminished social networks (Beck & Beck-Gernsheim, 2002). New media technologies may give rise to social networks precisely in the absence of defining characteristics of class, ethnicity, gender, and even personal condition (Thiel, 2005; Lenhart, Kahne, Middaugh, Macgill, Evans, & Vitak, 2008). Despite the speculations and studies of the anonymity offered by new media and the erosion of class boundaries through various modes of consumption, we reiterate the post-structuralist attention to the making and remaking of power in micro and macro processes. Butler's (2000, p. 13) theory of performativity invites us to look at how the agent is produced through performance in relation to how she or he presents self as a social subject. Butler writes:

> The theory of performativity is not far from the theory of hegemony in this respect: both emphasize the way in which the social world is made—and new social possibilities emerge—at various levels of social action through a collaborative relation with power. (p. 14)

So-called democratic technologies that facilitate "equal" participation, in fact, work through new or reconfigured hierarchies. The particular symbols of such "democracy" or "equality"—to continue with our example of the big ticket reality game show, *anyone* can make it—work together to create the universalization of a particularity of a dominant culture (Butler, 2000). Indian youth are called to such terms of "universality"; images of what is universally desirable are promoted with utmost clarity. What is nebulous and even absent are the structures to support the journey to those images of achievement.

To explain, despite strong pressure within families to get an education, the Indian government has failed to provide jobs for the thousands of youth who graduate college every year. Jeffrey (2008) writes that "Rising educated unemployment is a key feature of the lives of young people in India and other areas of the globe, and of growing concern among governments, international organizations and activist groups" (p. 739).

Multinational organizations step in here, with their own terms and conditions, demanding from the thousands who apply for a single position, a certain "universal" name, dress, and code of conduct, as we have seen in the case of call centers in India in a variety of studies (McMillin, 2008a; Pal & Buzanell, 2008). Aspiring applicants transact with their local conditions to answer that call, their daily practices undergo translation to align them to "universal conditions." During these transactions, transgressions of conservative norms may occur, resulting in "moral panic" and a tightening up of ideological boundaries.

"Moral panic" is a rather mild phrase applied to the widespread anxiety of parents, legislators, and public interest groups regarding the unpredictable behaviors of youth in response to popular culture. S. Mazzarella (2007) charts the ways in which youth have been framed in popular media in the United States: as juvenile delinquents in the 1950s as a result of their so-called susceptibility to depictions of sex and violence in comic books, television, and rock 'n roll lyrics; and as misogynistic criminals in the 1980s and 1990s because of their perceived enslavement to sexist and violent hip-hop and rap lyrics and music videos. Such strategies are propelled by the recurring anxieties of "the immorality of young people, the absence of parental control, the problem of too much free time leading to crime, and the threat which deviant behavior poses to national identity and labour discipline" (McRobbie 1991, pp. 182–183). They legitimize discipline and punishment of youth, without adequate engagement in the conditions that produce such media artifacts and that solicit ardent response. Boethius (1995) writes that

> The new media challenge the prevailing cultural values and the authority of the cultural powers-that-be as regards determining what is considered good and bad culture. The media habits and cultural preferences of youth challenge the foundations of norms. ... Children and youth often feel (as do women) dependent, suppressed and bound. (pp. 48–49)

While "moral panic" may be an apt phrase for a wide range of behaviors when "a person or group of persons emerges to become defined as a threat to societal values and interests" (Cohen, 1980, p. 9), the right-wing response to youth in India in general and Bangalore as a global city in particular may at best be characterized as militant.

Almost two decades after the proliferation of private foreign and indigenous satellite and cable television networks, and the opening up of markets to foreign investment, Indian youth are experiencing a tightening up of norms as never before. While urban teens may interact every day with remote contacts through social media such as Hi5!, Facebook, and Orkut, and "live" in real time as their friends and family all over the world, in their own neighborhoods, conservatives prowl, ensuring no single woman is on the streets after dark. So intensified have anxieties of the religious patriarchal right become that on January 24, 2009, a group of women relaxing with male friends in a pub in the southern city of Mangalore was brutally attacked. The "pink chaddi" or pink panties campaign was immediately launched on Facebook, where supporters across the globe could join the *Consortium of Pub-Going, Loose and Forward Women* and virtually deliver a pair of pink panties to symbolically shame the Shri Ram Sena, the group behind the attacks. In response to the outpouring of support virtually and on the streets, more women were attacked in Bangalore during February and early March 2009, for their "Western" modes of dressing (most commonly, jeans and blouses instead of the Indian *salwar kameez* or *churidhar*, although some reported attacks even while clad in Indian clothes). NDTV.com journalist Maya Sharma (March 1, 2009) wrote that the harassment of young women had led to the formation of activist groups such as Fearless Karnataka who were planning to stage a protest on March 8, International Women's Day. At the heart of their protest was the casual response of the police force who dismissed the attacks on women as just another case of "eve teasing." The strong message from the authorities was that young girls and women should not dress provocatively to warrant such attacks. It is evident that the interconnections made possible through globalization are also utilized to renew dastardly acts of violence against populations who were using those very interconnections to articulate agency.

How we understand the agency expressed by youth in globalizing times then has to be textured by the recognition that these youth have much to *lose* by voicing that agency. They are all too aware of the limits of their expression. These limits are communicated through various levels of television, whether the state-sponsored (and supposedly autonomous) Doordarshan, or the private regional and foreign satellite and cable networks.

Keepers of Capitalist-Patriarchy

Since its very first telecast in 1959, Doordarshan was used as an ideological tool of the central government, to promote notions of national identity and progress, notions that are redefined and manipulated, depending on which political party is in power (Mitra, 1993). Mankekar (2002) and Rajagopal (2001) have documented the role of the Hindu fundamentalist Bharatiya Janata Party (BJP) in the telecast of the Hindu epics *Ramayana* and *Mahabharata* in the late

1980s. The epics are extensively cited as examples of the educational, informational, and commercial potential of a national mass medium. To simplify greatly, serials, sitcoms, and game shows generally privilege upper-class Hindu males, construct middle-class Hindu females as submissive, and caricature ethnic minorities. Programs generated within a patriarchal, conservative context squarely place the responsibility of family, community, and national development on women (Mankekar, 1999). Doordarshan faced stiff competition with the arrival of private satellite and cable television that were coincident, but not necessarily because of, India's 1991 economic liberalization policy. Many Asian governments were unprepared for the sudden influx of Star TV programs (their permission was not sought even though required by ITU and WARC regulations). Yet the network (wholly owned by Rupert Murdoch by 1994) endured with its "multidomestic" rather than "global" strategy, in that it promised content that would be respectful of local cultures, engaging in such strategies as dubbing and subtitling to ensure programs resonated with local audiences. Other foreign channels such as CNN, TNT, and Cartoon Network (owned by Turner Broadcasting Services), ESPN (owned by Disney), HBO Pacific (owned by Time Warner), and MTV and its local clone, Channel [V] (owned by Viacom), soon followed suit (Sinclair 1998). Channel [V] borrows its strategies from MTV and, just as the latter "effaces the boundary between past and present in drawing indiscriminately on film genres and art movements from different historical periods" (Kaplan, 1987, p. 144), Channel [V] is also postmodern in its juxtaposition of videos of traditional Indian nationalistic songs and of pop, remixes of rap, Bhangra, reggae, and hip-hop by Indian and Western artists. Doordarshan responded to Star TV's competition for urban audiences by abandoning, for the most part, its objectives of education and information, and focusing, through aggressive commercialism, on entertainment. Its metro channels in urban centers of each state now compete not just with the foreign language English channels, but also with the private, regional, vernacular language television networks such as Sun TV in Chennai, Raj TV in Hyderabad, and Asia Network in Trivandrum. Regional channels are by no means free of ideologies of class, gender, caste, and religion in their programs. Yet, they are more appealing to urban youth because they also, to a greater extent than Doordarshan, provide diverse representations of women, youth, and progress. The greater incidence of female veejays and talk show hosts paves the way for the expression of female leadership and desire and subverts the limiting gender hierarchies all too evident on Doordarshan. Realism on private regional channels is conveyed through a recognition of the assertive, hip, urban woman; of the carefree, ambitious urban male; and of the presence of multiple choices of consumption, lifestyle, and career facing this population. Top-rated programs are reality dance and song competitions, and call-in music programs, cloned across channels.

In the current highly competitive media environment where mergers and acquisitions are as common as in advanced capitalist environments such as the United States, Kumar (2006) writes that the "middle vision" (p. 51), which is the hybrid, nationalist, and techno-aggressive voice of Doordarshan, continues to hold authority and provides a "synthetic sense of reality" (p. 92). Indeed television does offer a certain reality (in terms of characters and existents), representation (in terms of production techniques), and ideology (such as patriarchy and capitalism) that serve as crucial links between and among producers, texts, and audiences (Fiske, 1989). It is this reality-quality that bleeds televised sexism into the streets, gathering momentum from entrenched sexist and patriarchal structures, and creating confrontations between the keepers of the system and those who struggle to subvert it. Examples of such confrontations blotch India's television history. An early one is the controversial *Nikki Tonight* talk show of the mid-1990s on Star TV that was cancelled after a guest called Mahatma Gandhi a "bastard bania" (a Gujarati trader, or more colloquially, a miser). The host was roundly criticized and the Rupert Murdoch–owned network had to issue apologies for this unthinkable transgression.

Feminist scholars of international communication and globalization such as Mohanty (2003) and Kandiyoti (1991) argue that women and modernity, in patriarchal societies, occupy opposing realms. Greater economic opportunities for men are accompanied by further subjugation of women and the latter often face the backlash of technological progress in their confinement to the private sphere, as we see graphically in the 2009 attacks on women in Mangalore and Bangalore. The Indian film industry has churned out myriad women-centered narratives that can hardly be considered progressive; the overwhelming trend has been to provide depictions of how a woman should be kept in her place. Notable exceptions are the 1930s "Fearless Nadia" series played by the daughter of an Australian officer in the British colonial army. Nadia often masqueraded as a male action hero in such films as *Toofan Mail*, 1932; *Flying Ranee*, 1939; and *Son of Toofan Mail*, 1947 (Thomas, 2005). As efforts at independence intensified, nationalistic films emerged that upheld the poor farmer (e.g., *Do Bigha Zameen, Mother Earth*) and the poor urban resident (e.g., *Footpath*, 1953; *Pyasa*, 1957). Village and community life were portrayed as ideal while wealthy lifestyles were vilified as corrupt and "Western" (Gangoli, 2005). Nationalist efforts soon after independence focused on the development of women and subalterns, yet framed them as populations to be disciplined and spoken for. Postindependence cinema portrayed women as courtesans or prostitutes. Various fictional and quasi-fictional women were represented as virtuous and strong in character. They were exploited by men and invariably died at the end of the movie when their real identities were exposed (e.g., *Adalat*, 1957), or when they were shunned by their families for being prostitutes even though they were forced into the industry at a young age (e.g., *Pakeezah*, 1971; *Umrao Jaan*, 1981). The clear message of these films, a message that can be readily traced in contemporary Bollywood cinema (especially in the remakes of courtesan films) and on state-sponsored and private television networks, is that women can be economically productive. Yet their money and bodies are tainted, making suspect women who can be economically independent in real life. As India makes huge strides economically and even politically where more and more women attain administrative power, cinema narratives provide powerful and aggressive roles for men (Banerjea, 2005), and restrictive roles for women. They are tragic heroines who are pure in heart and mind. They can be rescued or abandoned; their fates depend on the men in their lives (Chakravarty, 1998). As Kumar (2006) contends, television in India does offer freedom of viewing a variety of programs within the privacy of one's home, yet binds the viewer in its promotion of ideologies that sustain the social order.

In the brief description of Indian television history and its current character (certainly not reducible to one sexist construction but with enough common traits to be discussed generally here) we see the ongoing tension between universality and particularity. For example, the very articulation of agency by young men and women, sharing a drink in a bar in southern India as their counterparts would likely do in the Western hemisphere, was used to violently punish them into conforming to particular and local norms of propriety. Butler (2000, p. 14) warns that the "universal" is actually what is particular to a dominant culture. Therefore the "universality" of youth sharing a drink in a bar was regarded by Hindu fundamentalists as a corrupting particularity of an alien culture requiring erasure and replacement with the universal (in essence, highly particular) local norm of young girls staying at home after dark and certainly not interacting with non-related men before or after marriage.

Televised narratives offer venues of performativity and facilitate ways in which the viewer's social world is constructed. The circulation of symbols of possibility and agency on the global screen has to be anchored with how they are appropriated and resisted at various levels. More importantly, they have to be evaluated for the avenues they signal for youth in a country such as India, where middle-class anxieties are produced through complex interwoven systems of caste, patriarchy, global-local capitalism, and colonialism. Through the internalization of these varied and interrelated structures, middle-class service of the very system that caricatures it is possible, even desirable. Within such a complex environment where televised patriarchy resonates with lived patriarchy, and patriarchy itself is tied to consumer identity where products are clearly gendered to promote desirable male and female behavior, the question of how teens negotiate structure to express their individual and unique identities becomes an intriguing one.

With India as the current hotspot for global circuits of labor and industry, we turn to an in-depth exploration of teens groomed at various levels, in multiple ways, to serve as a global super labor class. The euphoria of Indian youth meeting the global labor challenge is tempered by the dismal predictions of William Cline, economist of the Peterson Institute for International Economics, that India's population will increase by 450 million and its agricultural production will decline by 30–40% by 2080 as a direct result of climate change (cited in Kamdar, 2008). Youth have been directly in the line of the fallout of aggressive capitalist expansion. Television, as still the primary mass medium connecting youth all over the world, brings to its young consumers not just stark stories of crises, but tantalizing distractions to channel public concerns into private gratifications. We can put into context, from this macro view, the micro anxieties of young teens in Bangalore as they witness emerging opportunities and disappearing niches, depending on where they are located in the global economy.

Locating the Teens

In this study, we focused on urban teens who had access to a variety of media. Of course we can make a strong case that all youth everywhere in India are implicated in processes of globalization that include capitalist expansion along neocolonialist lines. However, to most closely look at the correspondence between the interpellations of the popular market and youth themselves, we selected only urban teens. This direction in fieldwork was bolstered by observations made in the 2003–2004 *TV Characters* project discussed extensively in Chapters Three and Four, where it was clear that the rural teens were entering the discourse and practice of globalization from a very different vantage point. Further study among rural teens to explore how they are drawn into expanding markets and how their lives are altered at a variety of levels in response would be fascinating, but beyond the scope of the current project.

Although the primary objective was to provide a thick description of viewer's responses to television, general descriptive statistics are provided for an overview of demographic and media ownership details. For all interviews, polyvocality and self-naming were sought as far as possible. As Zavella (1996) and Wolf (1996) suggest, respondents were asked to name their positions and identities as partakers of global, local, and national television. Zavella (1996) writes that self-naming will lead to insight on how connotations based on class, race, and ethnicity define the informant's sense of self. Giving "voice" to the subjects may result in a picture of how they want to be represented rather than how they really are (Lal, 1996). However, as Briggs (1986) notes, reflexivity of research results will help determine how audience's observations of themselves may be interpreted. Each lengthy interview was conducted more as a conversation between interviewer and respondent. Interviews took place invariably in the respondent's home, after the interviewee chatted with parents and shared tea and savories with them. As parents (or usually mothers if interviews were conducted in the middle of the day) went about their household chores, the interviewer and respondent would talk at length about various issues as outlined by the questions used in the first phase of the *TV Characters* project. The difference in this study was the focus on the role of interlocking family and social structures that shaped the teens' perceptions of self and future goals. The interviewer's insider status in the various communities from which respondents were selected created a strong base of trust and confidence. The combination of survey and focus group discussion allowed for reflexivity and resulted in data that was rich in breadth as well as depth.

In general then, to provide an overview of who participated in the 2005 study of the 26 respondents, 23% could be considered from a low-income bracket, that is with monthly incomes between Rs. 5,001 and Rs. 10,000[26] (USD 114–227). Twenty-seven percent could be considered from a lower middle-income bracket, with monthly incomes from Rs. 10,001 to 25,000 (USD 228–568). Four percent could be said to belong to the middle-income bracket with monthly incomes from Rs. 25,001 to Rs. 30,000 (USD 569–682) income bracket, and forty-six percent of the respondents could be considered to be from an upper-middle-income bracket with monthly incomes above Rs. 30,000 (USD 683) per month.

Defining class is not a straightforward process in India. Vickers and Dhru-varajan (2002) detail a variety of ways in which class is defined in countries of Asia, Africa, and Latin America. For example, land ownership is an important factor, not just socioeconomic level as is the standard measure in Western soci-eties. This means that many women in tricontinent countries are considered classless, because they are denied ownership even though they may be the primary workers on the land. In India and Japan, the caste system is robust; untouchability based on caste plays a significant role in how class is accom-modated. Communal affiliations have to be taken into consideration, such as religious, ethnic, and language identities. As Dickey (1993) elaborates in her study of cinema audiences in Tamil Nadu, India, class intersects with caste, sect, and religion. Therefore, as we have seen in the examples of Shubha and Ambika in the 2003–2004 *TV Characters* study, the urban or semiurban poor may see themselves as people who have nothing, who once belonged to land but who are now at the mercy of industrialists. They may recast these realities into a sense of fate, as the plight of people who were born to suffer. In this way, upper class people are regarded as "big people" or "rich people." In such a com-plex system, no one class emerges as a hegemonic class in the Gramscian sense and Dickey (1993) argues that "[O]pposition between classes has equally to do with values and aesthetics as with economic inequalities and relationships" (p. 11). Indeed, young men in India are acculturated into the importance of social connections and accumulation of goods. Caste plays an essential role in qualifying what opportunities educated young men actually can avail as C. Jeffrey, P. Jeffrey, & R. Jeffery (2008) demonstrated in an ethnographic study of villagers in Uttar Pradesh. We emphasize here that as we process the narra-tives of the urban teens in this study, we should keep in mind that the cultural definitions of class are as "real" and lived as the economic.

Where the subject chose to have the interview was also considered an important element in fieldwork since the objective was to ensure that subjects were as comfortable as possible with the process. The goal of critical ethnog-raphy is to facilitate a space that the subject is at ease in and where her or his "voice" can emerge with authority. This is based on the recognition that

> voice is an embodied, historical self that constructs and is constructed by a matrix of social and political processes. The aim is to present and represent subjects as made by and makers of meaning, symbol, and history in their full sensory and social dimensions. Therefore, the performance of possibilities is also a performance of voice wedded to experience and history. (Madison, 2005, p. 173)

Class anxieties emerged most clearly from those at lower-income levels. Teens in this bracket exhibited a painful self-consciousness in their embarrassment at having mothers who could not converse with the interviewer in English, or in having homes that did not contain conventional living room furniture such as a sofa, armchairs, and fan. For example, 15-year-old Swati (female) lived in quarters reserved for lower ranks of the Indian Air Force. The three–four-roomed houses invariably consisted of one bedroom, a bathroom, a tiny kitchen, and a small living room. Sixteen-year-olds Ravi Sagar (male), Shantanu (male), and Preeti (female) lived in similar accommodations. When contacted for the interviews, these teens organized a two-step process where the interviewer was first invited for a meal of *pulkhas* (fluffy soft bread made fresh over an open flame) and cauliflower *palya* (spiced side dish) at 16-year-old Deepti's (female) house in the same quarters before moving on to fellow resident 16-year-old Himanshu's (male) house, where other teens from the same building had gathered. Himanshu's living room had a few chairs and therefore presented an "appropriate" interview setting according to the teens. In this way, these lower-income respondents could offer hospitality to the interviewer, and at the same time, construct for themselves an insularity around their class positions that, they believed, the interviewer could not penetrate. Their responses to questions on television and identity could then be provided and received as whole systems of meaning in themselves, untethered to the messiness of their class positions. Interestingly, *after* the hefty meal and interviews, the distance between interviewer and respondents seemed to have collapsed—many invited the interviewer to their homes. Sixteen-year-old Neelam, for example, wanted the interviewer to see the special altar set up in her house to celebrate the Hindu god Ram's return to the historical city of Ayodhya celebrated through the Sri Rama Navami festival. She said that she initially did not want the interviewer to visit her home because she was embarrassed and thought the interviewer would laugh at the lack of furniture in her living room. Sixteen-year-old Ravi Sagar (male) and 14-year-old Ravi Kant (male) said that the interviews helped them, for the first time, to look inward and understand themselves better. As Ravi Kant put it, "From this interview I came to know what *real* I am." Although the interviewer could speak the local languages, the teens, regardless of their fluency in English, preferred to use this language, perhaps to mark for their own selves, the authenticity and legitimacy of the interview. The use of English as the language for all interviews will be discussed later in this chapter.

Although not asked in the initial questionnaire about demographic details, many respondents specified the subcommunity they belonged to in terms of religion. That is, instead of using the generic "Christian," "Hindu," or "Muslim" labels 8% listed themselves as Catholic while 27% described themselves as Protestant, for a total of 35% Christian respondents. Similarly, 8% wrote that they were from the Scheduled Caste of Hindus (the lower castes of the agricultural, butcher, sweeper, and scavenger communities, for example), 15% labeled themselves from the upper-caste Brahmin community, and one wrote that he was a Hindu Reddy, while 39% merely stated they were Hindu. No Muslims were included in the study because they dropped out after initial contact.

Kannada language was spoken by just one respondent, remarkable since the interviews were all conducted in Bangalore, the capital of Karnataka state where the native language is Kannada. A primary reason for this is that Bangalore is also a highly cosmopolitan city with laborers, industrialists, defense personnel, and professionals migrating to the city from all parts of the country. Hindi, then, was the language spoken by a majority of the respondents, 46% in all. Telugu was spoken by 19% of the respondents, Tamil by 23%, Coorgi by 4%, and Malayalam by 4% of the teens. The diversity in language is indicative of the diversity of regions represented by the subjects. Thirty-four percent was from the northern state of Uttar Pradesh, while four percent each was from the northeastern state of Orissa and the northwestern state of Rajasthan, respectively. The southern states of Andhra Pradesh, Kerala, and Tamil Nadu were represented by 23%, 4%, and 15% of the respondents, respectively.

As could be expected, the high number of Hindi-speaking teens came from families of Air Force and Army personnel and therefore went to the Kendriya Vidyalaya School in the Defence Research and Development Organization (DRDO) complex (46% in all). Of the other respondents, 23% went to Bishop Cotton's School, 8% to St. Joseph's European High School, and 15% to the Ujjwala High School (a low-income school established by the Alembic Glass Factory for its laborers' children), and 8% went to the very expensive Indus International School.

The reach of channels is a good indicator of viewer preferences since subscribers are able to choose, to a certain extent, the types of channels reaching their homes. With access to almost 40 channels, the students in this study varied widely in their viewing preferences. Responses were textured by language and religious differences. As part of Doordarshan's must-carry rule, all received the network's primary, Hindi language news and entertainment channels, DD1 and DD2, respectively. DD's regional language channels

(DD3–10) were far less subscribed to, with the most popular being DD9 (a Kannada language channel, an obvious choice since Kannada is the native language of Bangalore) and the least, DD6 (an Oriya language channel, a language of a northeastern state).

Most (78%) of the respondents had a radio set at home and 100% had televisions, among which 77% had cable connections. Only 8% had VCRs, 39% had stereos, 77% had computers, and 69% had DVD players. Cable connections included a variety of English language channels such as Disney, Cartoon Network, HBO, CNN, and ESPN; a few vernacular language channels such as the Telugu language Gemini, the Kannada language Udaya TV and Ushe TV, and the Tamil language Sun TV (based on the predominant language spoken in the neighborhood). Hindi language Zee channels were common in all cable homes. Participants watched television between one and two hours (31%) or three and four hours (31%) per day. Twenty-seven percent watched television between two and three hours per day and only twelve percent watched television for more than four hours per day. Most cited the English language channels such as HBO, Cartoon Network, Discovery, Pogo, and Animal Planet as their favorites. Sitcoms such as *Caroline in the City* and *Friends* were named most frequently as the preferred shows to watch while Hindi language soaps such as *Jassi Jaissi Koi Nahin* and *Kyunki Saas Bhi Kabhi Bahu Thi* were named among the least favorites for their maudlin and violent plot lines. Obviously the diversity of backgrounds of the respondents translated into very different viewing experiences and extremely interesting patterns of teen identity.

Doubt and Mistrust

Every single respondent in this project seized the interview as an opportunity to talk about her or his frustrations with parents. A strong disconnect existed between the freedom and mobility of characters on television and their experiences at home. Prominent topics of disagreement were academic performance and leisure time. Boys described how they were hit or slapped by fathers as punishment for low grades or for loitering in the streets when they should have been doing homework. Girls talked about how parents distrusted them; they were scolded if they talked to a boy on the street and were denied privacy at home. Such observations are not uncommon among Indian youth as demonstrated by Verma and Sharma (2003) in their study of 100 teens in urban India. Although they resented the strict controls, many in this study conceded that such control was for their own good and was their parents' way of showing them love.

Also, each talked about being part of a large family, where relatives either lived close by or within the home itself. Cousins shared similar experiences; uncles, aunts, and grandparents served as buffers. These supportive relationships put parental discipline in perspective for some, making it a necessary and bearable burden. The focus on academic performance is important to contextualize in urban India.

As discussed earlier, defining class is a complex and intertwined economic (Sridharan, 2004) and cultural (Mankekar, 1999; Rajagopal, 2001) process. While there is a vast petty bourgeois class (those who own property or land), property alone is insufficient to sustain support for upcoming generations. This class generally resorts to the practices of the middle class, that is, to reproduce status through education, acquisition of skills, and social networking (Fernandes & Heller, 2006). An important part of these practices is also the consumption of English language media as a way to accrue the benefits of economic liberalization. The television choices of middle-class teens, who arguably could include all the teens in this study since their income differentiations were subjectively produced, should be seen as an extension of class practices. In crucial ways, cultural practices came together in a fundamental economic sense; enjoyment of English language programs was not a mere phenomenon of non-Western youth wanting to emulate Western youth. Acquisition of fluency in spoken English expanded opportunities for material advancement as well. Structures are not external to action, but are reproduced through activities of daily life. Media institutions use interpretive frameworks with conventional codes through which messages are meaningful to audiences (Hall, 1980). As has been discussed earlier, a limited range of television program format and content was available to the teens, yet resonated with their current need for freedom and control.

Spanning ages 13 through 16, all the boys were similar in their television preferences. They watched such networks as the Discovery Channel, Cartoon Network, Animal Planet, AXN, and Star Plus most often. They made fun of Hindi language soap operas and dramas, ridiculing the melodramatic acting and far-fetched narratives. Reasons for their preferences were straightforward: they liked watching action, tests of endurance and skill, and magic tricks. They also preferred male characters who displayed leadership and strength of character. The boys in general (18 of the 26 teens interviewed) enjoyed reading Harry Potter books, playing with their Playstations, and participating in neighborhood and school cricket, football, badminton, basketball, and swimming competitions. Fernandes and Heller (2006) argue that television and other media images produce an NMC identity in India that is integrated with consumption of products engineered through market liberalization. While Satish Deshpande (2003) contends that the middle class in India has not and possibly can never attain hegemonic status despite its vast numbers, it reflects the interests of the hegemonic elite. India's move through its history from a developmentalist to market state, and in the latter 2000s, from an ancillary to increasingly central role in the global economy, has positioned the middle class as a key player in the construction of India's new infrastructure. It is within this frame that we evaluate Indian teens' consumption of television, their accommodation of pressures at home, and their insecurities about themselves.

The Disciplined Self

Perhaps it would be too dramatic to equate the actual *experiences* of some of the teens to Foucault's (1977) description of the panopticon, yet the narrations were reminiscent of the discussion of the prison structure where only the guard could observe, the prisoner was eternally watched. Dirks, Eley, and Ortner (1994) discuss the micro workings of power that rather than just being located within repressive state apparatuses, power,

> has invaded our sense of the smallest and most intimate of human relations as well as the largest; it belongs to the weak as well as to the strong; and it is constituted precisely within the relations between official and unofficial agents of social control and cultural production. (p. 5)

The macro structures of hegemony are reproduced through the micro processes of daily interpersonal relationships (Morley, 1980), as was demonstrated in the respondents' narrations. The teens conveyed a clear sense of place; their environments were, for the most part, carefully controlled, with a specified schedule for leisure, schoolwork, religious rituals, and so on. Anand, a 14-year-old, upper-income Hindu boy feared getting shouted at by his parents the most. His father was always monitoring his study habits and would scold him if he didn't sit with his books for hours at a stretch. However, such interactions made him want to be a better person and study harder. If it weren't for his sister, Anand would not have any leisure time at all. He watched his favorite programs, played on the computer, and went out with his friends when his parents were out and his older sister supervised him. She even gave him a little money for his exploits. Generally feeling restricted at home, Anand's escape was the world of technology and shows on television that focused on technological innovations. He frequently watched the History Channel for biographies of prominent world leaders such as Bill Clinton, and the Cartoon Network for such animated serials as *X-Men* and movies as *Men in Black*. Like several of the boys in the 2004 study, Anand enjoyed *Friends* on Star World, and particularly liked the character Joey's sense of humor.

Ashwin, a 14-year-old, middle-income Hindu boy, was not so charitable in his opinion of his father. While his mother was kind, hardworking, and gentle, his father was a "rough man," he said, very strict when it came to his school-work. He said, "I always fear my father because when you are wrong, he's a very bad man. If once he is in a mood to hit me then he will—he will NOT change his mind." Despite this harsh assessment, he too was quick to add, "Actually I believe that he [is] doing the right thing. He is trying to (steer) me in the right path." Ashwin believed his elders were always correct and that their greater experience in life qualified them to advise him and punish him when necessary. His loved sports and watched the Sports Channel and ESPN Sports regularly. Cricket, football, and basketball were his favorites. Unlike his peers, Ashwin's favorite television character was the female lead Jassi, in *Jassi Jaissi Koi Nahin*. Jassi, also highly popular among the teens in the 2004 study, played the Indian Ugly Betty; she was spunky and set right all dilemmas that came her way. Although treated badly by her peers, Jassi was good to all around her. Ashwin believed she set an important example for him; her kind and gentle ways discouraged him from retaliating against the boys who bullied him at school. Jassi's character would be greatly improved if she were more attractive, he said. Soon after the interview with Ashwin, Jassi did indeed undergo a transformation and became a model. This point is taken up in the next section, in the discussion of the experiences of the girls in this study.

Robert, a 13-year-old, upper-income Christian, echoed the sentiments of his peers. He said his father was very authoritarian and was "determined to do everything and he *needs* strict discipline and obedience (from me) and he wants us to pass in the exams." Like Anand and Ashwin, Robert felt a personal sense of responsibility not to let his father down, "We don't want him to put his head down and walk in shame. We always want him to put his head up and be proud of us." He shared his secrets with his grandmother who advised him to be submissive to his father and treat his friends well. Robert enjoyed the Cartoon Network the most, especially such characters as Bugs Bunny, Daffy Duck, Sylvester and Tweety, and Tom and Jerry. He believed he had a "personal connection" with a character named Steve on the Cartoon Network because "he teaches so many things that I wish I could be like him, I could teach people about love (and) friendship." He and Steve were similar because "he is very kind to people and he helps people in a time of need and he is always fun loving and he never gets angry at anyone, he is always cool about everything, he is never short-tempered." Robert recounted several instances where he helped his classmates with their math homework or on the playground, following Steve's example of being helpful to others. Interestingly, Robert described his father as the opposite of Steve. His father was strict, short-tempered, and although helpful, made Robert work hard for his rewards.

Getting hit by their fathers was a common and accepted occurrence among most of the boys interviewed. As Vishnuram, a 14-year-old, upper-income Hindu boy put it, "(My father) is a jolly type. But when I do some mischief, he hits me. But that is okay because it is my mistake. And plus, he plays with me when he is in a good mood." All the boys talked about how kind their mothers were and how they could rely on their mothers, grandmothers, and other women in the family to act as intermediaries.

Michael, a 15-year-old, upper-income Christian, believed his father was right in being strict. If his father were permissive and kind, Michael could grow up to be a spoiled brat. His father enrolled him in badminton and allowed him to start a newspaper route so he could save for a Playstation. He said his father constantly urged him to "be tough," which made him seek out such programs as *Fear Factor* on the AXN channel. He was full of awe for contestants who would eat bugs or be submerged under snakes to win the grand prize of $50,000. But his favorite television character was David Blaine for his amazing feats of magic. Michael and his father shared a passion for magic and together they tried to master card and sleight-of-hand tricks.

Tarun and Vineet, both 16-year-old boys in this income bracket, also preferred English language programs such as *The Practice*, *Friends*, and *Everybody Loves Raymond*. Tarun's mother insisted that he volunteer at the local retirement home every week, so as to stay grounded. Vineet, on the other hand, shared that he was an only child. He was often on his own and was suspicious of the relationship between his uncle, who helped managed the family estates, and his mother. His mother was very upset that he smoked, and so he had given it up temporarily. Instead, he was abusing drugs, without his mother's knowledge of course. Speaking at length even after the interview questions were answered, Vineet seemed to just want a listener. He talked about pressures at school. He said the interview was probably the only time someone had expressed interest in who he was as a person.

Most of the boys were insecure about their appearance and believed they were too thin, too fat, too dark, or too short. Being kind, helpful, trustworthy, and friendly were characteristics mentioned by most of them when asked to describe their strengths. Their fears were sometimes childlike. One mentioned his fear of the dark and his inability to sleep without a light. Another mentioned he worried he would fracture his leg. He did everything he could to avoid situations where he might have an accident. While a few described their anxiety over school exams, most discussed schoolyard bullying as something they deeply feared.

To stand up to physical threat, several mentioned developing their bodies based on global icons of strength, such as Arnold Schwarzenegger or the wrestlers on *WWE*. Sixteen-year-old Mahesh talked about going to the gym to develop his muscles like these characters, while another sixteen-year-old, upper-income Nishwin modeled Tom Cruise and Bollywood star Shah Rukh Khan. He said:

> Cruise really handsome, really hot, has the hair and body and looks; even James Bond has all the gadgets and is really rich. And Khan in India is everything, he is like God, he is good, handsome, and he is everywhere, in TV ads and programs. Whenever I have a hair problem, I have pictures of Sharukh Khan and Tom Cruise and I try to copy them. And when you see the movie you understand what they are trying to say. And in the movie *Chalte Chalte*, Sharukh Khan said love is nothing but only if you love one person, just because you love one person you don't have to marry her. And even if you do get married, it doesn't mean that love lasts.

The immediate relevance of Hollywood and Bollywood romance and action blockbusters for Nishwin's life is just one example among many. The self-consciousness of low-income teens and their class embarrassments should be placed here within the backdrop of the contemporary trend in Bollywood and Tollywood to churn out stories that privilege the upper class hero. Contrary to films in eras past that glorified the struggles of the peasant and that placed salvation of the human soul in the simplicity of village life, the trend now is to mirror the business-class lives of Punjabis within India and abroad, the biggest sponsors of the films themselves. Through an analysis of films in the 1990s and 2000s, Sudhanva Deshpande (2005) contends that

> The consumable hero is the creation of the liberalized market. To the extent that liberalization itself is a relatively recent phenomenon, having been set in place only in 1991, the consumable hero has no history. His class acquired jobs with perks, high disposable incomes, a jet-setting lifestyle and shopping holidays overseas only from the

mid-1990s or so. The person who has no history has no memory. More precisely, he has no history that he cares to recall. (p. 202)

The hero offered up for teens in globalizing environments sets up important guidelines for what is desirable and what signifies their entry into an adequate standard of living. The combination of heroes-with-capital and strict parents who regard that very capital as threatening to their child's journey toward a secure future created an ongoing tension that was always unresolved. Icons of progress and agency should also be seen as signs under which a range of behaviors is legitimized. Butler explains in *Giving an Account of Oneself* (2005) that violence is enacted under, for example, the sign of "self-defense" whereby one may justify aggression. The choice of violent and ultra masculine proto-types by particularly the male subjects in this study echo desires to conquer the violence they faced at the hands of their fathers, whether verbal or physical. These choices resonate with those of the young boys in the first phase of the *TV Characters* study discussed in Chapter Three. We recall Mario's declarations in Munich that he would beat people up if they interfered with his activities. Perhaps Mario would find consolation in knowing that in Bangalore, Nishwin felt the same way: "I have a very short temper. I just find myself clobbering people who harass my friends or girlfriend and I find myself in the principal's office. It is not good."

It is important to qualify here that from the time spent in the homes of these teens and through a review of their notes and photographs, conditions of their upbringing could be related to the average middle-class Indian home. But then as we have tracked through this book, the average middle-class youth is answering a global call to perform in *addition* to conventional pressures of staying out of debt, balancing family needs with social relationships, and so on. Through a fascinating psychoanalysis of how the "I" comes into being, Butler (2005) explains that, as we see in Nishwin's statements, guilt exacerbates the sense of omnipotence, under the sign of its critique. The violence that some of the male respondents faced at the hands of their fathers was not a mere pun-ishment nor did they themselves inflict violence on others as a simple act of revenge. What is actually occurring is far more complex. The act of violence itself exposes an inescapable vulnerability, an insecurity that is not possible to resolve. It provides a way through which the subject can understand how completely bound he is to the people within that immediate, close context, and within himself. The situations that the teens faced provided a "horizon of choice" (p. 101). At the same time, they grounded responsibility. As subjects, they were not entirely responsible for the situations they found themselves in, but those situations posed conditions under which they had to assume responsibility. The very fact that those conditions were not of the subject's making dictated that he had to heed them.

And so we see that these narratives revealed intricate lives and personalities, mature fears about the future and childish fears about the dark or personal safety. The boys reached out to programs that took them far beyond their immediate contexts or capabilities. Through television they could do amazing things such as stay under water for a week, like David Blaine, chase aliens like *The Men in Black*, win lots of money like the contestants on *Fear Factor*, be respected despite average looks like Jassi, and be popular and funny, like Joey on *Friends*. Although they grudgingly conceded their fathers were right in hitting them or scolding them into good behavior, it was obvious they each felt diminished and stifled by such strict parenting. Their mothers represented ambiguous support—they could be strict like the fathers or they could be soft and nurturing—the boys weren't sure what they could expect at any given time. They did seek out programs that brought them a larger-than-life sense of self. Strikingly, such a symbolic "self" seemed to emerge *for them*, for the most part, from foreign channels rather than state-sponsored national or private, vernacular language networks. The combination of strict parenting and preferences for foreign television programs that represented escape is not a simple cause and effect relationship. What this combination demonstrates is that the two go hand in hand; the tightening of parental control could very well be in retaliation to the democratic possibilities unraveling on the small screen that are threatening to the authoritarian environment, particularly in the face of limited opportunities for the rapidly growing middle class.

In the responses of the girls who participated in this study, we see the ideological positioning of their mothers, as keepers of a tightly controlled middle-class patriarchal system. Whether they were from low- or middle-income households played a crucial role in the latitude they were given at home. Girls from middle and upper-income households believed they were highly constrained in their activities. Girls from lower-income homes faced greater latitude, yet were keenly aware of how they would be "talked about" in the neighborhood if they so much as looked at a boy. Mothers reminded them every day about the strict norms of appropriate female behavior. As Fernandes and Heller (2006), Sridharan (2004) and others have noted, conservatism and capitalism go hand in hand. Indian teens, whether male or female, can be groomed for the global marketplace through essentialized, genderized channels. Fernandes and Heller (2006) write:

> The seemingly contradictory impulses of exclusionary nationalism and globalization (from Ram Rajya to "India Shining") are reconciled by affirming the essential and inviolate character of Indian civilization. This fusing of core values and progress provides a basis for integration in a rapidly changing world and provides comfort and even a rallying point to conservative lower middle classes. (p. 509)

Ram Rajya refers to the Hindu fundamentalist elite who have, throughout India's postindependence history, circulated notions of Hindutva or Hindu supremacy resulting in violence against ethnic and gender minorities throughout the nation.

All the girls participating in this study discussed their chores within the household and the expectations their parents placed on them regarding their academic performance. While the boys discussed strong pressure to succeed academically, the girls talked at greater length about the strict norms for interacting with boys. For example, Versha, a 15-year-old North Indian girl from an upper-income family, discussed her consternation at the conservatism of her parents. She said she was not supposed to speak to boys. Even though she didn't do anything "wrong," that is, converse with a boy or enter into a relationship with him, her mother continuously needled her on all she did outside the house. Versha was exasperated at her mother's lack of trust:

> She thinks some kind of affair is there (and) she tells me don't do all this. I mean I try to satisfy her that I am not *that* type of a girl. And people around me also know about me (and know) that I am not that type. She does not try to show me that she (believes) in me. But that confidence I want really from my parents.

She said her mother wanted to "pull her down" and would keep pointing out to what she had done wrong instead of recognizing what she had done right. It seemed natural then for Versha to select such shows as *Meher* (DD National) and *Kayamat* (Star Plus) that portrayed "bold" girls. In fact, Versha used the word "bold" repeatedly to describe the protagonists and discussed at length how she wanted to be bold like them. *Meher*, she said, was the story of a "girl who is fighting against all her problems ... she is a good person ... and she loves her sister. She is *really* bold enough to face *anything* and *everything.*" Through the story line, Versha learned that although "we have so many rivals we have to learn how to fight against them."

Kayamat was also the story about a wronged girl who reentered her family circle with a new face, after being presumed dead. The protagonist, Anamika, was courageous in uncovering the mystery surrounding her "death" and in her faith in God. Only her father knew who she truly was, because of the strong bond they shared. As it became apparent that the mother-in-law "murdered" Anamika, Versha said that she wanted to be as forthright and relentless as Anamika was in the serial. This was because

> a person *has* to be (bold) after her marriage. Now we see that so many daughters-in-law are (getting) *killed* by their fathers-in-law and mothers-in-law and she *fights* against them. You *have* to be bold; she has everything: she is beautiful, she is good, she is talented, she can do *anything*, whatever she wills. That's the same case with Meher. So you *have* to be bold like them, that's what I feel.

Other domestic dramas on Zee TV were too far-fetched and lacked the realism of Versha's favorite soaps discussed earlier. She said:

> I want to be actually a *very* bold person. And like Meher and Anamika, I have to fight against all the problems I have ... I want to be a pilot, I want to touch the sky, *feel* the goodness, I want to be at the *highest* in the Air Force. *Wherever* I am (even) if I don't become a pilot, I have to be the *highest*, not below anyone.

Versha's frustration at being held back by the conservatism of her family and the restrictions on girls in general was felt by Cora, a 16-year-old, low-income, Tamil-speaking girl, who lived in a suburb south of the city center. Deeply religious, Cora spent every Saturday afternoon cleaning the church and getting it ready for Sunday services. Despite her popularity and her visibility at the church, she said, "Inside I am afraid because I should not bring a bad name to my father." Her position at the church encouraged boys and girls her age to interact with her and strike up a conversation. They would ask her about the nature of her work and whether she was getting paid. Cora narrated an incident where a few boys questioned her about her job while she was sweeping her yard. Although she talked to them over the brick compound wall, a neighbor saw her conversing and reported it to her uncle and father. They both admonished her for speaking publicly to the boys because that meant she could be misconstrued as a girl without morals. She said,

> From that day, that's my biggest fear. See, I have done *nothing*. There is *no* wrong in me. But still people think I am doing wrong, I can't do *anything* (about it). So my biggest fear is that wherever I go I should not bring a bad name to my family. That's the fear I have, I should not *lose* myself.

To grossly simplify, to "lose oneself" would mean losing one's virginity. An Indian girl could be judged to have "lost herself" even with an innocent interaction with a boy, as we have seen graphically demonstrated in the attacks on women in Mangalore and Bangalore recounted at the beginning of this chapter. While Versha sought Hindi language serials with strong female leads, Cora was content to watch God TV and other religious channels with her family. She regularly watched prayer services conducted by evangelists like Paul Dinakaran (a Tamilian like herself) and Joyce Meyers. When her parents were not home, she watched the Cartoon Network and Animal Planet. For entertainment, the family watched Tamil movies on television, particularly those featuring the actor Vijay. Cora was often teased because she liked Vijay so much, but she dismissed such teasing saying that he acted in only family-oriented movies:

> His films are good (they are) not too vulgar also, good family stories, so that even our whole family can see. Nice, good comedy. When we see his films even our parents and all see it (and) he talks about (the whole) family like brothers and sisters, like that it is very good.

Kirthana, a 14-year-old, Telugu-speaking, upper-income girl, although less pressured about her interactions with boys than some of the other girls in the study, also preferred serials that featured women in dominant roles. Her favorite was *Jassi Jaissi Koi Nahin*, because of the realism in the serial. Like Versha, Cora, and most of the other girls interviewed, Kirthana exhibited sophistication in her understanding of the production qualities and the plot lines of the program. She did not care for shows that were outlandish such as *Talash* and *Kanch*, and thought *Jassi* was effective for its "naturalness." She liked the protagonist because "she is a very good actress ... and then the serial seems very natural as if it is happening to a real (person), it is happening *really* and it doesn't seem like a serial." Also, Jassi's transformation into a beautiful and rich model from her plain and averagely successful persona boosted her popularity considerably. Kirthana said she didn't like Jassi earlier when she wasn't good looking, but in many ways, Jassi's change paralleled her own. Kirthana had moved to her current neighborhood only a year ago and had found the transition very difficult. She was teased by her peers in the new neighborhood, was very lonely, and often cried when she came home from school. But just like Jassi, she gradually grew more confident, could stand up for herself, and now was popular among the teenagers in the area.

These examples are but a few among several deeply fascinating accounts of teen girl life and dreams in Bangalore. Keeping in mind that the responses were incredibly diverse and intricate in their depictions of the realities of the respondents, it is also safe to say that broad patterns emerged. First, as evident in the responses included here was the girls' fear that they would "lose themselves" or be regarded as wayward girls who talked to boys. Second, the girls felt frustrated that their actions were frequently misunderstood even by those who knew and loved them. Third, they all sought television programs that portrayed women in leading roles. Strong women were most often found in Hindi and Kannada language prime time serials, where heroines negotiated complex family relationships while being, for the most part, assertive *and* compassionate. Like the girls in the 2004 *TV Characters* study, the girls in this analysis were quite mature in their television preferences, rarely choosing the animated programs that were so popular among the boys.

Producing the Body for Labor

In urban India, choices abound on television and in the local market. The consumer can access the very latest foreign programs on HBO, ESPN, BBC, CNN, and Star Plus, and not have to contend with a lag of several years in soap opera or drama storylines as was the case just a decade ago. National and regional private channels bring sophisticated shows with complex plot lines and well-developed lead characters. Slick advertisements showcase global and local products that are available in local markets. The overt preference for regional and foreign programs over national points to a subversion, by the urban youth in this study, of the government's hegemonic imposition of monolithic notions of Indian nationhood through Doordarshan. Viewers were reproachful of narrow definitions of nation as Hindu and as upper middle class, and preferred alternative representations of individual and group identity through the regional and global channels. No doubt the latter did not stray too far from hegemonic gender or class constructions, but provided a wider range of characters and plots. Commenting on the early evidence of transnational relevance in local contexts, particularly authoritarian and conservative ones that claim hold over national imaginations, Morley and Robins write (1995, p. 116):

> Globalization is, in fact, also associated with new dynamics of *re*-localization. It is about the achievement of a new global-local nexus, about new and intricate relations between global space and local space ... the new global context is recreating a sense of place and sense of community in very positive ways, giving rise to an energetic cosmopolitanism in certain localities. ... If globalization recontextualizes and reinterprets cultural localism, it does so in ways that are equivocal and ambiguous.

The localization of programs on foreign channels (where, for example, Star TV airs Indian pop on its Channel [V] or dubs Western serials in Hindi on its Star Plus channel) and the globalization of local programs on regional channels (where, for example, Udaya TV presents a version of *The Newly Wed Game* through its Kannada language *Adarsha Dampathigalu*) created a genre in hybrid programs (see Kraidy, 2003) that was a breath of fresh air from Doordarshan's traditional Hindu-centric formats. In such an inherently hierarchical society where class, caste, gender, religion, and ethnicity provide fertile ground for subtle and volatile power struggles, ideologies of the same on film and television find strong consent and support. Besides, private and national networks draw heavily from the Indian film industry. With independent productions prohibitively expensive, the Indian television industry across the board relies on films to fill programming time. The result is a glut of film music–based programs, countdowns of top favorite film clips, interviews with actors, talk shows that incorporate film-based competitions, and so on. The space for truly pathbreaking serials and dramas is consequently, quite limited. Indian television and film are embedded cultural institutions; they should therefore be seen as dialectical media, communicating with local systems of patriarchy and capitalism and interacting with global systems that reinforce and bolster their potency.

As demonstrated in the teens' responses, family control was a formidable force. No matter what choices were available outside the home, within it, parents dictated, to a large extent, daily routines, study habits, leisure activities, and choice of friends. The teens sought programs that allowed them to transcend these tight controls. Boys lived vicariously through the daredevil contestants on reality shows and fantasy animations. They were easily entertained with slapstick cartoons. Girls explored beyond their conservative boundaries through female protagonists who weren't afraid to speak their minds. We cannot be too enthusiastic about such "innovative" serials, however. For example, Jassi, the plain-looking heroine of *Jassi Jaissi Koi Nahin*, had to morph into a beautiful model to widen her appeal. Anamika in *Qayamat* had to reenter her oppressive environment with a new face, to get to the root of her tragic "demise." These women required dramatic transformation themselves to change the status quo. In Kannada language serials on Udaya TV such as *Mangalya* and *Mahabayi*, the female leads were no doubt independent and bold, yet fulfilled their very restrictive obligations as wives and daughters as well. As has been pointed out in critical analyses of such U.S.-produced shows as *Desperate Housewives* (ABC), narratives on outspoken women are seen as progressive when, in fact, they depict the woman's compatibility and desire for her own subjectivity and entrapment within the status quo (McCabe & Akass, 2006).

Parents, media, and religious and educational institutions work together to ensure the child is independent enough to look her or his interpellator in the eye, but is at the same time never fully in control. Into such a system enter more and more multinational corporations, with refined research strategies of their own to understand exactly how to conduct a profitable enterprise within. The labor market is theirs for the taking: an ideally groomed, obedient, and eager-to-please proletariat. The latter have learned how to be diligent and how to accept strict discipline even though they are not comfortable with it. Television programs provide avenues for rebellion and outspokenness, yet the desirable outcome is that the protagonist remains popular and compassionate to everyone. At the same time, we have to recognize the agency that television offers girls like Versha where she can dream of becoming anything she wants to because of her favorite Meher on television. Versha and Cora also had strongly supportive fathers, a significant influence in a patriarchal environment. Previous fieldwork on call center workers showed that young men and women were quite vocal in demanding better work conditions such as longer breaks and better health benefits (McMillin, 2007). Also, a more recent study among 150 college girls between 16–20-years-old in Bangalore indicated that they were learning about critical and feminist theory as part of their curriculum. They were skeptical of prime-time Indian television serials across channels that presented "silence" or "quiet endurance" as desirable female qualities. *Jassi Jaissi Kohi Nahi* in particular resulted in varied and heated responses, most of them critical of the protagonist's power to exert control over her circumstances (McMillin, forthcoming). Fernandes and Heller (2006), although analyzing ideological constructions of class and their economic and social consequences in India, make a relevant point for our assessment here on the gender differences within the middle class:

> even as liberalization unleashes the discourses of merit, ability, achievement, and mobility and the world is said to become flatter, the fractions of the NMC deploy their positional assets with ever greater assiduousness and the logic of class struggle relentlessly delivers inequality. (p. 513)

This study reminds us how undeniable parental influence is and how strong the grasp of family is in nonmediacentric environments. It makes a strong case for attention to context in international audience studies. All teens in this study fell into a broad conceptualization of the middle class, a class that is increasingly at the center of Indian political and economic discourse. The definition of the middle class in India has undergone another complication through globalization. India's role in new circuits of labor as seen in the particular case of information technologies has generated a surge in the professional middle class who enter these circuits as skilled service providers. Whereas government institutions such as public sector banks and colleges and universities would be considered the workplaces habited by India's middle class, now the NMC streams in and out of multinational companies and foreign banks. It is this class that is implicated in the discourse on globalization (Fernandes, 2004). The practices of its children are touted as evidence of a nation gone wild, giving rise to right-wing activists who resort to violence to make their point that the Westernization of this class of youth will eat the heart out of a "pure" and "chaste" India. The young girls and boys interviewed in this study conveyed some of the stresses of a population that is both the poster child for national progress and the scapegoat for its defilement.

On another note, despite regular reminders of class distinction in the teens' daily lives where each teen lived in a household that employed a maid or two or more, invariably had a private vehicle, whether two wheeler or a car, and had a variety of appliances such as the television set, computer, and in many cases, a washing machine, it is remarkable that all of them believed their socioeconomic class had nothing to do with how they perceived their abilities. The project of secularism in India where children are taught in school at a very young age that all people are equal and that Mahatma Gandhi's *ahimsa* or nonviolence principle is the path to follow quite effectively erased from the young respondent's vocabularies, articulations of social inequity. They, almost as one, vigorously expressed that how much money or status their families possessed did not come in the way of their interactions with friends and neighbors. All were created equal. Yet as we saw in the ways in which interviews with low-income teens were organized, class status played a key role in how teens presented themselves. While verbally subscribing to a dominant discourse of equality, in material terms, these respondents "staged" the site of the interview so that elements of this "equality" were highlighted, not the conditions that set them apart from the interviewer. From their reception of various news shows and panel discussions on television, they were aware that a formal interview environment should rightfully include chairs and a table, at the very least. In these engineerings of environment and hospitality, we see assertions of agency even within the recognition that agency is diminished. These observations underscore the need to receive youth narratives not at face value, but as reminders of young people's ideological positions, where they can deny the relevance of class even as they silence their "uneducated" mothers or, in the case of upper-class teens, as they lift their feet up while the maid mopped the floor.

Language of Currency

Configurations of the workplace, changing power, and gender relations, use of new technologies have all been regarded as contingent upon the development of a well-adjusted youth labor force (Lesko, 2001). Youth participation in national economies as both laborers and consumers has precipitated a variety of new media technologies and consumer goods. Youth then no longer participate across the world in global programming or products but are also linked through interdependent and outsourced labor markets. The systematic training of urban Indian teens in the English language and the ongoing focus on science and technology serves both the perpetuation of the middle class and the goals of the national elite in positioning India as a serious player in the global marketplace.

English-speaking teens in urban centers such as Bangalore or Hyderabad could probably pass unnoticed in downtown Chicago or New York. How does our recognition of their signifiers of global identity change when we know that conversational English is now a mandatory requirement in their public high school curriculum to prepare them for an outsourced job market feeding multinational giants? Do we see the use of English as just the choice of an urban teen or as a response to a globalized economic environment that is reaping the benefits of entrenched colonial structures? Chow (1998) rightly points out to the systematic devaluation of national languages in colonial contexts by both colonizers and national elites. Such devaluation represents both racism and *classism within racism*. That is, while the study of native languages is never against the law,

> in order to head toward the upper echelons of society, one would, even (and especially) if one was a member of a colonized race, have no choice but collaborate with the racist strategies that were already built into the class stratification informing the management, distribution and consumption of knowledge. (p. 163)

Through this, we understand that the fluidity and mobility awarded by neocolonial processes simultaneously limit the ways in which the postcolonial native can participate. In India the British colonial legacy of English as the language of administration and upward mobility works in tandem with contemporary media structures to groom workers for a neocolonial marketplace. Ashcroft (2001) argues that classes on spoken English confer upon students an acceptance of English as the language of currency, upward mobility, and academic success. In this sense, and connecting with the stress of high school students at the interschool debate described at the beginning of the book, we understand Fernandes and Heller's (2006) comment that "The rapid proliferation of private schools and in particular the mushrooming of a multitiered system of private engineering and medical colleges marks a new stage in the composition of the middle class" (p. 514). Access to and success in high-quality education continues to be the overriding concern of middle-class families, requiring such practices within the household, as has been described by the teens in this project. We see then, how performativity comes to be "a cultural ritual, as the reiteration of cultural norms, as the habitus of the body in which structural and social dimensions of meaning are not finally separable" (Butler, 2000, p. 29). Identity is not constituted merely through difference and itself is not binary, but emerges from a field of relations. Television works in tandem with local institutions that follow the logics of global capital, to create the world within which Indian youth draw meanings and conclusions about their future.

This chapter has demonstrated that a formal analysis of the logics of identity constitution requires an understanding of the processes by which they are created and dismantled. Although the discussion of youth responses followed gender differences, the overarching theme was the strong pressures within the household to conform to socially prescribed gender roles. These norms work with other systems such as education, market, and religion to produce the obedient child and worker. Gender and class, therefore, were used as points of departure for analysis, as delineated by Laclau (2000, p. 53):

> We gain very little, once identities are conceived as complexly articulated collective wills, by referring to them through simple designations such as classes, ethnic groups and so on, which are at best names for transient points of stabilization. The really important task is to understand the logics of their constitution and dissolution, as well as the formal determinations of the spaces in which they interrelate.

The teens' own social and family contexts resonated with televised structures offering an easy cultural correspondence between real and televised environments. Girls' respect for fathers, older brothers, and other males in their lives was symbolic of their rootedness in a patriarchal society. Frustration among the girls that their morals were questioned each time they so much as glanced at a boy was evidence of the ruptures between the worlds they and their parents inhabited.

The analysis showed that hegemony works under certain conditions: an uneven distribution of power, and a subversion of particularities through universalisms. That is, Indian teens could be trained for the multinational workplace by maintaining the particularities of their local environments but by desiring the universalities offered through the media and market. Two possibilities follow, as delineated by Butler (2000). First, the particular can reject the universal; in this case, conservative parents can reject their children's desires to be free and express agency according to universal ideals unraveling on television. Second, the universal can reject the particular as seen in the example of the conflation of Louisiana Governor Bobby Jindal with *Slumdog* hero Jamal. Each can therefore reject the other while simultaneously requiring the other to function. Subjects do not just occupy positions within structure but also fill in structural gaps, as we see time and again in the explanations of young boys and girls that discipline by their parents, no matter how harsh, was necessary to produce them as good citizens. To explore further how distance between universal and particular is maintained and to examine the role of the researcher when that very distance is revealed to be a space of violence for the teen subject, we turn to the last two chapters in this book.

· 6 ·

CIRCLES OF LIFE

When keynote speaker Roy Disney said that his global empire *created* childhood, over 300 youth delegates at the 2007 Fifth World Summit on Media for Children (5WSMC) held at the Sandton Convention Center in Johannesburg, South Africa, rose to their feet and cheered. The irony of Disney's commanding presence in one of the poorest nations of the world may have been apparent to media scholars and political attendees at the Summit, but was emblematic of the diegetic power of film (Bordwell & Thompson, 1997) where the youth delegates could feel, in some way, that they shared the story worlds created by the media super power. As Roy Disney talked in simplistic terms about the global relevance of the conglomerate's movies, Mickey Mouse and Pooh lit up the massive screens in the background, disarmingly blundering through a variety of circumstances, rendering invisible Disney's formidable and intricate synergistic production and distribution industries that seal its success in far-flung markets.

Disney wrapped up his comments while the "Circle of Life" video from *The Lion King* incorporating over 25 different languages unfurled on the screens. The movie has been extensively criticized for "sanitizing" its narrative from any references to the people of the African continent. The audience related, as had countless others across the world, to "universal" hierarchies of power and privilege. Such hierarchies have been critiqued for their elevation of "a specific content to a global condition, making an empire of its local meaning" (Butler, 2000, p. 31). Just one aspect of this "specific content" is evident in the ordering of accents in the movie, which as Lippi-Green (1997) argues serves as a pedagogical device for young viewers to differentiate between the good and bad guys. The American accents of central, "good" characters, the British accent of the antagonist, and the stereotypical Hispanic and African American accents of the supporting staff of the antagonist, all work to create systems of recognition and, simultaneously, *misrecognition* (Taylor, 1994), where groups who do not speak with the accent of the dominant group in the film are outside the circle of privilege. Disney's Buena Vista International ensured that the film debuted synchronously worldwide in June 1994, coinciding with the release of other products such as animated storybooks, videos, theme park features, clothing, and other accessories, in synergy with Walt Disney Publishing Company and Media Station Inc., to name a couple. The exchange value of these synergistic products take on a magical life of their own (Miller, 1994), creating a "universal" relevance for consumers, even if their own contexts are far removed from the world unraveling on film. It is no surprise that Disney's largest market outside the United States is India, whose rising new middle class (NMC), as described previously, may not have hegemonic status (Fernandes & Heller, 2006), but nevertheless serves as an important articulator of hegemonic goals (S. Deshpande, 2003).

Hegemonies, therefore, work by constructing a universality of discourse. The circulation and universalization of cultural hierarchies reveals an interesting process whereby subjects of neocolonial contexts "appropriate, or 'consume,' the dominant, 'hegemonic,' culture, discourses, and technologies, for purposes which may be very different from those of the disseminations of that culture" (Ashcroft, 2001, p. 44). Such consumption is only part of a variety of rituals that contribute to the complex neocolonial character where initiation to imperialist cultures occurs through myriad entrenched institutions, of which education is one. With the structures for cultural and power transfer in place (Pieterse & Parekh, 1995) within neocolonial societies, facilitation of the "global corporate curriculum" (Demerath & Lynch, 2008, p. 20) is relatively easy. Engineers of this curriculum such as Disney set up a "consumer-media culture ... as a competing pedagogy" (Willis, 2003, p. 23). Such a curriculum works powerfully not just by what it teaches, but what it leaves out. In fact, the curriculum glosses over such elements as "Third World sweatshops, child labor, corporate greed, the corporate colonization of public space and the popular psyche, waste and environmental damage" (Demerath & Lynch, 2008, p. 21). As Venn (2006, p. 89) pertinently poses, the important question here is "What 'grand narratives' establish the values that should determine 'worthwhile' existences?"

In this chapter, we undertake an intricate analysis of the possibilities of transformation even within the large-scale acceptance of narratives that limit the mobility of the subject seeking transformation. What we are highlighting here is not the structures of media power that contain and regulate the imaginations of young consumers across the world, as is the primary thrust of political economy analyses, but to point to the precise diegesis of global products such as Disney films that set up narrow norms of success and desirability for youth worldwide. We recognize that audiences everywhere can identify with the broad themes of individual struggle and victory, yet we avoid a formalist approach to culture and social relations as proposed famously by Lacan (see Žižek, 1993, p. 149) where

> conditions that are external to the thing are posited as internal and immanent to the thing. Furthermore, at the same time that external and arbitrary conditions are rendered as immanent and necessary features of the thing, the thing is also grounded and unified by this performative act of definition.

That is, we do not assume that the representation of a stereotypical, ethnocentric world by Disney industries is uncritically internalized by its consumers. As Butler (2000, p. 26) argues, Lacan's *point de caption* "where an arbitrary sign not only appears essential to what it signifies, but actively organizes the thing under the sign itself" (p. 26) leads to the risk of analyzing those characteristics that come to be associated with the sign as the reality itself or the ground for analysis. Butler discusses that identities are performative, not essential, offering avenues for resistance and agency. She poses a key question: "if we cannot see how something new might come of such invariant structures, does it help us to see how new social and political articulations can be wrought from the subversion of the natural attitude within which we live?" (Butler, 2000, p. 28).

And so our journey brings us to examining the transformative possibilities articulated by the very audiences that rejoiced with and related to the victories of the Americanized Simbha in *The Lion King*. The *Exploring Gender across the World* project (sponsored by the IZI and conducted by the author) was intended to address what "gender"[27] meant to children from different countries. While this was the primary question posed by the sponsoring institute and has been discussed elsewhere (McMillin, 2008b), the chapter delves into how avenues for change are articulated by the very subjects that reap immediate rewards from a neocolonialist system that constrains them psychically and materially, in the long term. It describes the main questions posed to delegates during the 5WSMC but through a discussion of the responses, draws out the intricacies of fieldwork within such a venue. The questions pursued by the IZI were as follows: What do children from across the world perceive to be the characteristics, rights, and freedoms of a girl and a boy from their region? Second, what constructions of gender do they perceive on television in their region? Finally, what examples can they provide of the "typical" girl or boy as portrayed on television?

As demonstrated in Chapters Three and Four, television, particularly programs originating from North America and Great Britain, provide teens around the world modes of conduct and desirability. Local television programs provide immediate relevance, yet there is a clear recognition among urban teens of which is the more desirable, which is the "authentic" and which is being mimicked, to achieve membership in a globalized environment. In all these studies we have been on a quest to see how the agent is produced, what factors define who emerges with authoritative subjectivity and who emerges with a sense of service to the global order. Youth in various locales discussed identities in somewhat essentialist terms. They related to characters on television within those essentialized frames. At the same time, the qualitative fieldwork drew out the complex intersections of place, class, culture, gender, religion, and so on, so that even among responses articulated along essentialist lines, we could assess that these were more because of the limited vocabularies and mediated images the teen had access to, rather than their lived experiences. Through this fieldwork experience, we continue to affirm that youth do not live outside ideology, but as ideological subjects, view—at times with incisive vision—avenues for transformation.

In the *Exploring Gender* project, the time available and the primary thrust of questions could very well have resulted in essentialist responses. We did not have the luxury of time that was possible in earlier fieldwork. The design of the project was undertaken with care, therefore, incorporating as many avenues as possible—oral, written, and pictorial, for delegates to express their views and experiences. Through a multilevel design, we were able to derive a description of what youth across the world watched on television, what concerned them about representations of gender, and what they wanted to see improved or changed in these representations. An activist component of this project was to develop suggestions for better youth television from primary audiences themselves. While it is beyond the scope of this book to delve into the political and cultural histories of the participants from various countries, what is attempted here is a description of the varying degrees of agency experienced by the young people textured by the conditions of their upbringing. We have already heard, at close quarters, the stories of teens in Bangalore, Johannesburg, Munich, and New York. We have seen that teens in Bangalore and Johannesburg had a very different sensibility about the world around them, because they were indeed experiencing, arguably more dramatically than teens in Munich and New York, changes in their neighborhoods, political and economic systems, and, as a consequence, their future prospects. In fact, it is striking that with the exception of one teen, none of the teens in New York talked about the aftermath of the terrorist attacks of 9/11, even though the interviews were conducted just a few months later, and questions specifically addressed issues of national and global identity.

The responses of the delegates here are interpreted and received using the guidelines of "critical ethnography (which) begins with an ethical responsibility to address processes of unfairness or injustice within a particular *lived* domain" (Madison, 2005, p. 5). What this means is that we delve beneath the surface meanings of the data that was collected and we unsettle assumptions about the positions occupied by the delegates. In its research design and goal of eliciting suggestions from teens to improve quality of television programming, the project could be considered *participatory action research*. Such methodology is derived from the field of development communication where the researcher partners with the community under study to help bring about social change. When used by anthropologists, such a method includes the conventional elements of ethnography such as prolonged time in the field and immersion in the community. Teen delegates comprised the community under study but obviously a lengthy stay in the field was not possible. Yet the critical framework used by the researcher and assistants brought this undertaking in line with the basic tenets of participatory action research (Barab, Thomas, Dodge, Squire, & Newell, 2004).

Surface Representations and Snapshots

The Fifth World Summit on Media for Children held in Johannesburg, South Africa, from March 24 to 28, 2007, aimed to integrate children's perspectives into strategies to produce better media for children worldwide. Approximately 86 countries registered for the conference, which itself was sponsored by a variety of media and community organizations such as the South African Broadcasting Corporation (SABC), the Independent Communication Authority of South Africa (ICASA), the Department of Communications, Telkom, and the Media Development and Diversity Agency. A variety of plenary sessions and workshops were created around the theme of "Media as a Tool for Peace and Democracy." Some examples of panel sessions were

"Sport as a Peace Builder," "Conflict Resolution in Quality TV for Children," "Indigenous Knowledge Systems, Language and Cultures," "Producing for Toddlers," and so on. The standing-room-only attendance at these sessions spoke of the importance of the topics and the eagerness of both producers and academics to work toward better quality media for children. Final estimations of attendance were at 1,700 adult participants and 400 children participants, most between 13 and 16 years.

Youth delegates were chosen through a variety of procedures; no single selection method was possible or even desirable. In general, publicity about the 5WSMC was circulated to numerous media organizations and educational institutions among various countries. Organizers received a flood of letters in response from institutions such as Youth Media and the Children's Press Bureau, forwarding names of students and media workers, many from impoverished backgrounds in African countries. A review of some of the letters of intent from youth delegates showed that many had been or were connected to activist groups either directly or indirectly involving the media. Delegates particularly from African countries had been oriented to issues of child sexual abuse and transmission of HIV/AIDS. Some had received formal training in print and broadcast journalism, reporting on human rights issues and interviewing high ranking officials on the same. The letters were a combination of personal information and general achievements; on the personal level, all indicated a strong desire to speak up with dignity and change what was regarded, in the words of one letter, "the world (as) such a cruel place for children." While a majority of the children were from African countries, several delegates were from countries of the Middle East, Europe, and North America, providing an interesting range of participants.

To provide a brief overview of the tenor of the Summit itself, it should be noted that as contended by various youth scholars (see, for example, Buckingham, 2000; Fass, 2008), vast differences emerged in how children talked and how adults talked about them. The celebratory rhetoric of various national officials at the opening plenary struck a stark contrast, for example, to experiences recounted by child soldiers. To cite a few, 17-year-old Tepita Voze Sando from Liberia, 16-year-old Caroline Zephil from Haiti, and 14-year-old Aseel Issa from Palestine spoke eloquently about what they had endured as child soldiers. Sando talked about his early training on how to rape and kill. His involvement in radio later on saved his life. Zephil described her painful journey from a lost child of the streets to a popular radio DJ in Haiti.

During the duration of the Summit, the SABC conducted workshops in the afternoons, titled "The Whistle Blowers," which engaged school children arriving by the bus load each day in highly animated sessions on HIV/AIDS and sexual abuse. Also, in the lower level of the Convention Center where the workshops were held, various media organizations rented stalls for exhibition of their programming. These exhibitors (which included CINEKID International, Amsterdam; Danish Film Institute; and RAI, Italy) provided an opportunity for media scholars, professionals, and students to obtain examples of children's programming around the world. Computer kiosks allowed for Internet connectivity and for blogging activity (see http://www.5wsmc.com/blog), providing a sense of events as they were happening.

The *Exploring Gender* project was conducted in one of the workshop spaces. Youth delegates arriving for the afternoon sessions were distributed by youth organizers[28] among various projects, of which this was one. With multiple workshops taking place simultaneously, the project could be conducted with 42 youth delegates from 10 countries, instead of over 100 delegates that was initially anticipated. It was clear at the outset that we could not delve into deep questions of context and television relevance for the participants in the time that was available (around two and a half hours). Also, because workshops were conducted coincidentally in large spaces segregated by cardboard dividers, we had the added difficult of low audibility. While these were challenges that were apparent only at the site and time of the project, in the months prior, extensive time was spent in developing the project design and manuals for training research assistants.

Training of six research assistants[29] took place the day before the project was conducted. Interviewers were introduced to the objectives of the study and coached on techniques of interviewing. Each was assigned to a table that would contain delegates from a certain region of the world. Care was taken to ensure that all assistants were aware that comments could not be taken as representative of the country or region as a whole. The organization of tables according to geographical region was therefore just for efficiency of data collection. Assistants were instructed to make sure that all delegates at their table (usually numbering around eight each), were seated and given a chance to introduce themselves. Drawing upon Quijada's (2008) observations that talking is a form of activism, much time was spent during the training session to understand youth positions as experts and activists. Power discrepancies were also an important part of the training discussion. The research design itself was problematized as representing rituals of signification that could exacerbate power differentials between the researchers and respondents in terms of ethnicity, credentials, and fluency in English. The focus therefore was on limiting the number of questions asked and increasing the time for discussion, essay writing, and drawing. We were keen to get as much expression from the delegates as possible, on the key questions of what worked and didn't work for them on television, and how they would like to change it. Assistants were oriented to the possibility that for many young participants, interactions with researchers and social workers may be one of few opportunities through which they could talk about their anxieties and desires. The challenge for researchers and those committed to social change was to "rethink not what is beneficial for youth, but how youth as active participants promote and advocate movements that rethink how youth and other marginalized groups are positioned while building a context to delve deeply into social justice" (Quijada, 2008, p. 218). In this sense, youth "talk" was regarded as a form of activism in that it could effect change even if just in the moment where the articulation of struggle is the first step to changing the conditions that produce that struggle.

The 42 participants were from Tanzania, Lesotho, Botswana, Poland, South Africa, Ireland, Sweden, Palestine, Qatar, and the United States. All assistants were fluent in English, yet English was not their native language as it wasn't for many of the delegates as well. Interpreters, particularly for delegates from Palestine and Qatar, were available and played a significant role in translation of both oral and written comments. Participants were organized into eight focus groups. Three specific phases characterized the project.

First after introductory remarks from the author describing the project, each interviewer explained the project a second time to respondents at the assigned tables. After members at each table had an opportunity to introduce themselves, research assistants posed two questions to each respondent: First, what bothers you most about how boys and girls are portrayed on television? Can you give examples? And second, what kinds of stories about boys and girls would you like to see on television? All comments were recorded.[30]

In the second phase, the delegates were asked to write their responses to three specific questions. The first asked them to describe their experience as a girl or boy in their country. They were instructed to think about experiences at home and school and provide examples wherever possible. The second asked them to discuss their favorite television program, providing details of the name of the program, the network it was broadcast on, and the language of broadcast. The third question asked respondents to explain why the show was their favorite, and reflect on what it conveyed to them about gender identity. Put simply, they were asked what the show conveyed to them about being a girl or boy.[31]

In the third phase, when the respondents completed their essays, they were asked to draw a "typical girl or boy" from their country, in accordance with the objectives of the sponsoring organization. The discussion in this chapter reflects on the disconnect between the "universal" and the "particular" not just in terms of the particularities of teens' experiences and the limited universal role models on television, but also in terms of the disconnect between respondents' experiences and theory in youth and media studies to address this complexity. The research questions themselves posed a potential risk in that, for example, instructions to the teens to draw a "typical" girl or boy from their country could result in further essentialization both in the framing of the question and the response that would be delivered. Because of the constraints of time, language, and audibility (where the noise from parallel workshops made parts of the discussion difficult to hear), what was available and recognizable, as a common currency, was, ironically, these very essentialist frames. Research assistants were especially instructed to be sensitive to differing definitions of "typical boy" or "typical girl." The goal was not to reach consensus but to provide space and time for the expression of diversity. To maintain a common currency of language within that relatable structure, questions were posed in this convention to *stimulate* further discussion, not set its limits (see Ang, 1996).

During the fourth phase, respondents compared their drawings and discussed similarities and differences in their perceptions of girls and boys from their countries. They then developed a list of generalizable qualities for their regions and transferred this gender profile onto a wall map of the world. How the data are used and discussed places an important responsibility on the researchers. The role of the assistants was to document all written, oral, and pictorial submissions. The researcher then transcribed all materials and organized them so that recommendations for change in youth programs could be conveyed to the sponsoring institution, which in turn would transmit that information to television producers around the world.

Who Were the Respondents?

A quick demographic analysis of the participants showed that more females (29 in number or 69%) than males (13 or 31%) were involved in the discussion groups. The age of the children ranged between 11 and 18 years, with most in either the 10th or 11th grades. English was the native language of more respondents (24%) than any other language, followed by Arabic and Swahili at 12 percent each. A rich variety of languages such as Sotho, Setswana, Zulu, Sesotho, Tswana, and Mdebele was cited as the primary language by several respondents, since more than half of the respondents (25 or approximately 60%) were from African countries. Conversations during focus group sessions (one hour in duration with around eight teams each consisting of five–nine youth) were intense and animated. The young respondents were eager to share their views regarding the research questions, specifically, what it meant to be a boy or girl in their country, what their favorite television programs were, what bothered them about the representation of boys and girls on television, and finally, what they would like to see on television.

Several studies have asserted that in societies newly experiencing capital-ism, socioeconomic class is integrally linked to users' consumption of global media products and general cosmopolitanism. For example, in his study of South African youth, Strelitz (2003) found that upper-middle-class white stu-dents were bigger consumers of American television, music, and film where-as lower-class black students preferred native language programs. McMillin's (2002) ethnography among urban families in South India showed that teens from higher-income families enjoyed and identified with characters in such serials as *Charles in Charge* and *Full House* while those in lower-income families were avid viewers of regional language soap operas and sitcoms. Similar con-clusions are drawn in Grixti's (2006) analysis of Maltese youth and Havens's (2001) exploration of Kuwaiti youth.

The transnational relevance of industrialized, capitalist contexts, where individuality is glorified, is problematic, according to Fass (2008). Writing spe-cifically with the ways in which a primarily North American adolescence is universalized, she contends that in keeping with the logic of aggressive market expansion, "youth soon became a distinct product in the arsenal of Western capitalism. Appeals to youthful sexuality helped to sell goods and the youth market became a special marketing niche" (p. 26). The conflation of youth culture with consumer culture has been widely studied as summarized in Chap-ter Two. In fact, studies that focus on youth consumerism tend to view such consumers as free floating and mobile (Grossberg, 1988).

For example, in the study of youth consumer culture in Johannesburg, Nuttall (2008) examines billboard advertising to show how these conspicu-ous spaces in the urban landscape play with racial conviviality in a society still segregated more than a decade after the end of apartheid. Neoliberal market discourse identifies youth consumers as autonomous agents of their own destiny. Demerath and Lynch (2008) demonstrate how an "authoritative subjectivity" (p. 182) develops in suburban, American high schoolers, through interactions with parents, peers, and an all-pervasive commodity culture grooming them for a neoliberal order. Less authoritative and more ambiguous is the subjectivity of Latina/o youth in a dominant white U.S. culture where representations lie in the realm of deviance and outsiderness (Valdivia, 2008). Important to note is that agency or authoritative subjectivity in a consumer culture is most significantly felt by individuals anchored in a dominant group. Theirs is the privilege and freedom to choose. For those on the periphery of social circles of power, this freedom may be recognized, but also apparent is their inability to exercise it.

Focus group discussions and written responses from the 42 teens[32] at the 5WSMC generally reflected these patterns. We detected here a strong correspondence between teens' perceptions of their gendered selves and their television choices. Young girls from Sweden, Poland, and Ireland wrote about how they were treated no differently from boys and that their discussions of feminism and equal rights in school underscored their fair treatment. One 15-year-old from Ireland said that it was "great to be a girl living in Ireland. We all have equal rights and we have right to education and to play. We have the UDHR (Universal Declaration of Human Rights) to protect these rights." She loved watching *Bones* on Sky 1 because of its female lead: "it is usually the guy that's the hero but in this show it's the girl." Her 12-year-old friend agreed that everyone had equal rights. Girls usually did better academically than boys at her school, but they were allowed to mingle and do the same activities. She was an avid follower of *Lost* (Channel 4, RTE) that promoted the idea that everyone should work together to help the community. Another Irish delegate, a 16-year-old girl, chimed in reiterating that "everyone is equal in Ireland." She cited *Friends* (broadcast on E4) as a great example of a show that resonated with her own desire for equality—it was a good representation of males and females living together and sharing interests. Although another 13-year-old Irish girl agreed with her friends that it was great to be a girl in Ireland, she did point to portrayals of women as "damsels in distress" on television with men as "heroes that save the day. Or the women stay at home and cook and take care of children, while the men go out to work." However, like the members of her Irish team, she believed *Friends* was a good representation of gender equality because the show had the same number of male and female characters. According to her, *Friends* did not resort to stereotypes because all the characters had "original and realistic roles." Both men and women were funny and took turns at being funny.

Teens from Poland varied in their responses. A 13-year-old girl wished girls were not treated as the weaker sex and instead, given as much importance as they were on her favorite program, *Desperate Housewives.* A 12-year-old boy objected to the responses from his Polish mates. He said boys were most often depicted as bumbling fools on television. Even in his school, his teachers assumed girls were studious while boys merely played around. An 18-year-old girl from Sweden discussed her awareness of women's rights—the history of feminism was an important subject at school. She in particular was treated the same as her brothers. *The Parliament,* a Swedish show that spoofed politics and gender differences, was her favorite. It really brought out the lighter side of divisive boundaries, she said.

In these brief responses we can already see the discrepancies between how ideologies are accommodated between adults and youth, and between media scholars and young consumers. Those very shows touted as examples of equality and feminism such as *Desperate Housewives* and *Friends* have been the subject of feminist critique. For example, McCabe and Akass (2006) write in the introduction to their anthology *Reading Desperate Housewives* that "At a time when women are allegedly more empowered, more liberated than at any other time in our history, we seem as desperate as ever" (p. 9). The story of each extremely slim, coiffured, and anxious woman and her peers, whether in *Desperate Housewives, Friend,* or *Sex and the City* includes parody and possibility, the tragedy is that it is not easy to discern which is which (see Bordo, 2003). Postfeminist treatments of women-centered television programs, constructing them as free agents who can subvert systems but never really choose to do so, send an important and arguably debilitating message to teens that where one is, is right where one should be; transformation may be possible, conditions may be ripe, but is it really *necessary?* We continue with our examination of articulations of gendered lives and television preferences among teens from the United States.

All U.S. participants were African American girls. They were struck by the lack of media coverage, whether local or national, that accompanied their selection as delegates for the Summit. They were from different states, yet all believed that they would have merited a newspaper article and a few seconds at least, on television news, had they been Caucasian. Their views on gender politics within their schools or on television were not as positive as their peers from Poland, Sweden, and Ireland. A 13-year-old expressed that in the United

States, *how* a girl was treated depended on how she "presented herself." It was up to the girl to prove that she was good in academics and sports. In general, she said, "my country shows equal opportunity for both girls and guys if you can present yourself like you actually know what you are doing." *DeGrassi* (syndicated in the United States on The N and MTV channels), a program she and peers in the group watched regularly, presented realistic situations that girls and boys experienced, she said. A 15-year-old, however, was not so sure that it was a girl's responsibility to define the terms by which she was treated. She said:

> It is hard to be a girl in the United States because girls are like objects and are used at a boy's discretion. A lot of times girls are called bitches (and) ... it comes from the media. At home I am given the typical girl chores of cooking and cleaning. My mother even says these are the things that girls are *supposed* to do and no one should *have* to do anything.

A show she watched frequently just confirmed her position that girls were "viewed as objects, bitches, whores, and sluts in the media; not all women are like that." A 17-year-old concurred that girls were expected to be beautiful and scantily dressed to be noticed. Another 17-year-old talked about the "double negative" of being a girl and an African American. That said, she was enthusiastic about the opportunities girls had in sport, with well-sponsored support for girl teams in basketball, tennis, softball, volleyball, and lacrosse.

Responses from teens in African countries were more similar to African American teens in the United States, than teens from Poland, Sweden, and Ireland. While they expressed ethnic and national pride, most discussed their difficulties in behaving according to restricted notions of gender. We are reminded here of Brown and Gilligan's (1993) contention that as young girls undergo the developmental changes of adolescence, they also experience a "loss of voice" (p. 6). Pipher (1994) argues that young girls practice self-censorship because they are unable to resolve the desire to speak and be heard with the variety of punishments that result from making their voices heard. Entrenched structures ensure that girls and boys have prescribed roles that they are socialized to at a very young age. Among the African teens, several girls chose to write poems to express how they felt about being a girl. They described their sadness at being taken for granted. Some were happy with the opportunities to excel at school. For example, a 17-year-old girl wrote,

> I am proudly South African. I know how to sing and to make a poem, to make a speech, to debate, and how to dance. When I'm (in) school there're lots of opportunities. Like

they take you to someone professional and give lots of information o(n) what you want (to) be in life. And they give you or build up your self-esteem and confidence.

For a few others, their vulnerability as girls was a primary concern. A 16-year-old South African wrote:

When you are a girl you get raped. At school the other boys will take advantage of you by wanting to rape you. At home you'll do all the stuff that (is) done at home like cleaning the house, (and) washing the laundry.

A 12-year-old from Lesotho felt similarly:

Girls are always raped. Girls always have to do the house jobs, (like) cooking and cleaning. At schools, girls have to sweep and wash the windows. Girls are classified as the weakest people, so boys take advantage of it. Boys are always chosen to do things that are first position and girls on second. That's why I say being second means you are the first loser.

Her favorite television program was *Chatroom* (on TV1) broadcast in both English and Zulu. The messages of the show, which were not to discriminate but to love and protect one another, were appealing to this young woman. The young girls talked about tales of sexual abuse, as we shall discuss later in this chapter, yet also discussed their own sexual identities. Many had been or were currently involved in sexual relationships. They could see the disconnection between their sense of agency in directing sexual pleasure and their objectification by some of the men in their lives. They had to walk a tightrope so as not to incur the wrong kind of attention; at the same time, they sought to express their own need for a loving *and* sexual relationship.

A 15-year-old from Tanzania was grateful that equal rights for boys and girls were mandated. Although girls in rural areas of the country still suffered, in her school and neighborhood, girls were treated well. Several from Tanzania, South Africa and Botswana wrote in their essays that although equal rights were talked about, they still performed traditional gendered chores in their homes such as cleaning and cooking, and were expected to be subservient to the men around them.

A 15-year-old girl from Lesotho said that

I don't think Lesotho has quite reached a state of equality. Girls are always expected to do domestic work. While boys on the other hand, do nothing. Even in schools for example, girls are always told to sweep the classes. In my family there are only girls and my parents are happy with their two girls. But I have noticed in my extended family that my female and male cousins are treated differently. My grandmother, being as old school as she is tells me that boys are the heads of the family as it is stated in the Bible. But in my experience because we are girls and my parents are educated enough to know that there is no difference between boys and girls so they are happy to have two girls. But in some if not most families it is not so easy.

Boys from African countries expressed that girls were given too much importance in their schools. A 14-year-old boy from Tanzania, for example, wrote that he was expected to do everything and earn for his family when he grew up. He was encouraged to study while the girls in his family were encouraged to give up school and help around in the house. A 13-year-old boy from Botswana felt the burden of being the oldest in his house. He had to teach his younger siblings not to drink or smoke despite the pressures in his neighborhood to do so. Another 13-year-old, also from Botswana, expressed in his essay that

> There is a female's union and women are celebrated which makes it tough for boys. Sometimes girls in my school are taken into the hall where they are entertained and they are given candy but boys don't receive nothing [sic]. Boys in my school are told to clean the entire school premises and wash the class windows in the whole school while the girls sweep the classrooms.

Segregation of duties at school was continued in the home. A third 13-year-old from Botswana said that boys were meant to work outside the home and earn money for the family while girls were forced to stay at home and work even if they desired an education. He said that,

> parents only allow boys to study because they (think) that boys are more intelligent than females and say that males are supposed to work and not girls so the boys should study because they are the people who are going to work.

His favorite program was *SpongeBob Squarepants* because the animated serial depicted boys and girls playing and working together.

The vast differences in how teen delegates from Poland, Sweden, and Ireland, and those from Botswana, Tanzania, Lesotho, and South Africa talked about their gendered experiences are worth examining here. We acknowledge that these teens do not speak for all peers in their countries. Nevertheless, in just these responses, stark variances in agency were obvious. These variances remind us that the nomadism (Fiske, 1989) so extensively theorized in "active audience" studies is a privilege of those with the cultural, economic, and social capital to be mobile. The young respondents from African countries expressed their boundedness to structure. At the same time, they also revealed a dependency on structure that was quite different among the teens from Poland, Ireland, and Sweden. Teens from these latter countries could relate what they were taught in school, in terms of the history of human rights and feminism, to their own experiences. They saw equality in the very shows that have been critiqued for perpetuating patriarchy. Symbolic female presence on the small screen in terms of number of characters, speaking roles, and comedic turns all translated into gender equality. For African American teens, the connections between sexist representations on television and in their real lives were more obvious, because it was reinforced by the discriminatory politics of racism. Being marginalized in overlapping spheres of gender and race quite likely instilled a keener sense of a hierarchical world than their peers. It is in the teens in African countries that we see not just an awareness of an unequal society, but the consequences of how inequities play out. Many talked about sexual abuse in their neighborhoods, many reiterated stereotypes about boys and girls, and affirmed their role as keepers of such structures even as they protested against its oppressive influence in their lives.

In this sense, they expressed an agency *in seeing* that the others didn't. Their comments are examples of minority discourse (see JanMohamed & Lloyd, 1990) that allows us to identify transformative possibilities in the face of the deadening pessimism of some postcolonial scholars who believe the subaltern cannot speak (Spivak, 1988). Or at least, that the subaltern has to speak in the language of her oppressor to be heard (Ashcroft, 2001). As discussed in greater detail later in this chapter, elementary school curricula (South Africa is just one example) includes strategies through which children can articulate abuse; the subaltern is trained to speak. Chow (1998) contends that minority discourse, in its recognition of the subordinated position, "is accompanied by a persistent belief in the possibilities of expression, articulation, and agency" (p. 3).

The comments show us that entrenched structures of gender have a powerful denuding effect on youth identity. At home and at school, when youth are performing rites of gender signification, television is regarded as an extended space of that signification, not a subverter of it. In the next section, we see that all the participants were quite critical about the stereotypical ways in which boys and girls were portrayed on television. Many of the comments that follow could perhaps be described as "counter-discourse" (Ashcroft, 2001, p. 32) in that they provide oppositional voices to the capitalist-patriarchy of the most popular television programs. Yet within these comments, we also detect a reaffirmation of those very same hierarchies the teens sought to critique.

Problematizing Youth on Television

As youth delegates talked about their freedoms and restrictions in living gen-dered lives, we looked for ways to turn these descriptions into suggestions for television producers, on how to make programs more relevant and useful for them. We approached this phase of the project with the knowledge that teens had already used as examples of progressiveness, those very shows that could be critiqued for sexism and racism. To avoid perhaps eliciting responses that would support the status quo, we posed our question in the form of a problem—that is, we asked respondents to comment on what *bothered* them about gender portrayals on television.

From their essays and conversations, it was clear that most of the par-ticipants were watching a mix of children and adult television. For teens from African countries, shows such as *Soul Buddyz* and *YoTV* on SABC, *UEFA Champion's League, Friends, Idol* and *SpongeBob Squarepants* on DSTV; *Missing* and *Wildroom* on SABC2; *Foster's Home for Imaginary Friends* on the Cartoon Network, and *Police Show, Silent Shout,* and *Home Affairs* on Botswana TV were favorites. Respondents from the United States enjoyed *DeGrassi, CSI, Court TV,* and *My Wife and Kids* on such cable networks as Cartoon Network and WB. Irish teens counted among their favorites *Friends* on E4 and *Bones* on Sky 1, while a Swedish teen identified *The Policeman* as her top-rated show.

A common element that emerged was that these shows were perceived to break gender and race stereotypes. For example, a 15-year-old girl from Tanzania wrote that Cartoon Network's *Foster's Home for Imaginary Friends* was about

(A) teenage girl called Frankie. She does a lot of work and is not stereotypically blonde and beautiful. She is more of a tomboy and has a lot of attitude. She is the one who fixes things around the mansion and comes up with ideas. It teaches me that girls do not always have to be the pretty, curvy, and dumb ones; they are smart and good at technical things.

Similarly, for a 16-year-old girl from Lesotho, *Missing* and *Wildroom* on SABC2 were favorites because they portrayed two women police and an equal forum for boys and girls, respectively. As briefly mentioned in the earlier sec-tion, a 13-year-old girl from Ireland believed that *Friends* was realistic and down-to-earth because,

It has an even number of men and women, it is not stereotypical, they all have original and realistic roles, it's realistic because it's about people trying to get a job, pay their rent, and make friends. It's also very funny and (shows that) both men (and) women can be humorous.

Bones was a favorite because the hero is a girl, an unusual occurrence, she said. Although many of these shows may be critiqued for their limited representations of diversity as discussed earlier, it is important to acknowledge that they were perceived to go against the grain for these teens. *Police Show, Home Affairs,* and *YoTV* for African teens provided information on how to protect oneself from theft and how to express ethnic pride. The latter two programs in particular broadcast national affairs in a format accessible to teens.

Almost all participants in this project could identify instances of sexism in the programs they watched on television. African American teens were critical about race representations as well. For example, a 15-year-old said that African American boys and girls made the news when they were part of a crime story. She discussed an incident in Scotland where a white male called her the "N" word. She was shocked that he was not mocking her, but actually thought it was perfectly acceptable to do so. She attributed this to the disparaging media coverage of African Americans and their treatment in the real world. A 17-year-old girl, also from the United States, concurred, saying that "black males are portrayed as thugs ... (and) girls have on these skimpy little bathing suits, shaking their butts and their bodies like they're objects and a lot of times, because of this, women are viewed like they're objects."

Males from the Middle East, specifically a 11-year-old and 14-year-old from Qatar and a 16-year-old from Palestine were critical about the scantily dressed women on television. They differed vastly in their reasoning and solutions from the African American girls, however. While the latter were critical about scantily dressed women on hip-hop music videos and their own subsequent racist and sexist treatment in public spaces, the former explained that their idea of better programs for women were those that focused on cooking and sewing. The agency that these two groups were seeking for women was quite different.

Teens from Tanzania agreed that scantily dressed women on television led to their poor treatment in schools and other public spaces. Boys noted that young boys are seen on television as criminals and drug addicts. A 14-year-old boy from South Africa said that "they," referring to the SABC, wanted to develop programs for children, yet focused on the negative aspects of the life of young boys. Girls were given wider exposure through such programs as Sisterhood on

ATV, but programs on boys usually centered on music and included celebrities, not real life. Another 14-year-old boy, this time from Tanzania, expressed that most programs represented what adults believed children's programs should be. He said children's opinions on what was interesting to them were not included in program development. He also discussed an interesting tendency within himself and his friends. He said:

> because adults who make us watch what the boys do outside on the streets, if they come to us and blame us that "you are smoking," you *start* smoking, I actually do it because *you* say I am smoking so let's make what you say into a reality. It's just that the media shows the bad side of boys and that influences the boys to do what they see on TV.

A 16-year-old boy from South Africa agreed:

> Yeah like most kids learn from TV, so when they see people smoking, raping, and everything, they also want to try and see how it feels, what it's like so they should stop doing these movies that encourage children to do bad things. Most people learn from the things they see on TV.

A 15-year-old girl from South Africa added:

> The thing is that those people (girls) who wear short skirts and our father(s) when they (see) them they feel (they want) to do something with them and ... those short skirts influence our fathers to be attract(ed) to those girls who do those things, so if they *stop* doing those things, I feel things will be sorted out.

And a 14-year-old South African girl commented:

> What TV is doing is creating a picture, that we are *nothing* but objects. Everybody can walk over us. So the picture they are painting is completely wrong. ... We are like sex objects. They cannot ignore us. ... we are losing ourselves. We are losing ourselves slowly but surely.

To use just one more example, a 16-year-old boy from South Africa said:

> Young boys rob our parents or kill our parents because of bad things they (see) on the TV or because of money. So that is not okay because those stories influence us as young children or as a young generation to kill our parents or to st(eal) our parents' money ... so that's not okay so when someone acts or we see someone carrying the gun you go and st(eal) your father's gun and you are going to kill someone like that boy on TV (referring to an actual news report). He just d(id) it because he saw it on TV. So it touch(es) the younger ones, yeah.

These media-determinist statements should be put into context. We receive them with the understanding of the performative nature of such fieldwork. The research project itself was staged in a systematic way where youth delegates were told the objectives of the researchers and were asked to think of themselves as experts on television in their lives. As social subjects, especially in the focus group discussions, the tendency was to echo the points made by the most strident in the group. Also, the first person to voice an opinion usually set the terms of the discussion with participants very rarely disagreeing to what was first asserted. It is essential for us to understand that "Human desire implores that we be listened to, apprehended, engaged, and free to imagine in and with worlds of Others" (Madison, 2005, p. 175).

The comments suggest that the programs the teens were watching in themselves drew determinist relationships between representation and behavior without adequate contextualization. Sensationalist news stories and documentaries on a variety of social issues often juxtapose cause and effect to create simplistic and oftentimes magical lines of connectivity between complex occurrences. The limitations of television itself as an educator, particularly in an era of transnational media networks that bring in competing well-produced and provocative commercially based formats from more privileged parts of the world, are obvious here. The points made by these teens should be seen as particularly useful for media scholars and youth educators in identifying other mediating systems, besides television, in providing modes for empowerment. The methodological constraints that texture how these comments are uttered and how they are received will be taken up in detail in Chapter Seven.

Youth Suggestions for Quality Television

In keeping with our intent of deriving suggestions for better television programs for youth, we asked the respondents to comment on what they *would like* to see on television. Some teens opted for a simplistic overturning of gender roles. These were from Sweden, Ireland, and Poland. If the norm was sitcoms and dramas that portrayed women as caretakers and nurturers while the men were action heroes, they wanted the opposite. Teens from African countries were more nuanced in their responses. Perhaps a factor of the authoritarian public service television environment where the educational and informational roles of television are overt, they sought a more activist and pedagogical function for television. In their responses we see their sense of authoritative subjectivity gain momentum in their discussions of self and interests. Their views should therefore be received as important and practical strategies for producing better television for children and youth.

An overarching theme that emerged across all group discussions was that there was a need for more programming, in straight *quantitative* terms, for children and teens. Respondents from Tanzania, Botswana, and South Africa in particular wished for a network channel that carried programs for children. Currently most such programs were carried on pay cable or satellite channels, outside the reach of much of the populations in their countries. Many also voiced their desire for programs during the day and prime time; for the most part, they were limited to adult programs.

A second dominant theme was better *quality* of programs. Defining quality was understandably more complex. For example, respondents from Lesotho and Botswana discussed more training programs and opportunities for advancement for those interested in media. They believed current children and youth programs that were indigenously produced were amateurish and unpolished. As a 15-year-old girl from Botswana put it, "I think we need *real* development in our TV programs ... I think we really need our own shows instead of getting our shows from other countries."

Better quality was also articulated as an increase in the positive portrayals of youth in general. Boys from Tanzania and Botswana discussed how young boys were represented as drug addicts, thieves, or murderers, contributing to the perception that they were a threat to society. African American girls from the United States wanted diverse roles for African American boys and girls in particular. They wanted more to be portrayed as aspiring doctors or lawyers, not just dancers in hip-hop videos or comedians. A 15-year-old Tanzanian girl expressed frustration at the victim narratives of women on local programs as well as the programs on the few foreign channels she received:

> What I really don't like is all the stories about girls who have been abused. What about the girls who have survived through their lives, who have survived tough times? The girls who have run away from their homes ... why don't they talk about that? Why don't they help them through television? Through *anything*, through any part of the media? Instead of talking about victims? Why don't they talk about survivors?

In fact, a 15-year-old South African girl added that portrayals of abuse, while raising the awareness of horrific violence perpetrated on young girls, may also increase such incidents. She said:

> They also show us our fathers abusing us and which is not right. The other boys com(e) up to see that and they also abuse us and maybe you got a boyfriend who wanted to do the same thing that the father (is) doing and maybe (he) see(s) the same way the father is doing to control the wife. ...

What this young girl was trying to convey was that educational programs may serve to reinforce the very behavior they are attempting to eradicate. This comment is right on target with research that charts the reverse effects of educational programs (see Singhal & Rogers, 2001, for example). What would work better for these teens were shows that depicted a balance, where girls and boys were shown as leaders. In other words, they wanted a greater diversity in roles.

Another way quality was described was in a wider range in program formats. In particular, several teens wanted to see more news and documentaries. A 16-year-old from Lesotho said:

> I feel that the children have a lot of stories and a lot of sadness and a lot of joy. And if somebody would just take a camera and record everything, it would be so great. We ... have so much to say and so much to share—heartbreaking and joyful stories if they could be brought to light and people could see what was going on you know. I just love documentaries.

Her friend, a 12-year-old girl, wanted more programs that explained the political conflicts in her country. She wanted more "live" news stories told in a way that a younger audience could be involved with what was happening in their country. Better quality would also mean more direct involvement with children in the production of programs. A 16-year-old girl from South Africa and a 15-year-old girl from Tanzania wanted programs on children participating with the government and children fighting for their rights, respectively. A 15-year-old boy from South Africa wanted to see "children really participating in the media whereby children do their own shows."

Finally, teens in the focus groups agreed that they sorely needed programs that were directly relevant to the development issues of youth. A 16-year-old from South Africa explained that she would "like to see the (programs) where they are teaching about puberty and they are teaching about virginity and about menstruation." A 15-year-old girl from Tanzania added that she wanted more "Shows about young people talking about their problems, what they think and what is going on with their lives ... so I would like to see a kids program about what they like, what they do, what's bothering them." Another 15-year-old girl from Tanzania said that she "would love to see the children involved in the government too (in programs) about rights about democracy; they should be included in the politics…" A 14-year-old girl from South Africa and 15-year-old boy from Tanzania agreed that they wanted to see more shows on their culture and heritage. In particular, they wanted to see child characters stand up and fight oppression. Documentaries that would teach them about how to resist oppression, particularly, segregation, would be very useful, they said. Overall, they agreed that they wanted programs that depicted the underdog's rise, from abuse and squalor, to affluence and power.

The synopsis of the respondents' descriptions of their gendered experiences, what bothered them about representations of boys and girls on television, and what they wanted to see on television provides a snapshot of life and experi-ences of young viewers across the world. The quotes included above only convey a partial sense of the passion and intensity with which the young respondents discussed their gendered identities and what they wanted to change on television. The comments also convey very differing ideas of what television *can* really do. Within a largely public service media environment that characterized the African countries most of the teens in this study were from, these respondents seemed to want television to be more accountable. Also, they were articulating many of the objectives of networks such as SABC, and reflected the rhetoric of the health awareness workshops conducted at the Summit itself. Teens from the United States, Sweden, Ireland, and Poland were less hopeful about the capability of television to change. While the teens from the United States were very critical not just of cable television but in particular with hip-hop videos featured on cable and elsewhere, they too did not perceive television to be a medium of change.

Hidden Stories

While we had workable suggestions to convey to producers, what we also had were graphic depictions of the specific conditions of teen life in various countries. Despite the concern that instructions to draw a "typical" boy or girl would result in narrow representations of gender, the respondents provided a rich variety of depictions. One young man from Tanzania drew himself with six-pack abs, stating that this was how he would *like* to look. Several drew themselves in name brand clothing, sunglasses, and necklaces. Yet others used the opportunity to write poems and draw pictures depicting deep pain. Several undertook this task and their use of this forum to communicate fears, injustice, and ethnic pride. What follows is a description of some of the drawings and a critical summary that raises questions for future comparative, cross-cultural, and international qualitative studies.

A 14-year-old girl from South Africa drew a picture of a girl with a flower-like cloud or hazy sun over her head. The girl is crying and an accompanying poem tells the tale of abuse:

> *Being a Girl Child*
> I remember those days
> W(h)ere we could play
> On the streets till late
> Without being sc(a)red
> But now things (have gone)
> From being better to worse
> Playing late means you will
> Not be home for days
> Someone (is) taking you
> Treating you like a(n) object
> Not a human being who
> Has feel(ings), just like him
> What is th(is) world
> Coming to, boys, uncles, fathers
> Take a second and picture
> If you would like (it) if
> Someone was doing
> It to you

Several girls from South Africa, Lesotho, and Botswana in particular talked about the unquestioned assumption by the boys in their schools and neighborhoods and the men in their lives that they were objects of pleasure. Words frequently used to describe themselves were slave, housewife, sex object, reproducer, and house cleaner.

A 14-year-old from South Africa conveyed her feelings through a short poem titled simply, "Poetry about the Girl." It read:

> I am a girl
> I know I am a girl
> Nobody is going to tell me my gender
> I am a girl

With breast
With hips
And with my beautiful face
And I know that somebody
Will say I'm ugly
But I am a girl
Thank you

She said being a girl was something to be proud of, except when one got pregnant and had to endure hardship.

From Botswana, a 15-year-old girl also expressed how she felt about being a girl through a poem:

What a little mis(s)ie you are
But what a(n) amazing disine [*sic*]
You(r) form all spoken sound
You give us the gift of state
You make eating a pleasure
Just a sip of you
Tells a story
Cold or hot
Salt or sweet
You make eating a pleasure
Sometimes you (p)ut me in trouble
Stop me from abusive stories
Train me to talk with love

Poetry produces an interesting challenge for the researcher trained in the methods of qualitative fieldwork including analysis of oral histories. Poetry should be seen as performative just as speech is, in the sense that it is much more than words on a page, or words out of a person's mouth (Fine, 1984). Oral narratives produce visual, tactile, olfactory, and aural sensations drawing the audience or the listener into a dynamic relationship with the producer. When what is to be interpreted is poetry, the most ethical and efficient way is to not interpret, but let the words speak for themselves.

Langellier and Peterson (2004) write in their analysis of oral histories that there are a few aspects to take into account. The first is to see the narrative as *embodying the physical contact among people* in that moment of production. The poems here should therefore be seen as produced within the 5WSMC environment where for days preceding and days following, each child delegate was given a clear indication that her or his voice was important, that somebody was going to do something about what she or he had to say. Perhaps the tales told were their own, perhaps they were about friends and neighbors. The sexual awareness education they were currently receiving at school and the fast-paced, high-intensity, SABC-conducted workshops at the Summit were all participants in facilitating the production of the written narratives, oral comments, drawings, and poetry. Second, the narratives should be seen as *situated*. That is, they are anchored to a certain history, culture, and power relation as expressed through language and ritual. Recognition of power relations cultivates a sensitivity to how narratives are constrained even as they are allowed to be told. The focus group discussions that involved the presence of researchers who were not from the context of the teens themselves, quite possibly constrained what could be told. The opportunity for written comments provided greater freedom in narrative. Also, the delegates were asked to only state their first names, if they chose to. Provision of gender, age, and country of origin was all that was needed for demographic information. Such a format awarded them a certain degree of freedom in telling their stories. Third, narratives should be seen as *discursive regularities* through four further considerations. A primary one is that they should be organized according to what is essential to its meaning and what is not. This is a tricky area because it relies on interpretation by individuals who may not be privy to inside meanings of the narrative. For example, in the poem from the 15-year-old girl from Botswana, we see two themes, one that addresses abuse and one that presents her as a sexual being, wanting to be trained as a lover, as deeply desired. Both components of this poem are intimate parts of the thoughts of the same person and cannot be seen as disconnected. In fact they provide a powerful reminder of just how vulnerable to abuse young girls are when the "I" of desire changes, without the subject's consent, to the "you" of objectification. A second aspect of narrative as discursive regularities is in its patterns of repetition and internal ordering that allows the researcher to classify themes. This process is evident in how the teen delegates' responses, taken altogether, are organized not just according to how they addressed the research questions, but also in how they were organized within themselves. Repetition was evident in every focus group, where, as stated earlier, the tendency was to follow the group leader. However, the reframing of questions over and over again and the distribution of the microphone among various participants resulted in new forms of dialogue and differentiations in opinions and knowledge with each round of questioning. Third, the researcher should pay attention to the position of the subject herself or himself and what qualifies the speaker to tell a story. The limitations on time and the paucity of information on each delegate prevented researchers from being able to get a sense of the context of the subject. However, in each participant's obvious recognition that her or his experience and comments were valued in this project and in the powerful context that the Summit itself offered where "stories of the native" were given credibility, there were no grounds to question the respondents' authenticity. Finally, the conditions of the narratives themselves have to be understood; that is, the process through which meaning is produced. The description of methodology and the space where the project was conducted provides a basic indication of some of the conditions. Further, because English was not the native language of most of the participants, each question was posed in multiple ways to ensure clarity as far as was possible. The difference in ethnicity, class, knowledge, and status between researcher and informant must all be seen as contributing to the conditions under which meanings were produced. Many of the comments are directly reproduced here to allow for reader interpretation and contestation.

The drawings of some of the participants from African countries had an interesting common element: a girl in the foreground either smiling or crying, but accompanied by a cloud and rain or a shadowy sun at best. While drawings by boys from African countries and girls and boys from European countries and the United States were stand-alone representations with the image taking center stage, those from Qatar and Palestine included some context. As with the girls from African countries, these renditions depicted a harsh and violent environment. The drawings showed young children going to school with war planes dropping bombs on them. These youth were closely chaperoned and further questions seeking explanation for the drawings were not feasible.

While the qualitative studies recounted in this book involved lengthy periods in the field, the *Exploring Gender Project* could be termed a *snapshot reception study*. Its strength lies in its inclusion of teens from various countries. The project provides a sense of the differences in political and cultural positioning of the teens and how they view the function of television in their lives. A great value of a crosscultural study, such as this one, is that it also demonstrates—in vivid terms—the vast discrepancies in privilege among the participants. The format of the project itself offered a space for them to "tell it like it is," yet we are reminded by Foucault's (1982, cited in Butler, 2005) pessimistic admonition that the truth alone is not capable of saving the subject. This is because the subject is not inherently constituted in truth, but in relation to structure and relations. Reflexivity then, which is what we are seeking in the respondents in this study, is not really possible unless the subject is capable of fully seeing herself or himself in relation to truth. This irony, Butler (2005) delineates,

> does not preclude the possibility that some change may happen along the way. After all, when one gives an account of oneself, one is not merely relaying information through an indifferent medium. The account is an act—situated within a larger practice of acts—that one performs for, to, even *on* another, an allocutory deed, an acting for, and in the face of, the other and sometimes by virtue of the language provided by the other. This account does not have as its goal the establishment of a definitive narrative but constitutes a linguistic and social occasion for self-transformation. (p. 130)

The project itself, conducted within the chaos of parallel workshops—within the grand venue of the Sandton Convention Centre—and including young people from parts of the world where such luxuries such as polished granite floors and bejeweled chandeliers were possibly inconceivable, served an allocutory function. Some suggestions offered by the teens were through the words and phrases used by the researchers in asking the questions. At the same time, most of the responses surged through with a raw honesty that was undeniable. The appropriation of the focus group discussions, to convey in as graphic terms as was possible, the violence within families and in neighborhoods perpetrated on young children, especially girls, was remarkable. The project, then, allowed for such utterances of a subjective "truth." It constituted a moment for self-transformation and social occasion. It may or may not be capable of saving the subject, more likely not, when we recognize that such salvation rests not just in the revelation of such truth, but in substantive change in the relationship between the subject and her or his truth engineered by social and political structures.

The challenge of limited time may be extrapolated to other qualitative fieldwork, no matter how long or how briefly the researcher is engaged with the field and respondents. This weakness lies in the role of the researcher herself or himself. When the project serves as a forum for catharsis, as we have seen in the case of the young girls from Lesotho, Botswana, Tanzania, or South Africa, the focus group discussions and essays could very well have served as a rare space where a survivor of abuse could be heard. What is the role of the researcher at this point? How does the researcher accommodate those seren-dipitous moments that beg flexibility in the research design?

These challenges are discussed in the concluding chapter where we engage in a reflection of the ethics of doing critical research on youth. The *Exploring Gender* project is presented here as an opportunity to raise questions about comparative study and stimulate further discussion about international audience research. We certainly should seek opportunities wherever possible to include a range of voices that would be next to impossible with the traditional sources of academic funding that are available, funding that often limits study to one country, or at the most two or three. The findings of this project add to our understanding of youth voices across the world. They provide a snapshot into teen lives in vastly different contexts. At the same time, they point to the similarities in the sense of vulnerability, self-consciousness, and limited agency that youth experience no matter where they are from. Very importantly, they give us some direction in what kinds of programming youth want to see. We learn that they want to be directly involved in content; they want to be shown as leaders and survivors, not losers, victims, and criminals; they want to see stereotypical gender roles subverted; and they want affordable, well-produced, indigenous programs.

We also learn that as adult researchers in youth media, we should be mind-ful to place youth voices in context, interrogating their own ideological positions as we interrogate ours. Fass (2008) cautions us in how we evaluate child and youth experiences around the world. Our own subjective positioning as readers is essential to recognize because the tendency, across the world, is to exoticize and even render primitive the narratives from teens in the global south. The norm is to generalize "youth," "child," "adolescence," and "childhood" to how it is experienced in middle-class Western societies. The equation of a particular Western childhood to a universally desirable childhood may result in the inter-pretation that the teens from African countries lacked any agency, and were helpless victims of their circumstances. Fass (2008) writes:

> We historians in the West and of the West have come to understand childhood through certain lenses, fashioned from Enlightenment ideas, Victorian images, and modern childrearing beliefs. ... globalization forces us to ask ourselves what our obligations are to these images and to these children. (p. 27)

Our obligations to these children include recognizing that local activist agencies are working hard to change circumstances that victimize children. As Madison (2005) and Shome (2006) have pointed out, critical fieldwork has to identify

various support structures, nongovernmental and otherwise, that work to eradicate oppression. Without such acknowledgment, respondents' comments sit
as sensational vignettes serving not much more than shock value. A further
critical study on the variety of activist organizations in each of the countries the
delegates came from would be useful to uncover not just strategies that work,
but those that perpetuate the very behavior they intend to stop.

This project used components of reception studies and qualitative fieldwork. It is an examination of the correspondence between televised and real
senses of self articulated by teens from various countries. As a participatory
research project, it placed emphasis on listening to the teens first, and then
guiding them to respond to questions about how to produce better quality television for youth. The focus was on establishing trust and respect and describing a shared intention (Barab et al, 2004). Reception studies have come under
critique for their quasi-ethnographic character and their often unconvention-
al adaptations to local contexts (Murdock, 1997). While they may include
the components of ethnographic fieldwork such as participant observation,
and interviews, they are suspect precisely for their flexibility and their circum-
vention of some of the rigors of ethnography as used in anthropology, which,
among other elements, requires long-term immersion in the field (Hastrup
& Hervik, 1994; Nightingale, 1996). Reception studies may use such methods as analysis of viewer mail (Ang, 1985) and participant observation and
interviews (Morley, 1980; Jhally & Lewis, 1992; Gillespie, 1995) to address
the use of communication technologies within the household and interrogate
the construction of identity in global and local media. The most strident criticism of analyses that follow the tradition of British cultural studies is that
they focus on viewing pleasure and fandom, with only tangential treatment of
structural context. As Bird (2003) discusses, rather than wrestle with questions of whether the viewer is active or passive, or whether ultimately the
media are good or bad for us, we need to directly engage in the issues or power
and control "that often seem to play around the edges of audience research"
(p. 167). The chapters so far have demonstrated just such an engagement.
We now move to the concluding chapter of this book, to assess the methodological and ethical considerations to keep in mind, when studying youth
cultures in globalization.

· 7 ·

REFLECTIONS AND DIRECTIONS

Peering through our window, we see that the train is pulling into the station once again. Perhaps this is our destination; more likely it is a brief stop before we travel on. It is time to smooth down our crumpled clothes, grab our belongings, and be pushed out through the door with other surging bodies. We savor a cup of tea at the station café; it is time to reflect on where we have been. We stepped off the beaten tracks at several points along our journey, entering intimate spaces of youth around the world. We climbed back on, connecting varied experiences to theory and recognizing the value of a critical perspective. Through stops and starts, through meanderings and introspections, we are now ready to discuss the interesting dynamic among theory, methodology, and results.

We use as our starting point, Madison's (2005) call for critical media ethnography, which may be defined as *"critical theory in action"* (p. 13, emphasis in original). Through a summary of observations made so far in the preceding chapters, this chapter provides a critical discussion of youth, media, and globalization. It addresses the importance of scholarly work on the processes by which youth, particularly in developing economies, are groomed to be service providers. Servility of the worker to a larger global order is a necessary condition for progress and upward mobility in her or his local context; media scholars and activists have an urgent part to play in laying bare structural inequities that facilitate the existence of one only through its submission to the other. We draw out the opportunistic possibilities of all sides of such interdependent relationships upon which globalization thrives and through which it is even possible. The researcher's insider/outsider status, the distance between educational levels between researcher and respondent, and the degree to which the researcher is "present" in the field—all these texture how fieldwork is conducted and what kinds of results are produced. The discussion therefore includes an exploration of power differentials in the field and ethical issues involved. Using the basic tenets of critical media ethnography, the chapter concludes identifying points to be considered in "studying" youth cultures ethically.

Where We Have Been

Chapter Two addressed the disconnect between experiences on the ground and theoretical approaches to youth, media, and globalization that abound in dichotomic positions. Binaries distance one extreme from the other, such as, for example, colonizer and colonized. They legitimize boundaries between the two and avoid analysis of the spaces of expression in between. In other words, the political refugees within the shades of grey go untheorized. "Youth" has been conventionally projected as a consumer category, as an assertion of independence, and as a labor market. Dominant trends in scholarship on youth and media are inadequate for postcolonial contexts, especially in the current moment of globalization when disciplined youth from developing economies are desired in the global marketplace. The need for dedisciplining in the field, or to even become undisciplined (Shome, 2006), has been underscored as perhaps the only way to move away from the Euro-Anglo-American dominance in academic disciplines. To attempt a transnational interdisciplinarity, Shome argues that we must first draw attention to the inequities of globalization and their specific geographies. Second, we must recognize that the ground we engage in is only what we see, to stretch observations to what we cannot is a disservice to those who are not included in our analytical ground. Third, observations and fieldwork must be produced within a recognition of the work produced by local grassroots networks.

The fieldwork experiences recounted in this book foregrounded to the extent that was possible the locale differences in the global order that the teens occupied. How they accommodated processes of globalization differed significantly as a result. Youth narratives themselves served as the ground for our analyses. These brought forth important ways through which we could address how agency was produced, yet care was taken to not unduly privilege the comments or romanticize them as *the* legitimate account of experience. Focus was on how this ground was informed by structure and vice versa. Also, in every venue, the work of local supporting structures, such as community beautification projects and media workshops in Johannesburg or religious affiliations in Bangalore, was acknowledged as meaningful influences in teens' lives that filled an important need in their quest for agency.

Emphasized is the importance of theory as well as methodology. If we were to use a developmental framework, we run the risk of reducing them to hormone-driven individuals and incomplete adults. This "incomplete adult" conception may prevent us from understanding youth in structural terms, as less powerful than adults. Even the most thoughtful ethnographies sometimes slip into the mistake of assuming youth to be on their way to a completed stage, and therefore do not give sufficient credibility to youth informants as authorities on their own lives.

Postcolonial theory provided a useful way to engage with power differentials in the field. As stated in the introduction to this book, the postcolonial critical perspective was effective even though the locales differed vastly in political history, because it focused on transformative possibilities within structural constraints. Globalization could then be studied as a process that offers agency even within a neocolonial trajectory. Each global city, be it Bangalore, Johannesburg, Munich, or New York, was an integral part of the respective nation's modernity project; teens interviewed in these venues could certainly relate to the fast pace of the city, accommodating, at various levels, its reconfigurations of landscape and demographics. Time spent in respondents' homes, schools, and community centers and our in-depth and meandering conversations for extended periods of time all brought forth a rich tapestry of diverse lives in very diverse locales. How youth partook of amalgamations of culture—the urban global intermixed with familial and religious rituals, for example—depended also on how well they were accommodated by the adults within their families. Adults set strong limits to teen freedom, serving, in most cases, as the first response to teen needs. While audience studies begin with the media as their vantage point, that is, they track audience responses and consequent behavior in relation to media, we witnessed that media served as only part of the many influences in an individual's life. Television, even in New York and Munich, was not a central aspect of teen lives. It no doubt, with other communication technologies such as the computer, cell phone, and radio, occupied an important space in their daily routine, yet was organized around other pressing agendas such as studies and family obligations. Commercial media culture played a significant role in how youth perceived themselves and their realities, yet these were only part of the complex, intermeshed groups they belonged to. Youth talk provided part of the ground for analysis and—placed within its national, historical, cultural, and material contexts—provided tremendous insights into the dynamic relationship between cultural practice and structural environment.

We expand here on the processes involved in the relationship between the subject and structure. Observations with various groups of teens showed that through the dialectical correspondence between the two, identity emerged, always incomplete, always in negotiation. The pull of family, peers, religion, and school was powerful; these should be seen as mediating systems in themselves, working with television (as just one component of an increasingly complex media system) that called the subject to different tasks and levels of performativity. How the subject answered, what latitude she or he had for an indeliberate response, translated into agency. Over and over, we saw that the subject could sit quite comfortably in the very structures that constrained her or him, justifying punishment for transgressions as *just the way it should be*. The material and emotional rewards for obedience were significant.

In general, teens were embedded in complex systems of shared responsibility, partnering with parents in running the household. Those of middle- and lower-income households in particular had mature concerns of succeeding academically so they could help financially. Many cared for siblings, all had chores and faced pressures at school with keeping up grades and fitting in with peers. All teens loved music, television, and hanging out with friends. Parents and close relatives, for all the teens, played important roles: they modeled hard work and perseverance, they demanded diligent attention to school, and they provided rewards for good behavior. And, as in the case of some of the Indian and South African teens in the *TV Characters* studies, punishment was tempered by large support systems. Grandparents, neighbors, even aunts and uncles who in some cases lived with the nuclear family in one large home, provided for the most part, recourse for the hurting teen. Comments made in interviews therefore should be taken as representations of multiple relations, not as contained truths in and of themselves. For those teens who talked about abuse in the *Exploring Gender* project, we observed that agency emerged just in the articulation of that occurrence. Their voices in the microphone, their words and drawings on paper, were, within the mechanisms of the research design, to be organized, catalogued, and reported somewhere. The performance of the investigative process worked in producing the conditions for some degree of agency.

Television was still, even during the mid 2000s when these studies were conducted (2003–2007, to be precise), a primary medium from where teens got their entertainment and information. Regardless of where they were positioned in the world (in terms of nation) or neighborhood (in terms of community, caste, class, gender, and so on), programs, both foreign and indigenous provided relevance for their own development into young adults. Across various countries, both boys and girls were in search of an inner strength that would allow them to rise above their existential struggles. Models of strength were offered through corporate structures that funneled teen desires into a limited range of characters. Examples of these were the *WWE* wrestlers, action heroes such as New York policeman John McLane (played by Bruce Willis) in the *Die Hard* series, or Captain O'Neill in *Stargate SG-1*. For some of the teens, the intellectual and comedic wit of Richard in *Caroline in the City* and Chandler on *Friends*, or the naivete of Phoebe on *Friends* and the impulsiveness of Lolle in *Berlin Berlin* provided lessons on how to manage conflict and toss aside self-consciousness. Silence and endurance in heroines of indigenous soap operas helped young girls in particular learn how to negotiate resistance without incurring the wrath of conservative systems.

While all the teens discussed future goals, their sense of whether they would really make it into their profession of choice was defined by how strong their local networks and economic standing were. For teens like Rabia and Nina in South Africa, involvement with media production groups provided a tangible transition to their dreams of working with television. For Verena in Munich, being the daughter of highly educated parents meant that she would go to university, regardless of her grades. For Ashok and Zohrab in Bangalore, things were not so clear; they could very well be fledglings of "Generation Nowhere" (Jeffrey, 2008), coined by a group of young men in Meerut, North India who, despite education degrees, did not have salaried work, and met once a month to lament their fate. Lacking propertied middle-class status, these members of India's NMC (Fernandes & Heller, 2006) would have to navigate India's affirmative action policies to secure seats in professional engineering, medicine, or business colleges, or settle for baccalaureate or master's degrees and enter into the information industry servicing primarily foreign clients.

This brings us to the differences among the respondents. Teens of color from Johannesburg and teens in Bangalore were clearly witnessing a different world. Their grasp of reality around them was textured by a heightened sense of a very hierarchical society. Local relationships and power differentials played a significant role in shaping each teen's sense of agency and self. Postcolonial theory helped us get to the heart of "cultural legitimation." Chow (1998, p. 162) defines this as

a procedure in which a first set of terms acquires validity and significance—becomes "viable" and "real"—through a second set of terms. Events, including the event of the production of knowledge, usually do not become "legitimate" until and unless they are being reinforced by other events that provide the grounds or terms of their validation or justification.

The process of cultural legitimation for Indian teens revealed an interpellatory dynamic where they struggled to resolve signs of globalized teenhood on television with constricting notions of appropriate adolescent behavior stipulated at home. The changing urban landscape of these respondents, engendered by new MNC tenants, primed them for techno-urban plots swirling around characters sophisticated and buff enough to manipulate the environment for personal gain. The manipulations were appealing as counterdiscourse; they also helped these young people acquire knowledge about themselves. Such mediated knowledge came to sit as a legitimate authority, shoulder-to-shoulder with other legitimate authorities in their lives, such as parents and elders.

Attempts to avoid essentialist descriptions notwithstanding, it was evident that teens talked about themselves, their friends, and favorite television characters through essentialist frames. These articulations helped us understand, with greater clarity, the ideological function of these positions. They served as veritable forces to carve out the individual's sense of agency. Confirming a wealth of scholarship on the intricate workings of identity along lines of difference (see Anderson, 1991; Hannerz, 1992, for example), these young people particularly those from upper middle classes who preferred Western programs, saw discontinuities between their lives and their immediate environments, but greater similarities with those depicted on Western television programs (see also Grixti, 2006). Perhaps we can surmise that television programs conveyed to them a social world order, allowing them to partake in global-urban teen rituals. Couldry (2003) urges us to be cautious bystanders of such rituals. As critical scholars, we need to examine the order *and* disorder that characterizes social life, not merely celebrate, in this case, television's projection of a certain order. While Couldry is interested in how people *act* around media celebrities and production spaces, his point that the study of media rituals must extend to the space and practices around it, is highly relevant and is demonstrated in the attention to the variety of engagements in the teen's life, of which television watching is one part.

The Ethics of Asking

The responses of the teens in the various studies recounted here should be seen as intimately informed by the relationship between interviewer and respondent.

Butler (2005) writes that when one gives an account of oneself, one is doing so in response to a question based on an ethical relation between the one posing the question and the one answering. It is rarely a reflexive process where one offers up a narrative. Butler writes:

> Moreover the very terms by which we give an account, by which we make ourselves intelligible to ourselves and to others, are not of our making. They are social in character, and they establish social norms, a domain of unfreedom and substitutability within which our "singular" stories are told. (p. 21)

The question of ethics becomes all the more pressing, as we take into account the differing power relationships between researcher and respondent. To avoid ethical violence against the subject, Butler (2005) explains that it is necessary to see narratives as never complete; it is not possible to establish a "prehistory" of the subject. Responsibility in how one gives an account of oneself and, by extension, how one listens to and receives accounts of others lies in admitting that there are limits to understanding and interpretation. This position of the researcher receives support among critical ethnographers and informed the methodologies used in all the studies described in this book. The tension between researcher subjectivity and objectivity can be appreciated through a discussion of what we mean by the grounded-entry approach we have adopted in this book. A *grounded entry* is not the same as using grounded theory although the basic premise is that we begin with empirical context to build theory.

As discussed elsewhere (McMillin, 2007), the late 1960s and 1970s were a time of theoretical ferment as scholars particularly in the humanities questioned the relevance and usefulness of methods of the social sciences that dictated much of media audience research. Over four decades ago, with *The Discovery of Grounded Theory*, Barney Glaser, trained in quantitative social research methods from Columbia University and subsequently in qualitative research methods at the University of Chicago, took a revolutionary step in advocating the development of theory from data, going against the overwhelmingly positivist theory-dictates-methodology trend in the social sciences. Grounded theory was a response to the rising skepticism of the romanticization of liberal individualism in symbolic interactionism and to the gaining strength of the two opposing camps of the "hard methods" of statistics and structural functionalism and the "soft methods" of ethnomethodology (Thomas & James, 2005).

Symbolic interactionism, as developed by University of Chicago social psychologist George Herbert Mead in the 1900s, proposed that individuals adapt to an ever-changing environment through a process of reflection and interaction with it (Mead, 1934). Herbert Blumer, also from the University of Chicago, built on Mead's conceptualization that humans develop through internal conversations among "I," "Me," and "Myself." The basic proponents then of symbolic interactionism are that first, individuals act on things that have meaning for them; second, such meanings develop from the social interactions one has with others; and third, meanings may be changed through the individual's interpretive process in dealings with others (Blumer, 1969). The researcher, through participant observation, must "[Lift] the veils that obscure or hide what is going on" (p. 39) to understand the respondents' point of view, from within her or his natural context. Grounded theory, as a methodological approach to the theoretical umbrella of symbolic interactionism, has been cultivated most significantly for the fields of health and education.

Grounding our approach to the study of youth and media globalization should not be confused with grounded theory that derives from a systems approach "to generate a theory that accounts for a pattern of behavior which is relevant and problematic for those involved" (Glaser, 1978, p. 93). Using empirical data from observations, grounded theorists attempt to generate universal concepts and paradigms; in a nutshell, they develop theory from data. Grounded action may follow where interventions are created to respond to macro organizational issues. As Stillman (2006) summarizes, "Grounded theory and grounded action are conceptual, theory-generating methodologies, and researchers using these methods are system theorists" (p. 500). The primary tenets of this approach are theoretical sampling, constant comparison, coding and categorizing, writing memos, and generating theories (Jeon, 2004).

This book provided a pathway by which we can theorize about youth and media use beginning with the immediate *lived experience* of the respondents themselves. It gives the researcher the "explanatory power" (Glaser & Strauss, 1967, p. 247) of the grounded theorist and the freedom to continue engagement with the field and subsequent evolution of theory. How this approach is different from grounded theory is that it recognizes the ideological entrapment of the researcher and researched. Whereas Glaser and Strauss (1967) believed that there is no inherent difference between qualitative and quantitative methodologies and approaches and that any sociologist could "discover" theory, this book problematizes context and scrutinizes ideological mechanisms that produce youth, consumer, researcher, research methodologies, and empirical data. Symbolic interactionism and grounded theory do not draw in centrally the question of power. As much as they were developed to counter limitations of positivist social science, they fall into the trap of assuming that the truth can be unveiled, that it exists external to ideological structures.

Criticisms of grounded theory are many. A primary one is that it reduces complex relationships and meanings to simple phenomena leaving little room for the richness of context or for explanations that the respondents themselves may be unaware of (Layder, 1993). It privileges procedure over interpretation where the attention to techniques of sampling may result in the tendency to hunt for data rather than really look at it and understand what it tells us about the relationships and realities (Robrecht, 1995). Another broad criticism is that its models of induction, explanation, and prediction may actually be inappropriate to the basic aims of qualitative inquiry (Haig, 1995) so that ultimately, grounded theory is just a clumsy way to bridge quantitative and qualitative modes of research. As Thomas and James (2006) write, it is impossible for a compromise or middle ground; the fundamental assumption that "discovery" of a "theory" is possible on the "ground" is problematic in that it also assumes something about the mind of the researcher, of social reality, and how knowledge can be uncovered. In other words, "the implication accompanying grounded theorizing is that the knowledge of these others has in some way to be sanitized for it to become transparent to rational people. The narrative has to be broken, 'fractured,' for sense to prevail" (p. 791). Such an assumption also results in an ahistorical approach to the study of consumer and viewing behavior, where colonial pasts have much to do with contemporary practices. As a strong caution against such tendencies to order behavior for the production of knowledge, this book, in its theory and methodology, has aligned itself with the mission of postcolonial criticism, which is to maintain theoretical sophistication while at the same time being vigilant to the "guises of imperialism" (Chow, 1998, p. 167).

Vigilance to these guises translated into following the flow of narratives not just in how the discussions were structured, but also in how questions were asked in the field. The interview process is fraught with unequal power relations. The interviewer has control in terms of status, schedule, research tools such as tape recorder and camera, and—most importantly—knowledge of questions and of outcome of the interview. To alleviate some of the distance in power, Briggs (1986) emphasizes the understanding of how language works: it is *referential* in that it identifies people, places, objects, events, and processes and it is *indexical* in that it is dependent on the context in which it is expressed. It is essential that the researcher has a sense of the communicative competence of the interviewee to be able to interpret the interview as a communicative event. Care was taken in each study to not just analyze the comments of respondents, but also to describe the context as much as possible, including a variety of elements to convey the features of the communicative event. Also important are features of the metacommunicative event that include nonverbal cues that may very well indicate the opposite position of what is being uttered. Jokes, literary and religious allusions, oral history, and so on are crucial to understand, making it a good idea to review notes or play back recordings to interviewees to check for accuracy and to provide room for additional observations. The researcher has to be aware that respondents bring their own goals to the fieldwork. For many, this could be a social event, an opportunity to strike a relationship or even secure some material benefit for the future. Preparation for fieldwork should include several levels as a result. These include background research, exploration of the culture and society under study, familiarity with language of the interview (Finnegan, 1992), and clear (to the extent possible) articulation of goals on both sides of the process. Lal (1996) cautions that in the overriding concern to give "voice" to the subject and diminish researcher control over data, the report may actually provide a picture of how the respondents *want* to be represented, not what really happened during fieldwork. All of these important guidelines for fieldwork were followed closely. With the exception of the *Exploring Gender* study, fieldwork followed multiple phases and methods as described in respective chapters, so that as much of the context as possible was gathered. We devote some space here to a discussion of how the results of the *Exploring Gender* study should be accommodated. Its value lies in its quick summary of a variety of perspectives and in the stories of abuse that surfaced.

The snapshot methodology that denied us a full understanding of the complex contexts these teens came from, nevertheless, gave us a vivid sense of the vast differences between the experiences of the teens from African countries and those from European countries, for example. However, the responses cannot be used as representative of the respective countries or regions. The short period of time, the selection of respondents through formalized screening procedures of the Summit itself, and the fact that English was not a native language for many of the research assistants and respondents should be seen as factors that limited the freedom with which responses were made and questions asked. Second, the definition of geographic "region" was vague and arbitrary. Broad profiles developed from any region of the world are problematic since they gloss over the rich diversity between and within countries. Although respondents wrote out summaries of their *perceived gender profiles* onto large, wall world maps, such profiles should be viewed as those that were generated from the small group of delegates present from that region. Many elements may be left out and existing elements may be problematized. Third, the *televised gender profiles* that the participants were encouraged to develop through consensus to be written on a wall world map as they did with the *perceived gender profiles* may have concealed more diversity in programs and opinion than they revealed. Ultimately, while the representation of perceived and televised gender profiles may be visually pleasing on a world map and can convey a sense of gender differences across regions, a more accurate analysis would include in-depth, qualitative analyses of youth responses from specific countries. The cultural distance between research assistants and respondents where, in some cases, the respondents had to explain colloquialisms that were incomprehensible to the assistant could lead to an "evaluative hierarchy" that reproduces a colonized ordering of the world (Caputo, 2000, p. 19). Madison (2005) cautions that in the representation of voices from societies that have experienced systemic violence both within their communities and externally, there is a tendency for the researcher to play an emancipatory role. While this is commendable, the danger is the reproduction of stilted and stereotypical images of the community under study. In highlighting the "problems" or the "injustices" experienced by a community, research, or participatory media projects stop at critique and do not acknowledge local systems that are working hard to change the status quo. The invisibility of local efforts serves to recreate hierarchies where stories of misery and violence receive international awards while further objectifying the victims in such stories. In this sense, critical ethnography, also termed "new ethnography," the principles of which were employed in all fieldwork described in this book, "must not only critique the notion of objectivity, but must critique the notion of subjectivity as well" (p. 8).

To stay faithful to context and make explicit the subjective positioning of the researcher, the *TV Characters* projects relied on elements of ethnography. All researchers either worked, lived close to, and/or grew up in the very neighborhoods where they conducted fieldwork. As delineated in the section on grounded theory, conventional anthropological inquiry has come under criticism for its expectations of researcher objectivity and detachment from subjects even if the researcher has been living with the subject for long periods of time (Amit, 2000). The privileging of "objective" is symptomatic of an academic alliance with linear models of studying human behavior representative of modern, industrialized, and capitalized environments (Okely, 1992). Venn (2006) argues that orthodox positivist conceptualizations of the ideological subject support the notion that a rational "truth" exists, that it can be uncovered through a science, and that the subject just needs awareness and education of her or his position to break out of it. Alternatively, "immersion in the field" itself is under debate because it produces the contradictory claims that immersion with the respondents' context and detachment from that very context are both required to produce untainted results (Callaway, 1992). The site of study itself also raises concerns among anthropologists who argue that one has to go "away" to pro- duce valid results, not study one's own people. On the other hand, some others contend that such a requirement may reproduce colonizing representations of the world, because it is essentially done through the outsider researcher's eyes. The continued tendency to centralize television and other media within the complex rituals in people's lives plagues both media anthropology and media studies. This is a matter of consternation for scholars who examine media usage in nonmediacentric societies.

What this book has offered is a way to address that very aspect—that media are only a part of people's daily rituals. Such usage is one element in the many practices that flow through an individual's daily routine. Qualitative studies, particularly international, comparative, and longitudinal ones, are scarce and difficult to execute. More qualitative studies are sorely needed to address impor- tant contextual questions and draw out the nuances in audience reception. It was beyond the scope of the studies related here to include the rich variety of media youth used. At the time of writing, cell phones and iPods were integrated aspects of upper-middle-class teen lives. Young people themselves would benefit from learning and understanding how their choices are informed by competing and overlapping structures in their lives. Such inquiry brings us all closer to understanding the myriad negotiations youth go through in a multimediated globalizing world.

The multilayered methodology facilitated engagement with the field (see Hörschelmann & Stenning, 2008) and scrutiny of what is constructed within the teen's realm of experience as knowledge, and how that knowledge is used to exert control on her or his world. Contrary to theorizations of adolescence as a fluid stage in an individual's life where global interconnected networks offer multiple choices of products and avenues for individual expression (Blackman, 2005), youth are very much bound to structures. Their activities and realities may not be reducible to any one identity position such as class, religion, or gen- der; these positions are performed through their television choices and their discussions of daily rituals. A holistic sense of where the teen was in her or his life was derived from observations of how they watched television, through journal entries and scrapbooks and interviews with families and friends. To get a sense of the diversity of youth audiences around the world, and working within the constraints of funding, and time, multisited audiences were studied (Gupta & Ferguson, 1997). The number of sites and the number of respondents were limited to allow for examination of contexts in depth. The focus on context and mediating systems other than television in producing the teen experience was more incisive because of this. The "multiple layers of representation" (Himpele, 2002, p. 314) of fieldwork facilitated the study of the "production of locality" (Appadurai, 1996, p. 181). By weaving back and forth, between narrative and context, the stories came to be situated within the particular, connected to other particulars. This is representative of the postcolonial framework's problematization of identity as reference points. Its value lies in its shift in

> the conceptualization of identity to an epistemological paradigm in which it is liminality, instability, impurity, movement and fluidity that inform the formation of identities. ... these notions are part and parcel of new discursive practices which are drastically transforming knowledge by stubbornly focusing our attention on what has hitherto been cast outside the boundaries of what can be known. (Chow, 1998, p. 166)

In the effort to move away from fixed identity positions we see that youth themselves are caught in the middle of the battle for fixity imposed by other constituents within their lives. Perhaps nowhere else is this battle more apparent than among the Indian teens. Their television watching cannot be received at a mere descriptive level, but has to be connected to macro processes of globalization that turn increasingly toward India not just for outsourced labor markets in production and support services, but in research and development as well.

The Continued Relevance of Postcolonial Theory in Globalization

Writing in 2004, 25 years after *Learning to Labour* was published, Paul Willis states that the relationship of class to culture continues to be an important analytical base in youth studies. Agents within a group may share a culture, but they are in relation with one another, relations that are predicated upon the variations in capital that they possess. Cultural practices have to be seen not just as the use of cultural products imbibed with symbolic meaning, "but also, in one way or another, useful for making sense of economic *positions* and *rela-*

tions" (p. 170). Ethnography continues to be the method that brings us closest to the ways in which objects and artifacts "are worked on, used, shaken and stirred for purpose in living ways through practices on the profane grounds of history" (p. 176). Willis' (2004b) comments have relevance for the youth discussed in this book. Their cultural practices were always in relation to structures of power. Although Willis allows for great flexibility in cultural play, arguing that relations between signifier and signified are always elusive, and that ethnography can only hope to come close to what they could mean, we see that in very authoritarian environments, meanings are concretized and used, as veritable products, to exert discipline and punishment. We also see that choices of cultural products are deliberate, not just random options of leisure, but purposeful preferences that embody an economic opportunity.

In the 2000s, television audiences across the world are witnesses to potent partnerships between nation-state and market; national and economic goals are intertwined in a way unprecedented before the advent of satellite television in the early 1990s. Cosmopolitanism is a nationalist project. The cultivation of the consumer is as crucial an imperative for governments as it is for private corporations (Abu-Lughod 2005). Robust formats such as game shows, film-based programming, reality shows, soap operas, and talk shows flood television networks, whether state-owned or private, global or local. Ideologies of gender and class endure in these formats because of their resonance with entrenched systems of patriarchy across national boundaries. Textual analyses of television from China (Zhong, 2002), India (Fernandes, 2000; McMillin, 2002), Hong Kong (D. H. Lee, 2004), Indonesia (Sutton, 2003), and Malaysia (Ang, 1996), to name a few countries, illustrate that males continue to be constructed as action and romantic heroes while females are represented in supporting roles, with limited freedom and agency. The aggressive consumer focus has been noted in such transnationally successful programs as *Pokemon* (Buckingham & Sefton-Green, 2003) and in provocative advertisements that crowd the world of youth (Klein, 2000). Televised stereotypes about gender invariably correspond with existing cultural stereotypes (Ex et al., 2002). Violence on children's television is packaged attractively where male aggressors are often portrayed as heroes. Females in leading roles may question boundaries but also provide reaffirmation of traditional practices. Munshi (2001) demonstrates in her analysis of the "modern woman" in Indian media that such a representation is a stereotype in itself. She wears the latest urban western fashions and is quite at ease in the most affluent shopping malls. Yet she is fiercely protective of her heritage, well-versed in ancient scriptures and saves her virginity for her husband.

The standardized sets and camera work of original and copied versions of game shows such as *Idol, Millionaire,* and *So You Think You Can Dance*; reality shows such as MTV *Real World, Amazing Race,* or *Survivor*; and drama-comedies such as *Ugly Betty, Desperate Housewives,* or *Life on Mars* produce heroes who inhabit an urban, technologically rich, action-packed world, where brute strength is essential to survive. Such a channeling of the rich diversity of human life into the fair-skinned, slim, intellectually superior, and exquisitely toned woman or man, resonates, as it did with the teens in the case studies, with deep desires for control and autonomy. The viewer's ability to emulate such ideals and the distance between viewer and hero depends also on the positionality of the former. Therefore, states Laclau (2000), "particularities ... without ceasing to be particularities, assume a function of universal representation. This is what is at the root of hegemonic relations" (p. 56). The universal is an "empty place" (p. 58), requiring these particularities to fill it up, and in doing so, creates essential structural effects.

The circulation of standardized formats around the world sits well with the imperatives of Occidentalism. Venn (2006) identifies these as the deployment of modernity along a linear trajectory with the goal of realizing the rational, unitary, self-sufficient, and autonomous subject; relentless commodification and inherent capitalism; and the assumption that such universalist and totalizing forces are superior to the rest of the world. Combining physical, epistemic, ontological, and symbolic violence, the native's story stays hidden, or it gets told through "universal" and standardized formats as we witnessed in the *Slumdog Millionaire* example.

The paradigmatic structure of the film effectively reduces darkness, filth, violence, and horrific poverty to the particularities of Indian society. Raised to universalism, are the bright lights, cleanliness, civility, and affluence, of the *Millionaire* show. Serving effectively as a metaphor for India as a majority-youth-populated country possibly shaking the labor foundations of the Western proletariat, particularly in the United States, the movie makes plain an important message: the lifeline is within reach. To access it, the young Indian laborer requires a transfiguration offered through a globalized process, which confers knowledge of the context, language, and accent of clients situated in industrialized metropolitan centers. As the movie itself unravels, the audience's relief at reaching the breathing spaces supplied by the mercifully familiar universal in the face of the extreme depravity of the particular, is palpable. It effectively offers up a range of "empty signifiers" (Laclau, 2000, p. 56) that fill the space between the particular and universal, that the particular *has* to don, to acquire cultural legitimation within the universal. Author Swarup, director Boyle, and music director A. R. Rahman together were able to convey the journey of not just Jamal to *Millionaire*, but the movie itself as a product, to the global stage through its use of culturally legitimized transnational actors, and synergistic television and film production and distribution systems. Although most prominently received as a story of love and hope, *Slumdog* also revealed to audiences everywhere the workings of cultural transformation, where salvation is possible through the gradual gentrification of the unwashed slumdog into an urban teen-with-capital. The opportunism of the particular is as important a motivating force in this relationship as is the hegemonic intent of the universal. Ultimately, as Chowdhury (2006) reminds us, in the interconnections and interdependencies of globalization, "Increased access to cultural material, moreover, has not translated into increased access to economic opportunity" (p. 129).

The ongoing efforts by various publishing houses to produce texts on conversational English for middle and high school students in India can therefore be seen as further gentrifying strategies to prepare Indian youth for the global marketplace. English language classes act as interpellating forces, conferring on their subjects an acceptance of English as the language of currency, upward mobility, and academic success.[33] In this sense, selections among middle- and upper-income Indian teens for English language television programs are not merely the outcome of a fascination for all things Western. They cannot be reduced to mere cultural residue of British colonialism. Such selections should also be seen as motivated by an obvious connectivity between play and work, between current leisure and future employment. A number of case studies have identified the incorporation of American sitcoms such as *Friends* and MTV music countdowns as part of the curriculum in call centers (Pal & Buzzanell, 2008; McMillin, 2007). The Information Technology Enabled Services–Business Process Outsourcing (ITES–BPO) market was expected to provide jobs for over 1 million Indians by the end of 2008 (National Association of Software and Service Companies, NASSCOM, 2003) and generate export revenues in excess of $60 billion by 2010 (NASSCOM, 2005). Viewing of U.S.-generated sitcoms and dramas has to then also be seen as important primers for such an industry that thrives on employee mimicry of its majority clients and owners. The promotion of the television *and* film hero from the working class to the bourgeoisie class as evident in the great variety of examples scattered throughout the book is not a matter of chance; it is a purposeful reflection of the times.

While highly profitable economically, making mimicry the logical career path of the opportunistic, we have to keep on the radar the unleashing of violence in response to that very opportunism. Religious fundamentalist groups such as the Shri Ram Sena employ extreme force to constrain urban teens within narrowly defined notions of gender-appropriate behavior. The hypocrisy is tragically obvious—opportunism is sanctioned only in economic terms because such transactions take place in the external material sphere. Within the cultural, inner, spiritual sphere, the boundaries are clear; possibilities limited to only what is hegemonically prescribed (Chatterjee, 1993). None of the Indian teens in the studies recounted here had experienced graphic sanctions on freedoms in the proportion of the attacks of fundamentalist attacks on young women described in Chapter Five. Yet the highly publicized workings of such groups, and the ongoing incidents of "eve teasing" that refer to a range of harassment inflicted on women all over the country, work as signifiers of the discipline and punishment that accompany globalization. M. Rogers (2008) argues that such depictions of hypermasculinity and patriarchy is precisely because of a loss of self-esteem that accompanies the rising economic value of the urban Indian woman in a globalizing marketplace. Rogers' fieldwork among inner-city college students in Chennai, Tamil Nadu, showed that just the ability to speak English, and the choice of young girls to wear "Western clothes" translated into a justification for men to harass them for their "immodesty" and "Westernization." Caste hierarchies exacerbated by the social subordination brought about by those who are unable to avail of gentrification strategies result in an outpouring of violence on those who are most vulnerable within the system, and at the same time who stand to gain most by global industry: young women.

It is clear then that when we discuss teens in developing, postcolonial economies, we have to understand the lifelines offered to them by a globalizing marketplace, the transformations they have to undergo to align themselves with the imperatives of such a marketplace, and the price they have to pay for their opportunism, exacted by the guards left behind of the old system. The young laborer flits within overlapping systems of power, attentive to opportunities for advancement, passionate about transformative possibilities of the system itself, yet mindful to not venture out too far and risk personal safety.

Willis (2004b) writes that worldwide, the working class has suffered with the reduction of quality and quantity of jobs available. Gonick (2006) notes that the shift in U.S. national policy from state building in terms of federal programs to support citizens during the postwar years to focus on *individual* development created a reflexive modernization. The century-long child saving policies in the United States and the social programs that accrued as a result of this approach

gave way to the zero-tolerance policies and the 1996 Welfare Reform Bill, push-
ing vast populations of children into poverty:

> The withdrawal of state services and support of youth come at a time of ongoing and
> significant disruptions to the circuit of production, reproduction, and consumption
> marking the traditional transition to adulthood. ... Changes in the economic order, the
> dismantling of postwar social structures, rising levels of youth unemployment, welfare
> and education cuts, and credential inflation, mean that young people have the difficult
> task of reconciling the contradiction between the reality of the structural constraints
> shaping their specific circumstances and the "promises " of wealth and well-being
> offered by an increasingly global society. (p. 5)

This was perhaps a foreshadowing of the job crisis in the United States at the
beginning of 2009. To keep youth studies relevant, the focus on structural
implications for cultural processes is crucial. Media scholars in particular, with
their inherent orientation toward examining the location of communication
technologies within society, tend to choose theories and methodologies that
track responses to such technologies. For example, youth participation in social
media such as YouTube, Facebook, and MySpace, and the media that make
these possible—computers, cell phones, iPods, Blackberries— are studied for
their potential to engender "new patriotisms" (Dolby & Rizvi, 2008, p. 7).
Young people are regarded as identifying themselves through consumption of
fast food, music, and so on, rather than class identifications, caste, or even religious identifications (Willis, 2003).

It is obvious that the political edge of cultural studies has to continue to
drive inquiry. It is provocative to think of disembodied spirits and deterrito-
rialized ideas in a global consumer context (Appadurai, 1990). Transnational
media flows, in particular, make possible participation in various rituals of selfhood, defaulting youth rites of passage to those unraveling on television. Youth
become signifiers of globalization; their agency and autonomy become an indicator of the progressiveness of their home societies. Yet suspension of analyses of
global consumer culture to the space above which consumption actually happens precludes an analysis of how exactly transactions are made not just between
consumer and corporation but within the consumer herself or himself. The case
studies provided insights into the various consuming contexts teens are rooted
in—their families, schools, neighborhoods, peers, and television worlds. They
were not necessarily swept into market narratives, more real were their immediate demands of school, home, and work. More studies that begin on the ground
are essential before we take off into the ethereality of global-local transactions.

The case studies underscore the importance of problematizing who has control over representation and how strategies for consumption are deployed. The discussions in this book also point to how now, more than ever, the interconnections of globalization need to be used for social change. Marx's organic view of capitalism and his extrapolation of development to the rest of the world through "the prism of the projected 'image' of modern Europe" (Serequeberhan, 2007, p. 125) has been critiqued extensively (see also Hall, 1981). Marxist analysis is itself attacked for being reductionist, for stripping down all phenomenon to its economic base, or as Willis (2004b) problematically puts it, a precultural level. Postcolonial studies have been assailed for their dematerialization of texts and ahistorical description of processes. All academic squabbles aside, the conditions of globalization demand a return to analysis of structural claims on culture. In making a case for revitalizing postcolonial studies through its Marxist roots, Bartolovich (2002) contends that

> What distinguishes a specifically Marxist critique, however, from a more general anticolonialism, is the insistence that cultural analysis of the everyday (and the extraordinary alike is inseparable from questions of political economy, in and outside the metropole; and that the critique of colonialism, and of the social order that has followed formal decolonization, is inextricable from the critique of capitalism." (p. 6)

Nimitz (2002) adds that Marx did fundamentally recognize that capitalism extracted from its laborers "blood and dirt" (cited in Nimitz, 2002, p. 69), making the process excruciating and exploitative whether on the core or periphery. Arguing for the continued relevance of Marxism for postcolonial theory, Nimitz states that Marx and Engels were always keenly interested in revolutionary movements and their interdependency. Social revolution may be initiated much easier in an underdeveloped than in a developed setting; however, it needs an interlinked momentum with that of an advanced industrialized capitalist country to be sustained. He notes,

> Their claim that socialist transformation could begin in the underdeveloped world but had to extend to advanced capitalist countries to be successful is more relevant today than ever. Evidence continues to mount that the post WWII Third World revolutionary process, often in the name of "Marxism," may have reached an impasse that can only be resolved in the advanced capitalist world—the site of material prerequisites. (p. 70)

These interpretations of Marxist theory provide clues for how we study youth and globalization; we need to focus on the interlinked nature of globalization, where histories and futures of economies—developed or developing—are inextricably implicated within one another.

We also need to pay close attention to the opportunistic practices of the colonized subject. Ashcroft (2001) observes that "The alternative to a passive subject unable to escape the formative pressures of imperial ideology is a subject who consumes the dominant culture in a strategy of self-fashioning and self-representation" (p. 40). In every one of the case studies we found examples of opportunism; we cannot let these examples sit as cultural practices, but use them to evaluate the interconnected structures that produce them as agents of change. Many of the teens showed that far from being passive victims of media or systems of patriarchy, they could inject a counterdiscourse; they had laid claim to the cracks in the system that offered possibilities of transformation. These negotiations revealed deliberate operations to manipulate dominant discourse to one's advantage. The danger is in holding up such "advantage" as a sign for the whole because it conceals the agents that truly benefit in an economic sense, from such operations. Ashcroft (2001) poses: "Does the fact of transformation, the capacity of colonized peoples to make dominant discourse work for them, to develop economically and technologically, to enjoy the 'benefits' of global capitalism, mean that the colonized have had a measure of 'moral luck?'" (p. 5). At a time when the world is experiencing the effects of the U.S. economic crisis and when educated and technologically skilled populations across the world are probably the only ones able to keep their jobs, the word "luck" cannot be used lightly. India could very well be a global superpower by 2033 as some might want to predict (Kamdar, 2008). Perhaps by 2050, BRICS economies combined will be larger than G6 in U.S. dollar terms, jumping up from 15% of G6 economies where they are right now (Wilson & Purushothaman, 2003). Young people everywhere could be more and more connected, preferring, as GenYers, the NetGeneration, or NextGeneration, whatever the current trendy catchword is, online relationships through social media than interpersonal ones (Hines, 2008; MacArthur Foundation, 2008). Globalization does not hinder the imperatives of authoritarian states; on the contrary, it offers more complex ways for economic participation while enforcing exploitative labor conditions. International alliances continue to be impotent in the "face of conflicts between national capitalisms" making war a recurrent feature of globalization (Chowdhury, 2006). More urgent than ever is the need for theoretical and methodological rigor in examining the *interconnections* of globalization themselves—how are they facilitated? What kinds of relationships do they engender? What economic possibilities do they create? Further, the culture-structure battle has to be overcome. Either position is damningly reductionist, and avoids analysis of the ways in which products become meaningful *culturally and economically* simultaneously. More theoretical scrutiny needs to be provided on *opportunism* in a globalizing world—what is the character of this opportunism? What mediating systems facilitate its trajectory? What ethical transformations are possible? Finally, the predictions of dramatic changes in the global economy in the next 50 years have implications on how youth are called to contribute in an ever-connected marketplace. *Place* continues to provide ontological relevance. Shifting power relations, increased wealth in the periphery paired with declining standard of living in the core notwithstanding, colonial pasts continue to inform the globalized present. The imprint of the past must not be erased in how we study the present.

NOTES

1. JoEllen Fisherkeller is Associate Professor in the Steinhardt Department of Media, Culture, and Communication at New York University. She has published in various communication and education journals and is author of *Growing Up with Television: Everyday Learning among Young Adolescents* (Temple University Press, 2002).
2. Firdoze Bulbulia is a media producer and director. She is Chairperson of the CBFA (Children & Broadcasting Foundation for Africa) and Secretary General of the CIFEJ (International Centre of Film for Children and Young People).
3. The study was sponsored by the Internationales Zentralinstitut für das Jugend- und Bildungsfernsehen, IZI (International Central Institute for Youth and Educational Television) at Bayerischer Rundfunk (Bavarian Broadcasting Corporation), Munich, Germany.
4. Follow-up fieldwork, sponsored by the IZI, formed Phase 2 of the *TV Characters* study. While many of the same questions from the first phase were used, the overall theme of respondents' anxiety in facing the upcoming 10th grade exams served as a base for new questions on labor identity. So, for example, teens participating in this study were asked more extensively about their plans for the future and the role family and peers played in influencing those plans. Television and other media usage emerged in these conversations as secondary influences.
5. The study was sponsored by the IZI.
6. Firdoze Bulbulia was the primary researcher in Johannesburg. Quotes and experiences of the six South African teens included here are derived from Bulbulia's report submitted to the IZI and from discussions at the *TV Characters* workshop in Munich, September 2004.
7. Fieldwork in Bangalore was conducted by the author and Susheela Punitha, professor emeritus of Bangalore University. Punitha identified an initial pool of 14 respondents in January 2004. After preliminary interviews with each respondent in February, nine were chosen for the study. Punitha monitored the scrapbook and journal activity for two months after which the author conducted participant observation and in-depth interviews with eight of the respondents (the ninth was unavailable). Tape transcriptions and journal and scrapbook analyses were conducted by the author. Materials from six teenagers were selected for discussion in the *TV Characters* study.
8. Petra Strohmaier and Anita Lakhotia of the IZI supervised fieldwork among the teens in Munich. Quotes and experiences of the six German teens included here are derived from the report submitted to the IZI and from discussions with Lakhotia at the *TV Characters* workshop in Munich, September 2004.

9. JoEllen Fisherkeller was the primary researcher in New York. Quotes and experiences of the six New York teens included here are derived from Fisherkeller's report submitted to the IZI and from discussions at the TV *Characters* workshop in Munich, September 2004.

10. Only first names are used, most of which are aliases, to protect privacy.

11. European Commission Audiovisual and Media policies, http://ec.europa.eu/avpolicy/reg/avms/index_en.htm

12. Interviews with Shubha and Ambika were conducted in Kannada, which is the author's and research assistant's native language as well. Their journals were written in Kannada and were transcribed by the author.

13. Tsotsi Films (2006). *Kwaito Music Origins*. Retrieved March 15, 2009, from http://www.tsotsi.com/english/index.php?m1=press&m2=kwaito

14. *Backstage* was dropped on 2007 due in part to conflicts between its various production houses and the e.tv channel. Also, the soap faced stiff competition from other prime time serials such as *7de Laan* on SABC2, *Binnelanders* on M-Net, and *Isidingo* on SABC3.

15. M-Net. (2005). *Carte blanche*. Retrieved March 10, 2009, from http://www.mnet.co.za/Mnet/Shows/carteblanche/About_Team.asp

16. Fourteen 10th Street Productions doing post on *The Pure Monate Show* (2004, September 8). Retrieved March 11, 2009, from http://www.bizcommunity.com/Account/196/66/1103.html

17. Originally under the capitol Wrestling Corporation and promoted under World Wide Wrestling Federation (WWWF) and subsequently under World Wrestling Federation (WWF) the company now promotes its simulated sports under World Wrestling Entertainment.

18. The exception was *Spiderman* where posters depicting the hero with goggles reflecting the twin towers were already in circulation and had to be altered post-9/11.

19. Rebirth Africa (2000). *Apartheid South Africa*. Retrieved March 11, 2009, from http://www.rebirth.co.za/apartheid_and_immorality2.htm

20. The Indian caste system is broadly divided into the Brahmins (the priestly or learned class), the Kshatriyas (the warrior class), the Vaisyas (the agricultural class), and the Sudras (the menial class). The menial class usually comprises of scavengers, tanners, and undertakers). Several classes are included in each caste. While originally based on occupation, caste is conventionally determined by birth. Specifically, social, intellectual, and physical capacities are believed to be biologically determined.

21. Bull (1993) identifies three factors that led to the establishment of the EU. First, the nation-state in several countries had failed to maintain law and order and protect its people from foreign attacks. Second, the division of Germany into the East and the West caused a weakening in economic ties with the West European countries. A single entity that could protect the citizens of European nations from the failures of the nation-state, and that could strive toward the unification of West European countries, was sorely needed. Finally, there was a global trend in establishing international organizations such as UNESCO and the International Monetary Fund (IMF). The Cold War and the following Communist bloc resistance to the principles of universalism propagated by these organizations resulted in the rise of region-based organizations such as ASEAN, NATO, and the EEC.

22. As stipulated by the Treaty of Rome, four major institutions contributed to the institutional base of the EC: the European Commission that consists of civil servants appointed by the

government of each country for a five-year period, the Council of Ministers that is an intergovernmental body and makes policies based on proposals initiated by the Commission, and the European Parliament that acts as a consultant and reviews proposals sent by the Commission before sending them off to the Council and finally, the Court of Justice, comprising 13 judges, which is the judicial component of the EC (see Bull, 1993, pp. 29–32).

23. The trek toward unity was led by two groups of people: the "federalists" who strived for a United States of Europe where the supranational interest stood superior to the national interest, and the "intergovernmentalists" who believed that common institutions among nations should be set up only to facilitate cooperation among nations while the nation itself remained autonomous. Federalism and its objectives of economic, social, and cultural integration were unacceptable because it meant for many countries, the deterioration of the nation-state. The federalists therefore sought the economic integration of the nation-states realizing that this would eventually lead to political integration. The compromise between intergovernmentalism and federalism (called functionalism or neofunctionalism) resulted in the establishment of the supranational European Coal and Steel Community (ECSC) in 1952, which supervised all European coal and steel production. The success of the ECSC led to the formation of the European Atomic Energy Authority (EURATOM) and the EEC in 1957. Thus, the EEC was mainly an economic community, but was driven by the goal of political unity (Wallace, 1995).

24. While the first attempts at European unity may be traced back to the 1920s, the first efforts toward this ideal actually began after the Second World War with the deterioration of the European nation-states. The postwar period witnessed the rise of regionalism in various parts of the world. The Cold War resulted in the division of the world into rival military units with the North Atlantic Treaty Organization (NATO) and its regional alliances on one side and the member countries of the Warsaw Treaty Organization on the other. The post–Cold War environment also encouraged anticolonial nationalism and led to the formation of the Non-Aligned Movement (NAM) and the regional coalition of Asian nations (Mayall, 1995).

25. Fieldwork was sponsored by the IZI.

26. At the time of writing, Rs. 44 = 1 USD

27. Other identity positions such as class, language, religion, ethnicity play a crucial role in the construction of gender identity. It was beyond the scope of this study to address all these positions and assess substantively, their interplay in how the respondents discussed their gender identities.

28. Keenan Harduth and Shaa'ista Bulbulia of South Africa were the youth organizers who helped secure the large space for the workshop and identify participants. All participants received a 5WSMC T-shirt and cap. The author thanks these organizers for their willing and cheerful assistance.

29. Research assistants included Anne Lassner, Corinna Kramp, and Elke Schlote, Maya Götz, Ole Hofmann, and Lisa Kuruvilla. The author thanks all assistants for their thoroughness and hard work. The complex project could not have been executed without their flexibility.

30. To ensure clarity of responses, each delegate was requested to state her or his name and country before attempting a response. Each question was posed one at a time, to each delegate in the group. When all responses to the first question were recorded, the second

question was posed and responses recorded in the same manner. Worksheets were provided to the research assistants for notes and observations.

31. All oral and written materials were entered into Ethnograph 6.0 for analysis of themes.

32. Names are omitted to protect confidentiality.

33. In this environment, the work of local translators who understand the ideological intent of the conversational exercises and the corporate environment for which they are produced is to be commended. Critically aware translators work within the imperatives of standardization set by the publishing houses to produce examples of transformative interactions in spoken English so that the non-native learner understands not just how to flow with the goals of the industry, but to inject counterdiscourse, if necessary (Susheela Punitha, 2009, personal communication).

BIBLIOGRAPHY

Abélès, M. (2007). Globalization, power and survival: An anthropological perspective. *Anthropological Quarterly, 79* (3), 483–508.

Abu-Lughod, L. (2005). *Dramas of nationhood: The politics of television in Egypt.* Chicago: University of Chicago Press.

Adhikari, M. (2005). *Not white enough, not black enough: Racial identity in the South African colored community.* Athens: Ohio University Press.

Ahluwahlia, P. (2003). The struggle for African identity: Thabo Mbeki's African Renaissance. In A. Zegeye and R. L. Harris (Eds.), *Media, identity and the public sphere in post-Apartheid South Africa* (pp. 27–41). Leiden and Boston: Brill.

Ahmad, A. (1992). *In theory: Classes, nations, literatures.* New Delhi: Oxford University Press.

Aksoy, A., & Robins, K. (1992). Hollywood for the 21st century: Global competition for critical mass in image markets. *Cambridge Journal of Economics, 16*(1), 1–22.

Alegi, P. (2008). Rewriting patriarchal scripts: Women, labor, and popular culture in South African clothing industry beauty contests, 1970s–2005, *Journal of Social History*, Fall, 31–56.

Algan, E. (2003). The problem of textuality in ethnographic media research: Lessons learned in southeast Turkey. In P. D. Murphy & M. W. Kraidy (Eds.), *Global media studies: Ethnographic perspectives* (pp. 23–40). New York and London: Routledge.

Althusser, L. (1971). *Lenin and philosophy and other essays.* London: New Left Books.

Amit, V. (2000). Introduction: Constructing the field. In V. Amit (Ed.), *Constructing the field* (pp. 1–18). New York: Routledge.

Ang, I. (1985). *Watching Dallas: Soap opera and the melodramatic imagination.* London and New York: Methuen.

Ang, I. (1996). *Living room wars: Rethinking media audiences for a postmodern world.* London and New York: Routledge.

Appadurai, A. (1990). Disjuncture and difference in the global economy. In M. Featherstone (Ed.), *Global culture: Nationalism, globalization and modernity* (pp. 295–311). London and New Delhi: Sage.

Appadurai, A. (1996). *Modernity at large: Cultural dimensions of globalization.* Minneapolis: University of Minnesota Press.

Appadurai, A. (2000). Grassroots globalization and the research imagination. *Public Culture, 12*(1), 1–19.

Appiah, K. A. (1996). Is the post in postmodernism the post in postcolonial? In P. Mongia (Ed.), *Contemporary postcolonial theory: A reader* (pp. 55–72). New Delhi: Oxford University Press.

Applbaum, K. (2000). Crossing borders: Globalization as myth and charter in American transnational consumer marketing. *American Ethnologist, 27*(2), 257–282.

Ariès, P. (1962). *Centuries of childhood*. Trans. Robert Baldick. London: Jonathan Cape.

Ashcroft, B. (2001). *Post-colonial transformation*. London and New York: Routledge.

Bachchan, A. (January 13, 2009). Day 265. Retrieved February 25, 2009 from http://bigb.bigadda. com/2009/01/13/day–265/

Balagopalan, S. (2008). Memories of tomorrow: Children, labor, and the panacea of formal schooling. *Journal of the History of Childhood and Youth, 1*(2), 267–285.

Banerjea, K. (2005). "Fight Club": Aesthetics, hybridisation and the construction of rogue masculinities in *Sholay* and *Deewar*. In R. Kaur & A. J. Sinha (Eds.), *Bollyworld: An introduction to popular Indian cinema through a transnational lens*. New Delhi: Sage.

Barab, S. A., Thomas, M., Dodge, T., Squire, K., & Newell, M. (2004). Critical design ethnography: Designing for change. *Anthropology & Education Quarterly, 35*(2), 254–268.

Barber, B. R. (1996). *Jihad vs McWorld: How globalism and tribalism are reshaping the world*. New York: Ballantine.

Barner, M. R. (1999). Sex-role stereotyping in FCC-mandated children's educational television. *Journal of Broadcasting & Electronic Media, 43*, 551–564.

Barnett, C. (2004). Yizo Yizo: Citizenship, commodification and popular culture in South Africa. *Media, Culture & Society, 26*(2), 251–271.

Beck, U., & Beck-Gernsheim, E. (2002). *Individualization: Institutionalized individualism and its social and political consequences*. London: Sage.

Beng-Huat, C. (2000). *Consumption in Asia: Lifestyles and identities*. New York: Routledge.

Bhabha, H. K. (1985). Signs taken for wonders: Questions of ambivalence and authority under a tree outside Delhi, May 1817. *Critical Inquiry, 12*(1), 144–165.

Bhabha, H. K. (1994). *The location of culture*. New York: Routledge.

Bird, E. (2003). *The audience in everyday life*. London: Routledge.

Blackman, S. (2005). Youth subcultural theory: A critical engagement with the concept, its origins and politics, from the Chicago school to postmodernism. *Journal of Youth Studies, 8*, 1–20.

Blumer, H. (1969). *Symbolic interactionism: Perspective and method*. Englewood Cliffs, NJ: Prentice-Hall.

Blumler, J. G., & Katz, E. (Eds.) (1974). *The uses of mass communications: Current perspectives on gratification research*. Beverly Hills, CA: Sage.

Boethius, U. (1995). Youth, the media and moral panics. In J. Fornäs & G. Bolin (Eds.), *Youth culture in late modernity* (pp. 39–57). London: Sage.

Bordo, S. (December 19, 2003). The empire of images in our world of bodies. *Chronicle Review*. Retrieved February 10, 2009, from http://www.apurnell.com/wilreadings/EmpireOfImages. htm

Bordwell, D. (February 1, 2009). Slumdogged by the past. Retrieved February 15, 2009, from http://www.davidbordwell.net/blog/?p=3592.

Bordwell, D., & Thompson, K. (1997). *Film art: An introduction*. New York: McGraw-Hill.

Botta, R. A. (2000). The mirror of television: A comparison of black and white adolescents' body image. *Journal of Communication*, Summer, 144–159.

Boyd-Barrett, O. (1998). Media imperialism reformulated. In D. K. Thussu (Ed.), *Electronic empires: Global media and local resistance* (pp. 157–176). London: Arnold.

Briggs, C. (1986). *Learning how to ask: A sociolinguistic appraisal of the role of the interview in social science research*. New York: Cambridge University Press.

Buckingham, D. (2000). *After the death of childhood: Growing up in the age of electronic media*. Cambridge: Polity.

Buckingham, D., & Sefton-Green, J. (2003). Gotta catch 'em all: Structure, agency and pedagogy in children's media culture. *Media, Culture & Society*, 25(3), 379–399.

Bulbulia, F. (2004). *TV characters and the formation of cultural identity: Case studies from Johannesburg, South Africa.* Internationales Zentralinstitut für das Jugend- und Bildungsfernsehen, Bayerischer Rundfunk, München.

Bulbulia, F. (2008). Race, class, and TV preferences. *TelevIZIon*, 21, E, 50–51.

Bulbulia, N. (1998). An overview of children's broadcasting in South Africa. In U. Carlsson & C. Von Feilitzen (Eds.), *Children and media violence* (pp. 231–237). Sweden: Nordicom.

Bull, Michael J. (1993). Widening versus deepening of the European Community: The political dynamics of 1992 in historical perspective. In T. M. Wilson & M. E. Smith (Eds.), *Cultural change and the new Europe: Perspectives on the European Community* (pp. 25–45). San Francisco, CA: Westview.

Butler, J. (1990). *Gender and the subversion of identity.* New Haven, CT: Yale University Press.

Butler, J. (2000). Restaging the universal: Hegemony and the limits of formalism. In J. Butler, E. Laclau, & Slavoj Žižek (Eds.)., *Contingency, hegemony, universality: Contemporary dialogues on the Left* (pp. 11–43). London and New York: Verso.

Butler, J. (2005). *Giving an account of oneself.* New York: Fordham University Press.

Callaway, H. (1992). Ethnography and experience: Gender implications in fieldwork and texts. In J. Okely & H. Callaway (Eds.), *Anthropology and autobiography* (pp. 29–50). New York: Routledge.

Caputo, V. (2000). "At home" and "away": Reconfiguring the field for late twentieth-century anthropology. In V. Amit (Ed.), *Constructing the field* (pp. 19–31). New York: Routledge.

Chakravarty, S. (1998). *National identity in Indian popular cinema 1947–1987.* New Delhi: Oxford University Press.

Chalaby, J. K. (2005). Deconstructing the transnational: A typology of cross-border television channels in Europe. *New Media Society*, 7(2), 155–175.

Chatterjee, P. (1993). *The nation and its fragments.* Princeton: Princeton University Press.

Chow, R. (1998). The postcolonial difference: Lessons in cultural legitimation. *Postcolonial Studies*, 1(2), 161–169.

Chow, R. (1998). King Kong in Hong Kong: Watching the 'Handover,' from the USA. *Social Text* 55(Summer 1998), 93–108.

Chow, R. (2002). *The Protestant ethnic & the spirit of capitalism.* New York: Columbia University Press.

Chowdhury, K. (2006). Interrogating "newness": Globalization and postcolonial theory in the age of endless war. *Cultural Critique*, 62, 126–160.

Clark, L. S. (2002). U.S. adolescent religious identity, the media, and the "funky" side of religion. *Journal of Communication*, December, 794–811.

Clark, L. S. (2005). *From angels to aliens: Teenagers, the media, and the supernatural.* New York: Oxford University Press.

Clarke, J. Hall, S., Jefferson, T., & Roberts, B. (1976). Subcultures, cultures and class: A theoretical overview. In S. Hall & T. Jefferson (Eds.), *Resistance through rituals: Youth subcultures in post-war Britain* (pp. 9–79). London: Hutchinson.

Cohen, S. (1987). *Folk devils and moral panics: The creation of mods and rockers.* Oxford: Blackwell.

Cole, J., & Durham, D. (2007). Introduction: Age, regeneration, and the intimate politics of globalization. In J. Cole & D. Durham (Eds.), *Youth, age and family in the new world economy* (pp. 1–28). Bloomington: Indiana University Press.

Colvin, R. (March 10, 2009). Obama plan sees extra pay for top teachers, may anger union. Retrieved March 10, 2009, from http://www.reuters.com/article/domesticnews/ idUSTRE52927W20090310

Coulter, A. (February 25, 2009). The Cal Ripken president. Retrieved February 25, 2009, from http://www.humanevents.com/article.php?id=30860

Curran, J., & Park, M. J. (2000). Beyond globalization theory. In J. Curran & M. J. Park (Eds.), De-westernizing media studies. London and New York: Routledge.

Demerath, P. (1999). The cultural production of educational utility in Pere Village, Papua New Guinea. Comparative Education Review, 43, 162–192.

Demerath, P., & Lynch, J. (2008). Identities for neoliberal times: Constructing enterprising selves in an American suburb. In N. Dolby and F. Rizvi (Eds.), Youth moves: Identities and education in global perspective (pp. 179–193). New York: Taylor and Francis.

Deshpande, Satish. (2003). Contemporary India: A sociological view. New Delhi: Viking Penguin.

Deshpande, Sudhanva. (2005). The consumable hero of globalised India. In R. Kaur & A. J. Sinha (Eds.), Bollyworld: Popular Indian cinema through a transnational lens (pp. 186–206). New Delhi: Sage.

Dickey, S. (1993). Cinema and the urban poor in South India. Cambridge: Cambridge University Press.

Dirks, N. B., Eley, G., & Ortner, S. B. (1994). Introduction. In N. B. Dirks, G. Eley, & S. B. Ortner, Culture/power/history: A reader in contemporary social theory. (pp. 3–45). Princeton, N.J. : Princeton University Press.

Dirlik, A. (1996). The postcolonial aura: Third World criticism in the age of global capitalism. In P. Mongia (Ed.), Contemporary postcolonial theory. New Delhi: Oxford University Press.

Diversi, M. (2006). Street kids in Nikes: In search of humanization through the culture of consumption. Cultural Studies and Critical Methodologies, 6, 370–390.

Dolby, N. (2006). Popular culture and public space in Africa: The possibilities of cultural citizenship. African Studies Review, 49(3), 31–47.

Dolby, N., & Rizvi, F. (2008). Youth moves: Identities and education in global perspective. London: Taylor and Francis.

Donadey, A. (2001). Recasting postcolonialism: Women writing between worlds. Portsmouth: Heinemann.

Doordarshan Audience Research Unit (1996). Nutech Pholithographers. New Delhi.

Drotner, K. (1992). Modernity and media panics. In M. Skovmand & K. C. Schröder (Eds.), Media cultures: Reappraising transnational media. London: Routledge.

Drotner, K. (2000). Difference and diversity: Trends in young Danes' media uses. Media, Culture & Society, 22(2), 149–166.

Durham, M. G. (1999). Articulating adolescent girls' resistance to the mediated feminine ideal. Psychology & Marketing, 19(2), 211–233.

Durham, M. G. (2002). Out of the Indian diaspora: Mass media, myths of femininity, and the negotiation of adolescence between two cultures. In S. R. Mazzarella & N. O. Pecora (Eds.), Growing up girls: Popular culture and the construction of identity (pp. 193–208). New York: Peter Lang.

Eagleton, T. (1991). Ideology: An introduction. London: Verso.

Eder, W., & Corsaro, D. (1999). Ethnographic studies of children and youth: Theoretical and ethical issues. Journal of Contemporary Ethnography, 28, 520–531.

Ellapen, J. A. (2007). The cinematic township: Cinematic representations of the "township space" and who can claim the rights to representation in post-apartheid South African cinema. Journal of African Cultural Studies, 19(1), 113–137.

Ex, C. T. G. M., Janssens, J. M. A. M., & Korzilius, H. P. L. M. (2002). Young females' images of motherhood in relation to television viewing. *Journal of Communication*, December, 955–971.

Fanon, F. (1965). *The wretched of the earth* [1961]. Trans. Haakon Chevalier. New York: Monthly Review.

Fanon, F. (1986). *Black skin, white masks* [1952]. Trans. Charles Lam Markmann. London: Pluto.

Fass, P. (2008). The world is at our door: Why historians of children and childhood should open up. *Journal of the History of Childhood and Youth*, 1(1), 11–31.

Featherstone, M. (1995). *Undoing culture: Globalization, postmodernism and identity*. London: Thousand Oaks and New Delhi: Sage.

Fernandes, L. (2000). Nationalizing "the Global": Media images, cultural politics and the middle class in India. *Media, Culture & Society*, 22(5), 611–628.

Fernandes, L. (2004). The politics of forgetting: Class politics, state power and the restructuring of urban space in India. *Urban Studies*, 41(1), 2415–2430.

Fernandes, L., & Heller, P. (2006). Hegemonic aspirations. *Critical Asian Studies*, 38(4), 495–522.

Fine, E. C. (1984). *The folklore text: From performance to print*. Bloomington: Indiana University Press.

Finnegan, R. (1992). *Oral traditions and verbal arts: A guide to research practices*. London and New York: Routledge.

Fisher, W. F., & Ponniah, T. (2003). Introduction: The world social forum and the reinvention of democracy. In T. Ponniah & W. F. Fisher (Eds.), *Another world is possible* (pp. 1–20). New York: Zed Books.

Fisherkeller, J. (2002). *Growing up with television: Everyday learning among young adolescents*. Philadelphia, PA: Temple University Press.

Fisherkeller, J. (2004). *TV characters and the formation of cultural identity: Case studies from New York: USA*. Internationales Zentralinstitut für das Jugend- und Bildungsfernsehen, Bayerischer Rundfunk, München.

Fisherkeller, J., & Freud, Z. (2006). Sie ist keine richtige Mutter: Wie Jugendliche in New York Geschlechterrollen mit dem Fernsehen verhandeln, *TelevIZIon*, S, 45–47.

Fiske, J. (1989). *Understanding popular culture*. London: Unwin Hyman.

Foucault, M. (1970). *The order of things: An archaeology of the human sciences*. Trans. from the French. London: Tavistock.

Foucault, M. (1977). *Discipline and punish*. New York: Pantheon.

Foucault, M. (1980). *Power/Knowledge*. New York: Pantheon.

Friedman, T. (2005). *The world is flat: A brief history of the twenty-first century*. New York: Farrar, Straus and Giroux.

Friedman, T. (May 21, 2006). Whole world grows into one big office. *News Tribune, Insight*, 3.

Gangoli, G. (2005). Sexuality, sensuality and belonging: Representations of the "Anglo-Indian" and the "Western" woman in Hindi cinema. In R. Kaur & A. J. Sinha (Eds.), *Bollyworld: Popular Indian cinema through a transnational lens* (pp. 143–162). New Delhi: Sage.

Ganti, T. (2002). "And yet my heart is still Indian": The Bombay film industry and the (H)Indianization of Hollywood. In F. D. Ginsburg, L. Abu-Lughod, & B. Larkin (Eds.), *Media Worlds*. Berkeley: University of California Press.

Gillespie, M. (1995). *Television, ethnicity and cultural change*. London: Routledge.

Gilligan, C. (1982). *In a different voice: Psychological theory and women's development*. Cambridge, MA: Harvard University Press.

Gilligan, C., & Brown, L. M. (1993). *Meeting at the crossroads.* New York: Ballantine.

Ginsburg, F. D., Abu-Lughod, L., & Larkin, B. (Eds.) (2002). *Media worlds: Anthropology on new terrain.* Berkeley: University of California Press.

Glaser, B. G. (1978). *Theoretical sensitivity.* Mill Valley, CA: Sociology.

Glaser, B. G., & Strauss, A. L. (1967). *The discovery of grounded theory: Strategies for qualitative research.* Hawthorne, NY: Aldine.

Gonick, M. (2006). Between "Girl Power" and "Reviving Ophelia": Constituting the neoliberal girl subject. *NWSA Journal, 18*(2), 1–23.

Gramsci, A. (1971). *Selections from the prison notebooks.* London: Lawrence & Wishart.

Grixti, J. (2006). Symbiotic transformations: Youth, global media and indigenous culture in Malta. *Media, Culture & Society, 28*(1), 105–122.

Grossberg, L. (1984). Another boring day in paradise: Rock and roll and the empowerment of everyday life. *Popular Music, 4*, 225–257.

Grossberg, L. (1988). Wandering audiences, nomadic critics. *Cultural Studies, 2*(3), 377–390.

Grossberg, L. (1992). *We gotta get outta this place: Popular conservatism and postmodern culture.* New York: Routledge.

Gunn, J., & Brummett, B. (2004). Popular communication after globalization. *Journal of Communication,* December, 705–721.

Gupta, A., & Ferguson, J. (Eds.) (1997). *Culture, power, place: Explorations in critical anthropology.* Durham, NC: Duke University Press.

Haig, B. D. (1995). Grounded theory as scientific method. *Philosophy of Education 1995: Current Issues* (pp. 281–290). Urbana: University of Illinois Press.

Hall, S. (1980). Encoding/decoding. In S. Hall, D. Hobson, A. Lowe, & P. Willis (Eds.), *Culture, media, language* (pp. 1972–79). London: Hutchinson.

Hall, S. (1996). Cultural studies and its theoretical legacies. In D. Morley & K. H. Chen (Eds.), *Stuart Hall: Critical dialogues in cultural studies* (pp. 262–276). New York: Routledge.

Hall, S., & Jefferson, T. (Eds.) (1976). *Resistance through rituals: Youth subcultures in post-war Britain.* London: Hutchinson.

Hall, S., Hobson, D., Lowe, A., & Willis, P. (Eds.) (1980). *Culture, media, language.* London: Hutchinson.

Hannerz, U. (1992). *Cultural complexity: Studies in the social organization of meaning.* New York: Columbia University Press.

Harrison, K., & Cantor, J. (1997). The relationship between media consumption and eating disorders. *Journal of Communication, 47*(1), 40–67.

Hastrup, K., & Hervik, P. (Eds.) (1994). *Social experience and anthropological knowledge.* London: Routledge.

Hay, J. (1996). Afterword: The place of the audience: Beyond audience studies. In J. Hay, L. Grossberg, & E. Wartella (Eds.), *The audience and its landscape.* (pp. 359–378). Boulder, CO: Westview.

Hebdige, D. (1979). *Subculture: The meaning of style.* New York: Routledge.

Hebdige, D. (1988). *Hiding in the light.* London: Comedia.

Herman E. S., & McChesney, R. (2003). The rise of the global media. In L. Parks & S. Kumar (Eds.), *Planet TV: A global television reader* (pp. 21–39). New York and London: New York University Press.

Himpele, J. D. (2002). Arrival scenes: Complicity and media ethnography in the Bolivian public sphere. In F. D. Ginsburg, L. Abu-Lughod, & B. Larkin (Eds.), *Media worlds.* (pp. 301–316). Berkeley: University of California Press.

Hoggart, R. (1957). *The uses of literacy.* Harmondsworth: Penguin.

Hörschelmann, K. & Stenning, A. (2008). Ethnographies of postsocialist change. *Progress in Human Geography*, 32(3), 339–361.

Hu, K. (2005). Techno-orientalization: The Asian VCD experience. In J. N. Erni & S. K. Chua (Eds.), *Asian media studies* (pp. 55–73). Malden, MA: Blackwell.

Hudson, B. (1984). Femininity and adolescence. In A. McRobbie & M. Nava (Eds.)., *Gender and generation* (pp. 31–53). London: Macmillan.

India no slumdog to West, filmmakers reply to Bachchan (January 19, 2009). *India Today*. Retrieved February 10, 2009, from http://indiatoday.intoday.in/index.php?issueid=89&id=25720&option=com_content&task=view&sectionid=4

Iwabuchi, K. (2005). Discrepant intimacy: Popular culture flows in East Asia. In J. N. Erni & S. K. Chua (Eds.), *Asian media studies* (pp. 19–37). Malden, MA: Blackwell.

Jacobs, S. (2002). How good is the South African media for democracy? Mapping the South African public sphere after Apartheid. *African and Asian Studies 1* (1), 279–302.

Jaffe, Alexandra (1993). Corsican identity and a Europe of peoples and regions. In T. M. Wilson & M. E. Smith (Eds.), *Cultural change and the new Europe: Perspectives on the European Community* (pp. 61–80). San Francisco, CA: Westview.

JanMohamed, A. R., & Lloyd, D. (1990). *The nature and context of minority discourse*. New York: Oxford University Press.

Jansen, J. D. (1998). Curriculum reform in South Africa: A critical analysis of outcomes-based education. *Cambridge Journal of Education*, 28(3), 321–331.

Jeffrey, C. (2008). "Generation Nowhere": Rethinking youth through the lens of unemployed young men. *Progress in Human Geography*, 32(6), 739–758.

Jeffrey, C., Jeffery, P., & Jeffery, R. (2008). *Degrees without freedom? Education, masculinities and unemployment in North India*. Palo Alto, CA: Stanford University Press.

Jeon, Y. H. (2004). The application of grounded theory and symbolic interactionism. *Scandinavian Journal of Caring Science*, 18, 249–256.

Jhally, S., & Lewis, J. (1992). *Enlightened racism: The Cosby Show, audiences, and the myth of the American dream*. Boulder, CO: Westview.

Juluri, V. (2003). *Becoming a global audience: Longing and belonging in Indian music television*. New York: Peter Lang.

Kamdar, M. (2008). India: Richer, poorer, hotter, armed. *World Policy Journal*, Fall, 95–104.

Kandiyoti, D. (1991). Identity and its discontents: Women and nation. *Millennium: Journal of International Studies*, 20 (3), 429–443.

Kaplan, E. A. (1987). *Rocking around the clock*. New York: Methuen.

Kearny, M. C. (2006). *Girls make media*. New York: Routledge.

Kenway, J., & Bullen, E. (2008). The global corporate curriculum and the young cyberflâneur as global citizen. In N. Dolby & F. Rizvi (Eds.), *Youth moves: Identities and education in global perspective* (pp. 17–32). New York: Taylor and Francis.

Klein, N. (2000). *No logo*. London: Flamingo.

Kraidy, M. M. (2003). Globalization *avant la letter?* Cultural hybridity and media power in Lebanon. In P. D. Murphy & M. W. Kraidy (Eds.), *Global media studies: Ethnographic perspectives*. (pp. 276–296). New York and London: Routledge.

Kumar, S. (2006). *Gandhi meets primetime: Globalization and nationalism in Indian television*. Chicago: University of Illinois Press.

La Pastina, A. C. (2003). Now that you're going home, are you going to write about the natives you studied? Telenovela reception, adultery, and the dilemmas of ethnographic practice. In P. D. Murphy & M. W. Kraidy (Eds.), *Global media studies: Ethnographic perspectives*. (pp. 125–146). New York and London: Routledge.

Laclau, E. (2000). Identity and hegemony: The role of universality in the constitution of political logics. In J. Butler, E. Laclau, & Slavoj Žižek (Eds.), *Contingency, hegemony, universality: Contemporary dialogues on the Left* (pp. 44–89). London and New York: Verso.

Lal, J. (1996). Situating locations: The politics of self, identity and "Other" in living and writing the text. In D. L. Wolf (Ed.), *Feminist dilemmas in fieldwork* (pp. 185–204). Boulder, CO: Westview.

Langellier, K. M., & Peterson, E. E. (2004). *Story telling in daily life: Performing narrative.* Philadelphia: Temple University Press.

Larson, M. S. (2001). Interactions, activities, and gender in children's television commercials. *Journal of Broadcasting & Electronic Media, 45*, 41–56.

Larson, R. W. (1995). Secrets in the bedroom: Adolescents' private use of media. *Journal of Youth and Adolescence, 24*, 535–551.

Larson, R. W. (2002). Globalization, societal change, and new technologies: What they mean for the future of adolescence. *Journal of Research on Adolescence, 12*(1), 1–30.

Layder, D. (1993). *New strategies in social research: An introduction and guide.* Cambridge: Polity.

Lazarus, N. (2002). The fetish of the "West" in postcolonial theory. In C. Bartolovich & N. Lazarus (Eds.)., *Marxism, modernity, and postcolonial studies* (pp. 43–64). Cambridge: Cambridge University Press.

Le Marcis, F. (2004). The suffering body of the city. *Public Culture 16*(3), 453–477.

Lee, D. H. (2004). A local mode of programme adaptation: South Korea in the global television format business. In A. Moran & M. Keane (Eds.), *Television across Asia: Television industries, programme formats and globalization.* (pp. 36–53). London and New York: Routledge Curzon.

Lee, F. L. F. (2004). Constructing perfect women: The portrayal of female officials in Hong Kong newspapers. *Media, Culture & Society, 26*(2), 207–225.

Lenhart, A., Kahne, J., Middaugh, E., Macgill, A., Evans, C., & Vitak, J. (2008). *Teens, video games and civics.* Washington, DC: Pew Internet & American Life Project. Retrieved January 15, 2009, from http://www.pewinternet.org/Reports/2008/Teens-Video-Games-and-Civics.aspx

Lesko, N. (2001). *Act your age! A cultural construction of adolescence.* New York: Falmer.

Lippi-Green, R. (1997). *Language, ideology, and discrimination in the United States.* London: Routledge.

Loomba, A. (1994). Overworlding the "Third World." In P. Williams & L. Chrisman (Eds.), *Colonial discourse and post-colonial theory: A reader.* (pp. 305–324). New York: Columbia University Press.

Lukose, R. (2005). Consuming globalization: Youth and gender in Kerala, India. *Journal of Social History, 38*(4), 915–935.

Madison, S. (2005). *Critical Ethnography.* Thousand Oaks, CA: Sage Publications.

Mankekar, P. (1999). *Screening culture, viewing politics.* Durham, NC: Duke University Press.

Mankekar, P. (2002). Epic contests: Television and religious identity in India. In F. D. Ginsburg, L. Abu-Lughod, & B. Larkin (Eds.), *Media worlds.* (pp. 134–151). Berkeley, CA: University of California Press.

Massey, D. (1997). A global sense of place. In A. Gray & J. McGuigan (Eds.), *Studying culture: An introductory reader.* London: Arnold.

Mayall, J. (1995). National identity and the revival of regionalism. In Louise Fawcett & Andrew Hurell (Eds.), *Regionalism in world politics: Regional organization and international order* (pp. 169–198). New York: Oxford University Press.

Mayer, V. (2003). Living telenovelas/telenovelizing life: Mexican American girls' identities and transnational telenovelas. *Journal of Communication, 53*(3)479–495.

Mazzarella, S. (2007).Why is everybody always pickin' on youth? Moral panics about youth, media, and culture. In S. R. Mazzarella (Ed.), *20 Questions about youth and the media* (pp. 45–60). New York: Peter Lang.

Mazzarella, S., & Pecora, N. (2007). Girls in crisis: Newspaper coverage of adolescent girls. *Journal of Communication Inquiry, 31*(1), 6–27.

Mazzarella, W. (2004). Culture, globalization, mediation. *Annual Review of Anthropology, 33,* 345–367.

McCabe, J., & Akass, K. (2006). *Reading Desperate Housewives: Beyond the white picket fence.* London: I.B. Tauris.

McCarthy, C., & Logue, J. (2008). Shoot the elephant: Antagonistic identities, neo-Marxist nostalgia and the remorselessly vanishing pasts. In N. Dolby & F. Rizvi (Eds.), *Youth moves: Identity and education in global perspective* (pp. 33–53). New York: Taylor and Francis.

McMillin, D. C. (2002). Choosing commercial television's identities in India: A reception analysis. *Continuum: Journal of Media and Cultural Studies, 16*(1), 135–148.

McMillin, D. C. (2003). Television, gender, and labor in the global city. *Journal of Communication, 53*(3), 496–511.

McMillin, D. C. (2005). Teen crossings: Emerging cyberpublics in India. In S. Mazzarella (Ed.), *Girl wide web: Girls, the Internet, and the negotiation of identity.* (pp. 161–178). New York: Peter Lang.

McMillin, D. C. (2006). Wenn wir aufhören, uns zu fürchten ... *TelevIZIon, S, 39–43.*

McMillin, D. C. (2007). *International Media Studies.* Malden, MA: Blackwell.

McMillin, D. C. (2008a). "Around sourcing": Peripheral centers in the global office. In R. Gajjala (Ed.), *South Asian digital diasporas and global technospaces: Culture and economics in cyberspace.* (pp. 249–263). New York: Peter Lang.

McMillin, D. C. (2008b). "We really need a new perspective": Teens talk about gender and television. *TelevIZIon, 21, E,* 54–55.

McMillin, D. C. (2008c). "When we stop being scared ...": Youth, culture, gender, and television in India. *TelevIZIon, 21, E,* 45–49.

McMillin, D. C., & Fisherkeller, J. (2008). "Teens, television characters, and identity," paper presented at the Popular Communication Division of the International Communication Association Conference, Montreal, Canada, May 2008.

McRobbie, A. (1991). *Feminism and youth culture.* Boston, MA: Unwin Hyman.

McRobbie, A. (1994). *Postmodernism and popular culture.* London: Routledge.

Mead, G. H. (1934). *Mind, self and society: From the standpoint of a social behaviorist.* Chicago: University of Chicago Press.

Meyrowitz, J. (1985). *No sense of place: The impact of electronic media on human behavior.* New York: Oxford University Press.

Miller, D. (1994). *Modernity: An ethnographic approach.* Oxford: Berg.

Mitra, A. (1993). *Television and popular culture in India.* New Delhi: Sage.

Mohanty, C. T. (1988). Under western eyes: Feminist scholarship and colonial discourses. *Feminist Review, 30,* 61–88.

Mohanty, C. T. (2003). *Feminism without borders: Decolonizing theory, practicing solidarity.* Durham and London: Duke University Press.

Mongia, P. (1996). Introduction. In P. Mongia (Ed.), *Contemporary postcolonial theory: A reader.* (pp. 1–18). Oxford: Oxford University Press.

Moran, A., & Keane, M. (2004). Joining the circle. In A. Moran & M. Keane (Eds.), *Television across Asia: Television industries, programme formats and globalization.* (pp. 197–204). London and New York: Routledge Curzon.

Morley, D. (1980). The "Nationwide" audience. London: BFI.Morley, D., & Robins, K. (1995). Spaces of identity: Global media, electronic landscapes and cultural boundaries. New York: Routledge.

Murdoch, G. (1996). Concentration and ownership in the era of privatization. In P. Marris and S. Thornham (Eds.), Media studies: A Reader (pp. 91–101). Edinburgh: Edinburgh University Press.

Murdock, G. (1997). Thin descriptions: Questions of method in cultural analysis. In J. McGuigan (Ed.), Cultural methodologies. (pp. 178–192). London: Sage.

Mutating; Hollywood blockbusters: Global release of new films aims to prevent piracy. (April 26, 2003). The Economist. Retrieved January 6, 2009, from http://www.highbeam.com/doc/1G1–100741154.html

Nightingale, V. (1996). Studying audiences: The shock of the real. New York: Routledge.

Nuttall, S. (2008). Youth cultures of consumption in Johannesburg. In N. Dolby & F. Rizvi (Eds.), Youth moves: Identities and education in global perspective (pp. 151–179). New York: Taylor and Francis.

Okely, J. (1992). Anthropology and autobiography: Participatory experience and embodied knowledge. In J. Okely & H. Callaway (Eds.), Anthropology and autobiography. (pp. 1–28). New York: Routledge.

Ong, A. (2004). Buddha is hiding: Refugees, citizenship, and the new America. Berkeley: University of California Press.

Pal, M., & Buzzanell, P. (2008). A case study in changing discourses of identity, identification, and career in a global context. Journal of Business Communication, 45(1), 31–60.

Paley, A. (May 17, 2006). Latest overseas outsourcing? Tutoring. News Tribune, A8.

Parsons, T. (1963). Youth in the context of American society. In E. H. Erikson (Ed.), Youth: Change and challenge (pp. 96–119). New York: Basic Books.

Pieterse, J. N., & Parekh, B. (Eds.) (1995). The decolonization of imagination: Culture, knowledge and power. London and New Jersey: Zed Books.

The pink chaddi campaign blogspot (March 7, 2009). Retrieved March 8, 2009, from http://thepinkchaddicampaign.blogspot.com/

Pipher, M. (1994). Reviving Ophelia: Saving the selves of adolescent girls. New York: Ballantine Books.

Postman, N. (1994). The disappearance of childhood. New York: Delacorte.

Price, M. E. (1995). Television, the public sphere and national identity. Oxford: Oxford University Press.

Prinsloo, J., & Janks, H. (2002). Critical literacy in South Africa: Possibilities and constraints in 2002. English Teaching: Practice and Critique, 1(1), 20–38.

Quijada, D. A. (2008). Marginalization, identity formation, and empowerment: Youth's struggles for self and social justice. In N. Dolby and F. Rizvi (Eds.), Youth moves: Identities and education in global perspective (pp. 207–221). New York: Taylor and Francis.

Rajagopal, A. (2001). Politics after television: Hindu nationalism and the reshaping of the public in India. Cambridge: Cambridge University Press.

Real, M. R. (1996). Exploring media culture: A guide. Thousand Oaks, CA: Sage.

Ricker, A. (1996). The Lion King animated storybook: A case study of aesthetic and economic power. Critical Studies: A Journal of North-South Dialogue, 10(1), 41–59.

Robertson, R. (1995). Mapping the global condition: Globalization as the central concept. In M. Featherstone (Ed.), Global culture: Nationalism, globalization and modernity (pp. 15–30). London: Sage.

Robrecht L. C. (1995). Grounded theory: Evolving methods. *Qualitative Health Research, 5*, 169–177.

Rogers, M. (2008). Modernity, 'authenticity,' and ambivalence: Subaltern masculinities on a South Indian college campus. *Journal of the Royal Anthropological Institute, 14*, 79–95.

Rogerson, C. M. (2006). Developing the fashion industry in Africa: The case of Johannesburg. *Urban Forum, 17*(3), 215–240.

Said, E. (1979). *Orientalism*. New York: Vintage.

Sanders, B. (1994). *A is for ox*. New York: Vintage.

Serequeberhan, T. (2007). *Contested memory: The icons of the occidental tradition*. Trenton, NJ: Africa World.

Sharma, M. (March 10, 2009). Attack-hit women of Bangalore vent ire on the Web. Retrieved March 12, 2009, from http://www.ndtv.com/convergence/ndtv/story.aspx?id=NEWEN20090085237

Shohat, E., & Stam, R. (1994). *Unthinking Eurocentrism: Multiculturalism and the media*. New York: Routledge.

Shome, R. (2006). Interdisciplinary research and globalization. *The Communication Review, 9*, 1–36.

Signorielli, N. (2001). Television's gender role images and contribution to stereotyping: Past, present, future. In D. G. Singer & J. L. Singer (Eds.), *Handbook of children and the media* (pp. 341–358). Thousand Oaks, CA: Sage.

Sinclair, J. (1998). Culture as a "market force": Corporate strategies in Asian skies. In S. R. Melkote, P. Shields, & B. C. Agarwal (Eds.), *International satellite broadcasting in South Asia*. (pp. 207–226). Lanham, MD: University Press of America.

Singh, P., & Doherty, C. (2008). Mobile students in liquid modernity: Negotiating the politics of transnational identities. In N. Dolby and F. Rizvi (Eds.), *Youth moves: Identities and education in global perspective* (pp. 115–131). New York and London: Taylor and Francis.

Singhal, A., & Rogers, E. M. (2001). *India's communication revolution: From bullock carts to cyber marts*. New Delhi: Sage.

Spivak, G. C. (1988). Can the subaltern speak? In C. Lemert (Ed.), *Social theory: The multicultural and classic readings* (pp. 610–614). Boulder, CO: Westview.

Sridharan, E. (2004).The growth and sectoral composition of India's middle classes: Its impact on the politics of liberalization in India. *India Review, 1*(4), 405–428.

Steinberg, S., & Kincheloe, J. (1997). *Kinderculture: The corporate construction of childhood*. Oxford: Westview.

Stillman, S. (2006). Grounded theory and grounded action: Rooted systems in theory. *World Futures, 62*, 498–504.

Strelitz, L. (2003). Where the global meets the local: South African youth and their experience of global media. In P. D. Murphy & M. W. Kraidy (Eds.), *Global media studies: Ethnographic perspectives* (pp. 234–256). New York and London: Routledge.

Strohmaier, P., & Lakhotia, A. (2004). *TV characters and the formation of cultural identity: Case studies from Munich, Germany*. Internationales Zentralinstitut für das Jugend- und Bildungs-fernsehen, Bayerischer Rundfunk, München.

Sutton, R. A. (2003). Local, global, or national? Popular music on Indonesian television. In L. Parks & S. Kumar (Eds.), *Planet TV: A global television reader*. (pp. 320–340). New York and London: New York University Press.

Thiel, S. (2005). "IM me": Identity construction and gender negotiation in the world of adolescent girls and instant messaging. In S. R. Mazzarella (Ed.), *Girl wide web: Girls, the Internet, and the negotiation of identity* (pp. 179–201). New York: Peter Lang.

Thomas, G., & James, D. (2006). Reinventing grounded theory: Some questions about theory, ground and discovery. *British Educational Research Journal, 32*(6), 767–795.

Thomas, R. (2005). Not quite (pearl) white: Fearless Nadia, queen of the stunts. In R. Kaur & A. J. Sinha (Eds.), *Bollyworld: An introduction to popular Indian cinema through a transnational lens*. New Delhi: Sage.

Thompson, E. P. (1963). *The making of the English working class*. New York: Vintage.

Thompson, J. B. (1990). *Ideology and modern culture*. Standford, CA: Stanford University Press.

Tomaselli, G. T., & Teer-Tomaselli, R. (2003). New Nation: Anachronistic Catholicism and liberation theology. In N. Couldry & J. Curran (Eds.), *Contesting media power: Alternative media in a networked world*. (pp. 195–208). Lanham, MD: Rowman & Littlefield.

Tomlinson, J. (1997). Cultural globalization and cultural imperialism. In A. Mohammadi (Ed.), *International communication and globalization*. London: Thousand Oaks and New Delhi: Sage.

Ul Haq, M. (2003). *Human development in South Asia 2003: The employment challenge*. New Delhi: Oxford University Press.

Usdin, S. (2005). Soul City, South Africa: Partnering with the media and civil society in achieving social change. *Exchange, 1,* 18–20.

Valdivia, A. N. (2008). Popular culture and recognition: Narratives of youth and Latinidad. In N. Dolby & F. Rizvi (Eds.), *Youth moves: Identities and education in global perspective* (pp. 179–193). New York: Taylor and Francis.

Venn, C. (2006). *The postcolonial challenge: Towards alternative worlds*. London and New Delhi: Sage.

Verghese, N. (2004). Pokemon monstrous hit in India too: Funskool. *Business Line*. Retrieved March 19, 2009, from http://www.thehindubusinessline.com/2004/03/12/stories/2004031201440600.htm

Verma, S., & Saraswathi, T. S. (2002). Adolescence in India: Street urchins or Silicon Valley millionaires? In B. B. Brown, R. W. Larson, & T. S. Saraswathi (Eds.), *The World's Youth: Adolescence in Eight Regions of the Globe*. (pp. 105–140). Cambridge: Cambridge University Press.

Verma, S., & Sharma, D. (2003). Cultural continuity amid social change: Adolescents' use of free time in India. In S. Verma & R. Larson (Eds.), *Examining adolescent leisure time across cultures: Developmental opportunities and risks* (pp. 37–51). San Francisco: Wiley Periodicals.

Verma, S., Sharma, D., & Larson, R. (2002). School stress in India: Effects on time and daily emotions. *International Journal of Behavioral Development, 26,* 500–508.

Vickers, J., & Dhruvarajan, V. (2002). Gender, race, and nation. In V. Dhruvarajan & J. Vickers (Eds.), *Gender, race and nation: A global perspective* (pp. 25–64). Toronto: University of Toronto Press.

Walker, C. (1996). Can TV save the planet? *American Demographics, 18*(5), 42–48.

Walkerdine, V. (2003). Reclassifying upward mobility: Femininity and the neo-liberal subject. *Gender and Education, 15*(3), 237–248.

Wall, J. (2006). Childhood studies, hermeneutics, and theological ethics. *Journal of Religion, 86*(4), 523–548.

Wallace, William. (1995). Regionalism in Europe: Model or exception? In L. Fawcett & A. Hurell (Eds.), *Regionalism in world politics: Regional organization and international order* (pp. 201–227). New York: Oxford University Press.

Weissman, R. (2008, November/December). The system implodes: The 10 worst corporations of 2008. *Multinational Monitor, 10,* 10–22.

Wilk, R. (1994). Colonial time and TV time: Television and temporality in Belize. *Visual Anthropology Review*, 10(1), 94–102.

Williams, R. (1958). *Culture and society, 1780–1950*. New York: Columbia University Press.

Willis, P. (1977). *Learning to labor: How working class kids get working class jobs*. Farnborough, UK: Saxon House.

Willis, P. (2003). Foot soldiers of modernity. *Harvard Educational Review*, 73(3), 390–415.

Willis, P. (2004a). Shop floor culture, masculinity and the wage form. In P. F. Murphy (Ed.), *Feminism and masculinities* (pp. 108–120). London: Oxford University Press.

Willis, P. (2004b). Twenty-five years on: Old books, new times. In N. Dolby & G. Dimitriadis (Eds.) with P. Willis, *Learning to labor in new times* (pp. 167–196). New York: RoutledgeFalmer.

Wilson, D., & Purushothaman, R. (2003). Dreaming with BRICs: The path to 2050. *Global Economics Paper No: 99, October 2003*. Goldman Sachs Group.

Wilson, T. M. (1993). An anthropology of the European Community. In T. M. Wilson & M. E. Smith (Eds.), *Cultural change and the new Europe: Perspectives on the European Community*. (pp. 1–24). San Francisco, CA: Westview.

Wolf, D. (1996). Situating feminist dilemmas in fieldwork. In D. Wolf (Ed.), *Feminist dilemmas in fieldwork*. (pp. 1–55). Boulder, CO: Westview.

Wong, C. H. Y., & McDonogh, G. W. (2001). The mediated metropolis: Anthropological issues in cities and mass communication. *American Anthropologist*, 103(l), 96—111.

Young, R. J. C. (2003). *Postcolonialism: A very short introduction*. New York: Oxford University Press.

Zakaria, F. (March 6, 2006). India rising. *Newsweek*, 34–42.

Zavella, P. (1996). Feminist insider dilemmas: Constructing ethnic identity with Chicana informants. In D. L. Wolf (Ed.), *Feminist dilemmas in fieldwork*. (pp. 138–159). Boulder, CO: Westview.

Zegeye, A., & Harris, R. L. (2003). Introduction. In A. Zegeye and R. L. Harris (Eds.), *Media, identity and the public sphere in post-apartheid South Africa*. (pp. 1–26). Leiden and Boston: Brill.

Zhong, Y. (2002). Debating with muzzled mouths: A case analysis of how control works in a Chinese television debate used for educating youths. *Media, Culture & Society*, 24(1), 27–47.

Žižek, Slavoj (1993). *Tarrying with the negative: Kant, Hegel and the critique of ideology*. London: Verso.

Zukin, S. (1996). *The culture of cities*. Oxford: Blackwell.

mediated youth

Sharon R. Mazzarella
General Editor

Grounded in cultural studies, books in this series will study the cultures, artifacts, and media of children, tweens, teens, and college-aged youth. Whether studying television, popular music, fashion, sports, toys, the Internet, self-publishing, leisure, clubs, school, cultures/activities, film, dance, language, tie-in merchandising, concerts, subcultures, or other forms of popular culture, books in this series go beyond the dominant paradigm of traditional scholarship on the effects of media/culture on youth. Instead, authors endeavor to understand the complex relationship between youth and popular culture. Relevant studies would include, but are not limited to studies of how youth negotiate their way through the maze of corporately-produced mass culture; how they themselves have become cultural producers; how youth create "safe spaces" for themselves within the broader culture; the political economy of youth culture industries; the representational politics inherent in mediated coverage and portrayals of youth; and so on. Books that provide a forum for the "voices" of the young are particularly encouraged. The source of such voices can range from in-depth interviews and other ethnographic studies to textual analyses of cultural artifacts created by youth.

For further information about the series and submitting manuscripts, please contact:

SHARON R. MAZZARELLA
Communication Studies Department
Clemson University
Clemson, SC 29634

To order other books in this series, please contact our Customer Service Department at:

(800) 770-LANG (within the U.S.)
(212) 647-7706 (outside the U.S.)
(212) 647-7707 FAX

Or browse online by series at WWW.PETERLANG.COM